What Your Colleagues Are Sa

M000025192

Teaching Kids to Thrive: Essential Skills for Success is a book that not only argues effectively for including social and emotional learning in every classroom, but also shows teachers how to do it. Debbie Silver and Dedra Stafford demonstrate how SEL instruction can be woven into all subject areas at every level of preK–12 education. They descriptively outline what SEL-friendly classrooms look like, and they provide a wealth of tools and strategies for educators who want to teach beyond the standards. I recommend this book for new and veteran teachers alike who want to help students learn to thrive both now and throughout their future lives.

—TODD WHITAKER
Professor of Educational Leadership
Indiana State University
Terre Haute, IN

Reading *Teaching Kids to Thrive* was like feeding my brain with Pop Rocks®! It had me captivated, wondering, and marveling . . . all at the same time. Debbie Silver and Dedra Stafford provide insightful research, actionable skills, and inspirational stories, while recognizing the voices of students and teachers at the turn of every page.

—DR. RUSSELL J. QUAGLIA, Executive Director
Quaglia Institute for School Voice & Aspirations
Portland, ME

There are some books that you pick up and just cannot put down. Well, this is one of them. If you are ready to move beyond grit, then *Teaching Kids to Thrive* is the linchpin needed in every school system. The authors provide relevant research to build their case and share easy and simple teacher-approved strategies that can be used immediately. Any stakeholder in education who wants to transform school culture must make *Teaching Kids to Thrive* required reading.

—SIMON T. BAILEY AND MARCETA REILLY, Authors
Releasing Leadership Brilliance

Debbie Silver and Dedra Stafford go to the heart of schooling students in this century—addressing the power of mindfulness and the value of empathy, and boosting the resilience of young people at a time when the world requires such a skill the most. Using relatable stories and strategies, the goal to help students *thrive* is central in every chapter. Like a favorite piece of music, the authors' passion for education is extremely contagious and memorable.

—JENNIFER BUCHANAN, MBA, MTA
President/Speaker/Author
Calgary, Alberta

Hoorah! Here is help with the overlooked aspects of teaching that matter most. Don't just read it—study it, live with it, and you too will thrive.

—**JOHN LOUNSBURY**, Dean Emeritus
Georgia College
Milledgeville, GA

"Good teachers teach subjects. Great teachers teach students." This often repeated quote of unknown origin typifies both the authors of this book and the intent of the book's content. In a world where "all data counts but all that counts is not data," Debbie Silver and Dedra Stafford provide guidance and important information on how teachers can teach students some of the most important of all lessons, things that do not become part of the data base which too often defines students. *Teaching Students to Thrive* guides teachers in how to incorporate essential social and emotional skills into daily routines. These are the essential skills students need in order to realize their potential not only as students but as successful and fulfilled members of society. As well as essential information, the authors incorporate practical activity guides to enable teachers to help their students become more successful in school and in life. Anecdotes, examples, and practical activities guide the reader to become more adept in incorporating social and emotional learning skills into everyday classroom environments. This book is a must-read for all teachers who harbor the desire to help their students develop the skills to successfully navigate not only school but life itself.

—**DUANE INMAN**, PhD, Professor of Education
Berry College
Mt. Berry, Georgia

In college courses, education students learn how to teach academic content. In *Teaching Kids to Thrive*, Debbie Silver and Dedra Stafford emphasize the importance of also teaching students. In a world changing at a pace rarely seen in human history, merely learning coursework won't be enough. Today's children need to be prepared to face challenges and have the capacity to flourish, regardless of what life throws at them. *Thrive* has teacher-friendly strategies and support that allow even the most experienced educators to see real cognitive, social, and emotional growth in their students.

—**CHERYL MIZERNY,** Educator and Blogger
It's Not Easy Being Tween
www.middleweb.com

Why should you read *Teaching Kids to Thrive*? Students today may be the most connected generation in history, but they can't find ways to connect with themselves. Debbie Silver and Dedra Stafford masterfully illustrate that Thrive skills can no longer be considered soft. This book evidences that learning how to control their bodies and emotions is every bit as essential to modern learners as understanding how to control the devices that students love so dearly.

—JARED COVILI, Author
Going Google: Powerful Tools for 21st Century Learning, Second Edition
Salt Lake City, UT

Teaching Kids to Thrive: Essential Skills for Success is an excellent practical guide for educators who want to apply the ideas of social-emotional learning to their classroom.

—LARRY FERLAZZO
Teacher, Author, and *Education Week* Teacher Advice Blogger
Luther Burbank High School
Sacramento, CA

Debbie Silver and Dedra Stafford have answered the question educators have asked time and again: "How, exactly, do I create a classroom culture conducive to growth, collaboration, and critical thinking?" The book explores the importance of resilience, empathy, persistence, and skills related to active listening, to creating the mindset that will nurture and accelerate the continuous-improvement process. These are not "soft skills" that live on the periphery of textbook-driven, correct-answer-seeking lessons. They are life skills students need to practice—and teachers need to model—on the road to success in school, college, the workplace, and in a democracy. This is an eminently practical resource with enough research, examples, frequently asked questions, exercises, stories, and humor for all educators; and all educators should have a copy of this book.

—RON NASH, Author/Consultant
Ron Nash and Associates, Inc.
Virginia Beach, VA

I am doing backflips over having this book in my life! I work with teachers every day, and every day I field questions on how to support learners in being open and present for learning. It is true—we are educating a different type of learner than those of earlier generations. And so our teaching must shift, remembering that we teach children, not curriculum. Debbie Silver and Dedra Stafford have written the guide to working with this new generation of students, one which begins with the social-emotional health of each learner. They tackle head-on the most challenging and real moments of teaching, creating a research-based, practical, tried-and-true (yet cutting-edge) handbook to simply and powerfully show learners how to ground and bloom. While this book focuses on students, the outcomes will bring joy, fulfillment, and gratitude to teachers. I have been waiting for this book without knowing it, and now it will be my go-to resource and recommended text on teaching students how to thrive in all educational settings and in life.

—PATTY MCGEE, Author/Consultant
Feedback That Moves Writers Forward
Harrington Park, NJ

There are no convenient, instant answers to solve tough issues in education, and no one "event" can make a difficult student easy to teach. Great teaching is hard work. This book lays out a brilliant process for building Thrive skills. Read the book. Practice the skills. Practice patience and perseverance. Enjoy the rewards.

—DR. MONTE SELBY
Educational Consultant/Author/Songwriter
Boulder, CO

Plain spoken and practical with enough neuroscientific research to support what teachers and parents have been sensing but didn't have the knowledge to articulate.

—DR. SUSAN GRANT, PhD, LLC
Neurolinguist
Timonium, MD

It is now time for student to truly thrive! Educators have been looking for a resource that puts the reality back in education. Debbie Silver and Dedra Stafford have done just that. The authors know about the importance of students understanding content, but they also realize that students must be optimistic, show integrity, understand empathy, and believe in gratitude. What we can learn from this book is that you may never lose a job in life because you're too smart; you get fired because you're not a nice person. Make sure you look at the book's examples and situations and try to change your practices within your classroom or school. Let's help our students thrive in all aspects of their life!

—JACK BERCKEMEYER, Educator, Author, Humorist, and Consultant
Berckemeyer Consulting Group
Denver, CO

TEACHING KIDS TO THRIVE

We would like to dedicate this book to all the great teachers who have always known that students need Thrive skills that go beyond the test. We thank you for your continued effort to prepare students for the aspects of their lives that go further than the three Rs. Additionally, we want to voice our confidence in today's kids, the adults who teach them, and the administrators who advocate for them. It will take all of us to ensure their ability to Thrive both now and in the future.

—Debbie Silver and Dedra Stafford

DEBBIE SILVER · DEDRA STAFFORD

FOREWORD BY RICK WORMELI

TEACHING KIDS TO THRIVE

ESSENTIAL SKILLS FOR SUCCESS

A JOINT PUBLICATION

FOR INFORMATION:

Corwin

A SAGE Company

2455 Teller Road

Thousand Oaks, California 91320

(800) 233-9936

www.corwin.com

SAGE Publications Ltd.

1 Oliver's Yard

55 City Road

London EC1Y 1SP

United Kingdom

SAGE Publications India Pvt. Ltd.

B 1/I 1 Mohan Cooperative Industrial Area

Mathura Road, New Delhi 110 044

India

SAGE Publications Asia-Pacific Pte. Ltd.

3 Church Street

#10-04 Samsung Hub

Singapore 049483

Executive Editor: Arnis Burvikovs

Senior Associate Editor: Desirée A. Bartlett

Editorial Assistant: Kaitlyn Irwin

Production Editor: Melanie Birdsall

Copy Editor: Melinda Masson

Typesetter: C&M Digitals (P) Ltd.

Proofreader: Lawrence W. Baker

Indexer: Molly Hall

Cover Designer: Rose Storey

Marketing Manager: Nicole Franks

Printed in Canada

Companion website icon courtesy of ©iStockphoto.com/Ylivdesign

ISBN 978-1-5063-2693-1

This book is printed on acid-free paper.

MIX

Paper from
responsible sources

FSC® C004071

17 18 19 20 21 10 9 8 7 6 5 4 3

CONTENTS

Access the website **www.teachingkidstothrive.com**
to find more classroom-ready activities,
author-recommended videos, websites, and other resources.

FOREWORD

A hinge is the primary mechanism used to swing a door open. Absent a hinge, the door remains a wall, blocking access to its other side. The Latin root of *cardinal* in "Cardinal Virtues," from Plato's *Republic*, is *hinge*. Plato's listed virtues, then, are the hinge necessary for passage.

Plato's virtues include *prudence* (the capacity to judge which decisions and actions to employ, given the factors of any situation, or to determine whether or not something is appropriate or inappropriate), *justice* (fairness), *temperance* (self-control, discretion, and moderation when warranted), and *courage* (fortitude, perseverance, and the ability to confront personal fears). These virtues have stood the test of time, finding their way into religions, civic duties, employee evaluation criteria, and our cultural narratives. To this day, we lift up individuals who exemplify these virtues as our heroes, for we are sure these are the keys to personal success.

Two thousand years later, Debbie Silver and Dedra Stafford identify the virtues of executive function, self-efficacy, self-regulation, perseverance, resilience, focus, integrity, and gratitude as critical elements to student maturation and success. They've tapped into the virtues river flowing through civilizations across time.

While knowing the difference between mass and weight or distinguishing among hue, tint, and shade may land on our must-know list for students in particular subjects at certain grade levels, we don't consider them nonnegotiable "vitals" to personal success the way we think being honest, taking initiative, and demonstrating self-discipline are.

Consider the situations our students will face and then discern whether or not a curriculum with little focus on self-efficacy, mindfulness, perseverance, self-regulation, executive function, empathy, gratitude, resilience, and integrity would prepare them for thoughtful, constructive responses that best serve local communities, let alone a robust and civil democracy:

- A community is divided over whether or not to let transgender students use the school bathroom and locker rooms labeled with the gender with which they identify. Tempers flare on both sides of the issue at a swim meet.

- Twenty-four-year-old Cecilia is a newly hired programmer for a local software company, but she's still living at home because she doesn't have enough money for a down payment on an apartment of her own yet. She claims the homeless in her community are a drug-addled drain on taxpayers, and every time we build them shelters or provide them with meals, we're perpetuating their drug problem, and no, she doesn't want any tax increase to pay for mental health centers either. Her father is aghast at his daughter's hypocrisy and lack of sympathy, and confronts her.

- Gary hates his job, but no jobs in his preferred field are available in his community. On top of that, his family is depending on his current job to pay for food, housing, transportation, and taxes, as well as for the health care coverage they receive. So, he slogs back and forth and endures each day at work, but he's exhausted and growing more resentful of his job and his family by the hour.

- If Nehri eats one more celery stick, she's going to scream. Her husband loses weight much faster than she does, yet she works out and watches her diet more. She's curt with her husband and grumpy at work. *The heck with it*, she thinks, *it's not worth all the stress. I'll start again next week.* Then she pops two donut holes in her mouth, slides the sausage-and-cheese pizza into the oven, and sets the timer for twenty minutes.

Teaching Kids to Thrive is the book many of us waited for our professors of teacher education to hand us but never received. We sat in courses and pored over historical foundations of schooling, puzzled over whether or not something was a goal or an objective, and tried to determine which theory of learning best described a teacher's interaction with her students. Silently, we pleaded with our instructors:

- *How do I get my students to pay attention and do their work?*
- *What if they get out of control in my class and don't respect me?*
- *How do I show them that I care for them without coming across as weak?*
- *What if they forget stuff all the time?*
- *What if they are always talking and interrupting me?*
- *What if they just give up?*
- *What if they ask me a question about a topic I'm teaching for which I don't know the answer?*
- *What if I don't get along with my faculty colleagues?*
- *How will I handle bullies in my classroom or among the faculty?*
- *What if students have scary, heartbreaking issues at home and I'm trying to get them to care about their schoolwork?*
- *What if the parents are real jerks?*
- *What if I fail my students as their teacher?*

Then, a year or so into our teaching practice and experiencing a particularly rough day of negative 'nesses—inattentiveness, forgetfulness, bitterness, messiness, grumpiness, and rudeness—we finally volcano, "I could really teach, if it weren't for all these kids!"

Even we veterans have those days. Silver and Stafford acknowledge that reality and give us the tools to not only understand the dynamics at play, but also respond to them effectively. I wish I had this book decades before now. I wonder what would have been different with my students' lives today if I had these insights back when I taught them. If I was now in the classroom, I would relish the opportunity to push my ego to one side, crawl inside these wonderful new perspectives, and use them sincerely with the new students I encounter.

I don't know if I have ever seen a book that gathers so many highly regarded and well-researched principles of social and emotional learning in one place and makes them so compelling and doable. The authors breathe life into what has been presented elsewhere as comatose or didactic. When we have questions about where to turn for more information on any one of these elements, Silver and Stafford have the resource ready. They are well read in the field, too: As I turn these pages, I'm compiling big lists of books and articles that are moving to the top of my reading lists.

Readers will want to have a pen for annotating the many silver bullet phrases and sentences for further thinking and sharing. One of the most telling lines of the book is "There is nothing worse than schoolifying something that is natural and essential to learning." Exactly! Silver and Stafford recognize that social and emotional learning awareness and practices are born from a clear understanding of how children—okay, any of us—learn and grow. This stuff speaks to the natural essence of what it means to be a human living in a community seeking connection, meaning, and hope.

The problem with many teacher and school discipline programs for building students' personal responsibility, focus, honesty, self-regulation, and integrity is that they are based on punishments and external validations that are effectively the Peanuts cartoon teacher's wah-wah-wahs. In an effort to help students mature, some of us actually deny the natural tools of personal growth at our ready disposal. What missed opportunities, and what harm done! And then we blame the child for his lack of focus, learned helplessness, and poor self-discipline, falling into deficit thinking in which the child is flawed and must be "fixed" by society with tools we don't have or understand. In these moments, we self-protect: We rationalize, grow callous, and remain impotent.

There's another path here. In these pages, students become full individuals instead of merely one more test to grade or seat to assign. There's specific talk about restorative justice, how to battle students' sense of entitlement, facilitating students' growing responsibility, teaching them how to focus and be mindful, and hard-core tenacity. There is nothing "soft" or nonacademic in teaching these skills, either. On the contrary, they are some of the most deeply challenging and academically oriented skills students will ever learn. College admission officers will tell you the same: A strong foundation in these skills is a greater predictor of success in higher education and career training than GPA and many other traditional indicators. Content knowledge is acutely relevant, but skills in self-regulation, perseverance, empathy, mindfulness, and executive function are the only ways we participate and progress. Admission officers are looking for evidence of these skills in potential students.

I shudder at the thought of driving a car while blind: How will I know where and when to turn or when to make minor adjustments in response to the quirky physics of steering a two-ton vehicle at sixty miles per hour in varied climates and road conditions and among just as quirky humans? How long will it be before I crash, and whom will I harm as I drive?

I have the same fear of teaching while ignorant of social and emotional learning practices; I just can't see how it can be done without undermining education's cause and harming students. In *Teaching Kids to Thrive*, we gather the fortitude to address these skills in our own classrooms and to bring them up in conversation with colleagues. Silver and Stafford make a perfect case for why we teach these skills and what it really looks like when we do right by them in the classroom. The Frequently Asked Questions and Thrive Skills in Action at the end of every chapter are worth the price of the book alone. It's rare for an education book to work so well as both compass and road map.

After reading *Teaching Kids to Thrive*, educators are going to see factors at play in academic learning that they didn't perceive before, and they will discover tools they never knew they had. Doors will swing open on critical hinges built for a lifetime.

Turn the page, step through, and see for yourself.

—**RICK WORMELI**
National Educational Consultant and Author

ABOUT THE AUTHORS

 **Dr. Debbie Silver** is a humorist, consultant, and retired educator with over thirty years of experience as a teacher, staff development facilitator, and university professor. As a classroom teacher, Debbie won numerous awards, including the 1990 Louisiana Teacher of the Year award. She speaks worldwide on issues involving education and is a passionate advocate for students and teachers.

Debbie wrote the best-selling books *Drumming to the Beat of Different Marchers: Finding the Rhythm for Differentiated Instruction* and *Fall Down 7 Times, Get Up 8: Teaching Kids to Succeed* and co-wrote *Deliberate Optimism: Reclaiming the Joy in Education*. Debbie is married to Dr. Lawrence Silver, and together they have five sons in five different states. They currently reside in Melissa, Texas, with their dog, two cats, and two aquatic frogs. You can read more about Debbie at www.debbiesilver.com.

Dedra Stafford is an educational consultant, trainer, and author. Her work has led her to speak in three international schools and more than forty states. Much of Dedra's time is spent supporting high-risk schools in an embedded capacity. With more than eighteen years in education as a former middle school teacher and district professional development specialist working with kindergarten through twelfth-grade teachers and administrators, Dedra understands the need for practical research-based strategies that can be implemented immediately in the classroom.

Dedra wrote *Podcasting: A Step-by-Step Guide for Creating Podcasts and Using Them in the Classroom* and was a contributing author for *The Nuts & Bolts of Active Learning Lessons*. Dedra is married to her best friend, Todd Stafford, and together they have a loving family of two sons, two bonus daughters, and three adorable granddaughters. You can read more about Dedra at www.dedrastafford.com.

ACKNOWLEDGMENTS

Debbie Silver:

I want to thank my friend, assistant, and co-writer, Dedra Stafford, for inspiring this book and insisting that we write it. Dedra always makes me want to be better than I am. She is one of the best "Thrivers" I know.

I want to give a shout-out to my eight grandchildren because watching them Thrive keeps me motivated to fight for a better world for all kids. It is my joy and my privilege to be your grammie, Charlotte, Gunner, Montana, Olivia, Liam, Kirby, Miles, and Kannon.

As always my thanks, appreciation, and love go to my best friend, my sounding board, my fellow sojourner, and my biggest cheerleader—Lawrence Silver. It is great to be married to another writer who is as weird as I am.

And finally, I am grateful to my Corwin family (all of you) and especially to the world's greatest editor, Arnis Burvikovs, along with Desirée Bartlett, Ariel Bartlett, Melanie Birdsall, and Melinda Masson. You five are truly a writer's dream team, and I am so thankful I have your unfaltering support. You truly help me to Thrive!

Dedra Stafford:

This journey began as a conversation with Corwin senior associate editor Desirée Bartlett, who challenged me to create the vision for a book that helped teachers go beyond the research to the practical implementation of the Thrive skills. Desirée Bartlett, Arnis Burvikovs, and the whole Corwin team, a heartfelt thank-you for working tirelessly to make this book a reality.

I want to also thank my family and friends for tolerating the countless hours this book has consumed of me. There are no words to say how much you all mean to me. I am a better teacher and a better person because of the impact each of you has had on my life.

Without a doubt, one of the greatest blessings in my life is my husband and "gardener," Todd Stafford. I thank the heavens for bringing us together to create this loving, loud, crazy family we call our own. Your never-ending love and support allow me to fly. I love you, more.

Lastly, with love and an abundance of respect, I thank the original consultants of the Nuts & Bolts Symposiums, who have had a lasting impact on education across the globe: Walt and Jan Grebing, Jack Berckemeyer, Debbie Silver, Rick Wormeli, Mark McLeod, Sharon Faber, Monte Selby, Kathy Hunt-Ullock, and Randy Thompson. You are the people I learned from, the people who inspired me, the people who guided me onto this path of speaking and writing, and for that, I'm humbled and grateful. And to the best nut of them all, Debbie Silver, you are more than my co-author and mentor; you are a trusted friend. Thank you for creating this book with me. Not a day goes by that I am not amazed at the talent, knowledge, and love that you possess and are willing to share. The list of what you've taught me is endless, and so is my gratitude. Since I have this opportunity, I want the world to know that so much of what I am and have become . . . I owe to Dr. Silver: S-I-L-V-E-R!

INTRODUCTION

Why Teach Social and Emotional Learning (SEL) in the Classroom?

In the world of school today, there is a relentless pursuit of attaining higher test scores. Educators and parents alike are caught up in the goal of gaining the competitive edge in making sure our students demonstrate specific academic competencies deemed crucial for later success in life. In the sprint toward these said capabilities, the pressure on educators, students, and parents is overwhelming. After all, mastering core curriculum is supposed to ensure our children's entrance into better colleges and/or careers, guide them toward financial independence, and fulfill the promise of the ever elusive guarantee for better lives. But sadly, it's just not happening that way.

The focus on a one-time winner-takes-all test environment often leads to feelings of entitlement (for those who measure up) or learned helplessness (for those who don't). School and district mission statements routinely tout the idea of building lifelong learners, but the joy of working hard toward a goal and the idea that learning never stops have gotten lost in the race to the top. We wonder if our educational system is taking the necessary proactive steps to help students wrestle with their current and future struggles. We question if our high-stakes, instant-accountability model truly serves their best interests not only for surviving in school but for Thriving in an increasingly ambiguous and volatile world.

As teachers and academicians, we have done our fair share of study on core curriculum issues, assessment, and accountability. However, our intent with *Teaching Kids to Thrive* is to explore key elements of learning that go far beyond subject matter knowledge and academic skill measurement. We want to talk about what it takes to help students—all students—move beyond merely coping and surviving. We want to teach them how to Thrive and how to navigate successfully whatever the future holds for them. We want to explore teaching social and emotional learning (SEL) skills as dispositions toward lifelong success.

Unless you teach in a sensory deprivation lab somewhere in the Antarctic, you are undoubtedly aware of the recent surge of interest in SEL in schools. With the passage of the Every Student Succeeds Act (ESSA), states are now required to include at least one measure other than test scores in their accountability systems, and many districts are turning to SEL components to fulfill this part of the federal law. An accumulation of research, documentation, and commentary in the past five years has come together to support the idea that SEL may have reached a tipping point for necessary inclusion in our schools.

Significant studies have shown that effective SEL programs in prekindergarten through Grade 12 give students as much as an 11 percent gain in academic achievement as well as building positive personal attitudes and enhanced shared interactions. Other studies find that students who are taught SEL skills are more likely to graduate from high school. Student populations, especially those identified as at-risk students, show a reduction in crime and delinquency both during school age and into adulthood.

Educators of students with special needs believe SEL helps their students in two ways. First, it promotes a consciousness and an inclusive attitude among their non-challenged peers. Second, it helps them develop their own emotional and social competence. For all students, SEL education provides the promise of multiple benefits on many levels.

Many teachers tell us they are committed to the idea of helping students learn and practice basic interpersonal and intrapersonal strategies, but they have no idea where to start. One of the most common questions we are asked is, "But what does this look like in my classroom?"

Often teachers see the influx of SEL standards as just adding another layer of responsibility to their already overflowing curriculum obligations. As veteran teachers, we totally appreciate those feelings. Our purpose with this book is to offer educators enough empirical research to justify incorporating SEL for every grade level in each discipline and to provide supporting activities, resources, tips, and guidelines that are classroom ready, teacher friendly, and teacher approved. We offer strategies and tools to help educators who are interested in teaching students the skills that will help them in their personal goals as well as with their interactions with others.

What Are the Thrive Skills?

We believe that specific terminology is vital to the understanding of concepts. Therefore, we want to be clear that we do not favor terms such as *soft skills* or *noncognitive skills* because we think these labels demean the importance of the proficiencies we are writing about. Referring to Thrive skills such as self-regulation, self-efficacy, responsibility, integrity, and others as "soft skills" seems to imply that they are somehow less valuable and less rigorous than academic skills such as basic grammar, math, history, and other subjects. Self skills and social skills don't necessarily trump academic skills, but the two are intricately entwined. SEL skills allow students to continue their struggles to learn the academic subjects and pay attention to their best ways for accommodating and assimilating new information. SEL skills also allow learners to communicate their interests and knowledge to others as well as handle troublesome interpersonal challenges.

Additionally, denoting self skills and social skills as "noncognitive" misrepresents them. Self-regulation, for example, has to involve a consideration and analysis of one's performance and mental state—a profoundly cognitive activity. Effective empathetic reactions result when individuals are able to assess another person's viewpoint as well as weigh options and make decisions. When referring to the particular set of skills and competencies we address in this book, we prefer to use *essential skills* or *Thrive skills*.

THRIVE SKILLS ARE MORE THAN JUST 21ST CENTURY SKILLS

21st century skills has become the shorthand terminology for skills students need to succeed in the current world as well as for whatever the future may hold. What the "four Cs" framework (communication, collaboration, critical thinking, and creativity) does not describe, however, is what underlies and enables these competencies. Examining those competencies is our purpose in writing this book. Today's learners do not know a time when the Internet didn't exist. They have been raised in the information-overload world, where we find ourselves over-connected to our screens and media and less connected to ourselves and the people around us. The multitasking selfie generation seems to have a deficit when it comes to the self and people smart skills of SEL. We want to equip teachers with a rational and practical implementation of SEL so that our students can succeed in this increasingly complex world.

THRIVE SKILLS ARE MORE THAN JUST *GRIT*

Angela Duckworth's popularized term, *grit*, is receiving a lot of attention in educational circles as a distinct character quality that to a large extent governs whether or not a student will ultimately achieve success. While separating this solitary trait as determiner of triumph is alluring because of its simplicity, it is also flawed for the same reason. Thrive skills encompass perseverance (often called grit), but they are much more than that. Bear with us here: Duckworth's study of grit came on the heels of Dr. Carol Dweck's groundbreaking research on mindset theory, which came from her (Dweck and associates) original study of attribution theory, which is supported by Albert Bandura's self-efficacy theory. Honestly, we are not trying to complicate matters, but rather we are clarifying our case that Thrive skills are complex, interconnected, and grounded in research that has been going on for decades.

In examining the many social and emotional skills important to student success, we chose those that have proven to be identifiable, malleable, and teachable. Our categories may vary somewhat from those of other researchers and educators (who also vary among themselves). We include what we consider the most essential self and social habits and skills that can and should be taught in classrooms and schools everywhere. *Teaching Kids to Thrive* provides an in-depth look at the following:

Chapter 1: Mindfulness

Chapter 2: Command and Control Functions

Chapter 3: Self-Efficacy and Growth Mindset

Chapter 4: Perseverance

Chapter 5: Resilience and Optimism

Chapter 6: Responsibility

Chapter 7: Honesty and Integrity

Chapter 8: Empathy

Chapter 9: Gratitude

As with most effective classroom activities, strategies, and tools, there is some overlap among the suggestions for classroom implementation. For instance, executive function is heightened by mindfulness practices, and perseverance and resiliency are improved through self-regulation and self-efficacy. The self and social skills work together to improve school climate as well as to give all learners the essential abilities they will need to enter the workforce, go on with formal education, and/or deal with future challenges as yet unknown.

TEACHING KIDS TO THRIVE OFFERS

- **SEL skills overview:** Gives a summary of the essential social and emotional learning skills needed to help students Thrive both now and in the future.

- **The latest research:** Incorporates the newest findings from neurobiology and explores their implications for classrooms.

- **Stories:** Abounds with anecdotes demonstrating how Thrive skills improve the academic, social, and emotional lives of students.

- **Implementation support:** Delivers strategies, tips, and tools to help teachers implement SEL training at any grade level.

- **Thrive Skills in Action:** Provides easy, inexpensive, teacher-tested activities for integrating Thrive skills in the classroom.

- **Additional resources:** The Taking It to the Next Level section on the *Thrive* website (www.teachingkidstothrive.com)

presents several resources for further activity ideas, websites, and supplemental tools.

- **FAQ:** Poses thorough and insightful answers to frequently asked questions.
- **Discussion questions:** Inspires deeper thinking for learning groups and individual reflection.

Taking This Book to the Next Level (*Thrive* Website)

Because the 21st century is fast-paced and ever changing, we have developed a website (www.teachingkidstothrive.com) to accompany *Teaching Kids to Thrive*. Our intention is for the website to serve as a living extension of the book. It contains up-to-date resources, several additional activities not found in the book, resources, video links, app suggestions, and activity sheets. We encourage educators to email or tweet us to submit your own activities and stories that support the Thrive themes. You can reach us via email at contact@teachingkidstothrive.com or via Twitter at @tchkids2thrive.

AFTER READING THIS BOOK, YOU WILL BE *MORE* ABLE TO

- Use mindfulness strategies to help students focus and access their inner strengths
- Help students build upon their existing ability to self-regulate and motivate themselves
- Guide students in developing their growth mindsets so they can visualize their goals and make plans to achieve them
- Cultivate an attitude and culture of perseverance in your classroom
- Incorporate resilience practices into everyday lesson planning and interactions
- Clarify what it means to be a responsible community member and help your students internalize how they can be responsible students and citizens
- Demonstrate how honesty and integrity can help build stronger relationships and foster a community of people who support one another

- Rethink your capacity for empathy and employ new tools and techniques for expressing empathy to students and colleagues

- Formulate an ethos of everyday gratitude so that students, regardless of their socioeconomic status, learn to honor the gifts they have and appreciate the pluses in their lives

- Use the strategies, tips, guidelines, stories, reflections, and inspiration from this book to ensure that your students excel not only in their academic skills but also in their Thrive skills, which lay the foundation for a healthy, whole, centered, and grounded young adulthood

Thriving Together

Integrating SEL in all schools will require that we as educators let go of a system ordered by control and immediate quantifiable markers in the form of grades and scores, but we believe we will see the ultimate benefit—producing more students who are future ready and able to Thrive no matter the circumstances. And the added bonus is that if we allow ourselves to practice what we teach, we educators will be better at Thriving, too.

We hope you will join us in this journey by sharing your thoughts, ideas, and resources.

MINDFULNESS IN THE CLASSROOM

SLOWING DOWN TO SPEED UP SUCCESS

For fast-acting relief, try slowing down.

—Lily Tomlin

We begin our study of Thriving in the classroom with an examination of *mindfulness*, a concept that can be used to support all the social and emotional skills we address in later chapters. Teaching mindfulness in the classroom has positive benefits, not the least of which is providing a realistic approach to reducing stress and focusing attention.

●●● DISTRACTED STUDENTS

The ninth-grade teacher tries to lead a discussion on basic concepts from the previous day's lesson, but it is going nowhere. Two students are slumped in their seats with earbuds peeking out of their hoodies, several are surreptitiously checking the smartphones shoved up their sleeves or sneaking glances at their smartwatches, and three are arguing heatedly about something one of them recently tweeted. The teacher surveys the disarray and says loudly enough

(Continued)

(Continued)

to be heard over the noise, "Okay, people, let's just calm down and take a breath—we've got a big review to cover for the upcoming test. I need you all to focus." The admonition is largely ignored, and the frustrated educator says to himself, "Just a few more days, just a few more days . . ." as he longingly looks at his desk calendar to check how many days remain until fall break.

In a classroom across campus, a primary teacher tries to rein in a rambunctious group of students by saying, "Okay, I've had it with the racket. Most of you are not paying attention. When I clap my hands, I want eyes on me. Stop fidgeting, stop looking out the window, and stop talking over each other." She claps. Calm momentarily prevails, but it takes less than fifteen seconds for the pandemonium to resume. The teacher chants in her mind, "School is out in three more hours, school is out in three more hours . . ." as she reaches for an Advil.

Later in their respective lounges, both teachers lament about how students today are distracted and unfocused. One says, "I'm up there doing everything but tap-dancing on roller skates trying to get their attention, and nothing works." The other tells his colleagues, "I don't know how I'm supposed to compete with all their distractions and diversions. It's like trying to hold thirty balls under water at the same time."

Both of these teachers could improve their classroom environments and their own psyches with an inexpensive, readily available resource called mindfulness. ●

Why Don't They Just Pay Attention?

Ask a group of educators about 21st century challenges to student learning, and among the top responses will be a lack of student attentiveness. Competing forces from outside the classroom as well as the wave of readily accessible digital devices have added a fresh dimension of distraction. Those obstacles are compounded by the enduring challenges of engaging students who come from poverty, dysfunctional homes, and/or life-challenging circumstances that make them unavailable for learning.

School is often a difficult place in which to Thrive. It can be a noisy, chaotic place that stresses students, teachers, and administrators alike. Today, schedules are packed tighter, recesses and breaks are often suspended, course selection and availability are limited, and accountability measurement tensions are amplified. Researchers refer to extreme stress overload as *toxic stress* and have determined that over time it actually reshapes the brain in negative ways. A 2014 paper from the National Scientific Council on the Developing Child compared stress overload to "revving a car engine for hours every day. This wear and tear increases the risk of stress-related physical and mental illness later in life" (p. 2).

Students of the 21st century live in a quick-fix world of instant gratification distracted by an onslaught of more information than any previous generation. They are bombarded with a never-ending stream of messages for most of their waking hours. Seldom are they given time to be still and think. Feeling the pressure of high-stakes tests, teachers rush students through the mandated curriculum like it is a sprint rather than a marathon.

Adults are quick to admonish students to calm down and take a breath, but it seldom occurs to us that the act of taking responsibility for calming oneself is a skill that must be taught. Generally, when we ask or tell kids to be quiet for a period of time, it is for our benefit and not for theirs. When they complain about being bored, we hand them something to distract them rather than encourage them to take advantage of the downtime to pause and reflect on their situation. The model we adults present is the overworked, exhausted, stressed-out grown-up who consistently complains that there's so much to do and so little time to do it. Rarely do kids experience an adult who says, "I'm feeling inattentive (or stressed), and I need to take a minute to calm myself and regain my focus."

Daniel Goleman, psychologist and author of *Focus: The Hidden Driver of Excellence* (2013) and other best-selling books on social and emotional learning (e.g., Goleman, 1995, 1998), says that he would like to see schools teaching exercises that strengthen student attention. He believes honing the ability to focus is a secret element to success that often gets ignored. When interviewed by Katrina Schwartz in 2013, he said,

> The more you can concentrate the better you'll do on anything, because whatever talent you have, you can't apply it if you are distracted. . . . This ability is more important than IQ or the socio-economic status of the family you grew up in for determining career success, financial success, and health.

If students don't learn how to shut out distractions and center their attention, they are at risk of suffering both academically and physically. They are setting themselves up for having serious problems in many aspects of their lives both now and later on. How do we help our students learn to slow down, think things through, and purposefully focus their attention?

Mindfulness: What It Is and What It Is Not

Since 2007, educators across the United States have been formally introducing students to a practice called *mindfulness* in the classroom. Most educators are familiar with the concept. It is hard to pick up a journal, attend a conference, or listen to a podcast about current trends in education that does not at least mention mindfulness. Type "mindfulness" into Google, and you get twenty-seven million hits. In 2012, Tim Ryan, a congressman from Ohio, published *A Mindful Nation* and received a $1 million federal grant to teach mindfulness in schools in his home district. Integrating the tenets of mindfulness practice in classrooms seems to have garnered increasing support.

Research has shown that helping students learn how to self-regulate their behaviors through mindfulness has a pronounced positive effect on classroom management issues in terms of reduced conflict and bullying as well as on individual behavior such as controlling impulsivity and attentional focus. Of course, mindfulness is not without its detractors, but the research on its positive impact on both social and emotional learning as well as on academic achievement is promising.

You may be in a school that practices school-wide mindfulness, you may already have a program in place in your classroom for teaching and practicing it with your students, or you may have just heard about it and want to give it a try. (And you may be reading this and asking yourself, "What is *mindfulness*? Is it just another *educational fix du jour*?")

Pause Your Reading and Try This

(Seriously, don't skip this part. Actually do it! It just takes two minutes.)
Take one hand and gently tap your thumb to each finger on the same hand. Think only about what you feel as you alternate finger taps. If your mind drifts to other things, just gently bring it back to your fingers. Notice but disregard all other fleeting thoughts. Focus on your fingertips. How do they feel right now? After a minute or two, relax your fingers and take note of any differences you feel in your hand. If you closed your eyes during this exercise, open them. Gently stretch your entire body and reflect on what just happened. If you have never done a mindfulness exercise before, congratulations—you've just completed your first one!

Mindfulness is not new. Generally, it is acknowledged as being based on age-old practices from the time of the Buddha, but some scholars believe that similar practices were advocated as well in Christian, Jewish, and Muslim teachings. Originally, it was grounded in religious practices, but most of today's researchers and practitioners are focused on the more secular applications of its short-term effect on self-regulation and its long-term impact on the neuroplasticity of the brain. The mindfulness practices we are advocating are not tied to any religious affiliation; they are proven ways to help adults and students alike prepare mentally to better handle distractors in daily life. They are not meant to be a new relaxation technique or a hippy-dippy esoteric fad. The activities we present offer students and the adults who teach them a way to calm the emotional center of the brain through nonjudgmental and nonreactive awareness.

The concept of mindfulness is gaining recognition in the fields of neuroscience and psychology and is also expanding its traction with educators and parents as a way to help learners grow and control their brains in a particular way. Mindfulness is a way of learning to be fully present in the moment without being distracted by past anxiety or future uncertainties. It is a way to become aware of our habitual reactions and emotional triggers as we practice a method for calming our minds and bodies. The basics are very simple but are not all that easy.

Using Mindfulness in the Classroom

In mindfulness exercises, we encourage students to practice limiting their focus to their breathing and/or a single concrete thing. The instruction will inevitably have students breathe deeply and think only about their breath as it enters and leaves the body—to focus on the here and now, not what might have been or what they're worried could be. The ultimate goal is to give them enough distance from disturbing thoughts and emotions to be able to observe them without immediately reacting to them.

In the beginning, the exercise should last no more than a minute or two. We tell our students their thoughts will naturally wander but to be aware of that and gently bring their attention back to the task at hand. We let them know they should not judge themselves or their thoughts but rather just take note of what is going on and redirect their focus. It is important to let them know this is not an easy process but it will become easier with practice.

We need to debrief students often in the beginning to get them to talk about how different things popped into their minds or maybe how they suddenly realized they have a pain somewhere or that they are hungry or cold or tired. Have a conversation with them about how the mind fills us with thoughts and messages that are not necessarily true but may just be a voice of concern or guilt or apprehension. For instance, a person should not say to himself, "Oh, I really shouldn't be thinking this particular thought. I must be a bad person." Instead, the learner might say, "Wow, that's a strange thought. I wonder where that came from," while continuing to return to the focused objective. Students are to notice but not judge thoughts. Tell them the goal is to watch your thoughts without identifying with them, much like sitting beside the road and watching cars go by. Sometimes you jump in one of them and it takes you down the highway, but then you remember your purpose, get out, and watch cars passing by you again.

Eventually, students will begin to be aware of body and mind messages constantly vying for attention. By increasing awareness of internal mental and physical states, mindfulness can help people gain a greater sense of control over their thoughts, feelings, and behavior in the present moment. By paying closer attention to the sensations they feel when they are anxious, angry, threatened, or the like, they learn to recognize certain triggers and also how to control their automatic reactions to those feelings. Ultimately, students learn to understand that they do not have to react or respond to every thought they have. They begin to realize they are strong individuals who can calm themselves, think things through, and consciously choose a course of action.

Beginning a Mindfulness Practice

You may already be practicing mindfulness yourself, and you may be experienced in integrating this practice into your classroom. Or you may be saying to yourself, "That's an interesting idea, but I have no idea where to start. I wonder how it's done, what it takes, and if it really works." In the Thrive Skills in Action section of this chapter, we offer a few of the more popular mindfulness activities along with some basic strategies we think will help you in any classroom. We highly recommend that you watch the video *Room to Breathe* as a staff development activity and discuss the possibilities for your school.

Sometimes teachers begin with a very simple breathing exercise. The breathing exercises in mindfulness are a strategic way to teach learners how to check in with what they are actually feeling. So many children are caught up in a state of constant stimulation and unexamined action–reaction response that they are oblivious to what is actually going on in their brains and the rest of their bodies. Intentional breathing prompts them to slow down, tune in to the present, and take a mental note of how they feel.

It is important to stress to students that this activity should be nonjudgmental. They need to try and push away any thoughts of self-labeling, shame, or guilt. The purpose of mindfulness is to simply acknowledge what is going on and be aware of it. Later in this book, we will examine how this awareness can bring about a higher sense of gratitude, more self-regulation, and better decision making, but first things first. Practicing the ancient art of mindfulness is a crucial skill for helping students improve their lifelong Thrive skills.

©iStockphoto.com/Wavebreakmedia

The movie *Room to Breathe* is about troubled students at Marina Middle School in San Francisco, California. The film presents a true story of the surprising transformation of struggling seventh graders in a school that has a high rate of disciplinary suspensions, overcrowded classrooms, and a markedly negative learning environment. One classroom of students is introduced to the practice of mindfulness meditation in an effort to provide them with social, emotional, and attentional skills they need to succeed. A teacher from the Mindful Schools organization persists in introducing them to mindfulness in spite of their initial resistance and markedly unenthusiastic response. She meets with the students for thirty minutes a week over a six-week period. Her first goal is to get students to become still and quiet when they hear a chime. Even that simple task seems to be at first unachievable for some. By the end of the program, she has the students applying the breathing techniques they learn in class to situations both inside and outside the school. At the end of the training, these same students report they are better able to control their anger, more focused on schoolwork, and more tolerant of each other, and they feel more in control of their futures. To watch the video, visit www.mindfulschools.org/resources/room-to-breathe ●

The important first step for teachers is to plan a time to implement mindfulness activities on a regular basis in their classrooms. There are plenty of YouTube videos, phone apps, articles, and other resources to help with specific procedures and routines. We present some of our favorites in this book and on the *Thrive* website (www.teachingkidstothrive.com).

implem.
resource

Research on Mindfulness in the Classroom

Yoga, Tai Chi, and Csikszentmihalyi's (1990) theory of *flow* are based on some of the same tenets of focused attention. Mindfulness as taught in schools usually focuses on concentrating, breathing, and making conscious choices. Ronald D. Siegel (2014), a psychologist and Harvard professor, cites study after study of hard science that supports the benefits to individuals (including children) who are being taught the practice of learning to pause and reflect before acting. He and other researchers have found that mindfulness practice over time actually changes the way the brain is formed. His catch line is Hebb's rule, "Neurons that fire together, wire together." In other words, people can actually help their prefrontal cortex to function more effectively over time with intentional practice of mindfulness.

constant
Revving
engine
example

Other neuroscientists also find that the permanent structure of the brain can be improved through mindfulness practices. World-renowned neuroscientist Richard Davidson at the Center for Healthy Minds at the University of Wisconsin–Madison, along with his colleagues, wants us to know three things: (1) You can train your brain to change, (2) the change is measurable, and (3) new ways of thinking can change it for the better (Wolkin, 2015).

Diversity
efforts

Davidson believes we can potentially influence the plasticity of our brains by focusing on skills and habits that benefit our well-being. Along with other measurable changes that have been observed, laboratory studies show the amygdala (center of our "fight, flight, or freeze" reactions and emotional control center) actually shrinks after sustained mindfulness practices. The connections between the amygdala and the prefrontal cortex are weakened, which allows less reactivity and paves the way for connections between areas associated with higher-order brain functions (such as concentration and attention).

Mindfulness is being studied as a countermeasure for use with students presented with such challenges as autism, attention deficit/hyperactivity disorder (ADHD), attention deficit disorder (ADD), and an array of behavioral issues. Carolyn Gregoire (2014) reports that mindfulness practices have resulted in "increased mindful awareness among both parents and children, and reduced parental stress."

While writing this chapter, we thought about how few times we actually practiced mindfulness as classroom teachers. Most of our classroom time was centered on lecture, group experiences, hands-on activities, and a rather frenzied pace to "get it all done" in our forty-five-minute class periods. Only rarely did we give our students time to disconnect from our fast-paced activities and hear themselves think. On one occasion, we took science students outside and asked them to select a tree that drew their attention, observe it, sketch it, and write something about it. Just sitting quietly and gazing at their tree selections had a profound effect on our middle-level students. Some actually had tears in their eyes as they begged to be allowed to just sit and be still for just a little longer.

We see now that in our efforts to hurry up and cover the mandated content we missed an opportunity to teach our students the important lifelong skill of being able to stop, breathe, and think about their thinking. The simple act of pausing to connect with one's thoughts in a focused, nonjudgmental setting can yield remarkable feelings of awareness and control. Simply being able to label feelings and realize one has a conscious choice about whether or not to act on those feelings is empowering.

So many of our students come to school after having experienced a tumultuous morning at home, bullying on the bus, or any number of distracting and upsetting factors. By giving kids a fresh start with a mindfulness activity, we help create better conditions for learning. As Argos Gonzalez, an English teacher at an alternative school in New York, put it, "If you don't address the noise in a kid's head that they bring from the outside, I don't care how good a teacher you are, you're not going to have much success" (Davis, 2015). The fundamental purpose is to help students learn to calm themselves and clear their minds so they can better focus on the lesson at hand. It is very much like training their "attention muscles."

Mindfulness is a commonsense lifestyle habit like brushing your teeth, exercising, or eating the right kinds of food. It is something that can be taught to every student. It offers educators a chance to reset the climate when chaos occurs or when tensions run high (for

In 2009, second-year principal Lana Penley was trying to find a way to heal the trauma caused when her 460 students and 50 staff members were herded from their burning school building to a sports field nearby. Later housed in a vacant school building across town for three years during the rebuild, Penley was concerned about the impact of the ordeal on her many at-risk students. The staff decided they would have to find a social and emotional curriculum to connect with the hearts of all who were affected. They tried many ideas from Goldie Hawn's MindUP™ program, but Penley noted the real change came from a simple shift in having teachers start each class in the morning with a few breaths to help students feel present. In the middle school, students did their breathing exercises after each passing period. Teachers began to embrace the concept of mindfulness and to use it for enhancing other Priority Academic Student Skills (PASS). The changes in tone and culture were dramatic. Discipline referrals dropped, teachers are happier, and this Title I school now has one hundred applicants for every open position (Schwartz, 2016a). ●

example, before a major test). Hopefully, schools will also embrace this relatively cost-free means of helping teachers and students develop positive, life-changing ways to think, relate to each other, and act in ways that help them Thrive. Jennie Rothenberg Gritz, in her article "Mantras Before Math Class," describes the beneficial effects of mindfulness practices in a school located in an area of San Francisco with the highest rates of violent crime. Within four years, the suspension rate dropped to one of the lowest in the city. "Daily attendance rates went up to 98 percent, and the students' overall grade point average showed marked improvement. This former troubled school now ranks first on happiness inventories administered throughout the district" (Gritz, 2015).

Implementation in the Classroom

How you address mindfulness needs to be the way that best suits you, your students, and your school.

At this point, those new to mindfulness usually ask questions like "But what does it look like in an actual classroom?" "What do I do if I have tables instead of chairs or no space for students to spread out?" "How often do I use it, and how long does it take?" Mindfulness in the classroom is an evolving practice that has only been used widely in the last ten years. The short answer to all those questions is that how you address mindfulness needs to be the way that best suits you, your students, and your school. Educators have chosen a wide array of making the concept work for their students. This is just a partial list of the variety of ways mindfulness has been implemented in classrooms:

1. Certified trainers are brought in at designated times during the week to work with students and teachers.

2. Teachers go through specific training and are then put in charge of leading their own students in mindfulness practices.

3. Classroom teachers set aside time every morning and every afternoon for mindfulness practices.

4. Middle and high school teachers begin each class with a few minutes dedicated to time for mindfulness. Thirty-minute sessions are offered three times a week.

5. A single forty-five-minute session is offered once a week.

6. A guided mindfulness practice is conducted in a high school for half an hour twice weekly.

7. In Britain, teachers follow a scripted program for nine lessons. Once students internalize the process, teachers and administrators use quick mindfulness practices whenever they think they are needed.

8. Schools in California and New York voted to add thirty additional minutes to the school day to implement a mindfulness program called Quiet Time (Gritz, 2015).

9. Counselors visit classrooms and conduct mindfulness activities.

10. Parents are encouraged to take mindfulness training offered by the school.

11. Regular mindfulness practice can be just moments of stillness or silence.

Mindfulness practice can be formal or informal. No matter how you choose to implement a mindfulness practice, the goal is to help students of all ages learn they can use it anytime they need to refocus their attention or reset their thoughts. They soon realize they have the power to check in with their bodies at any time, figure out what is going on, and restore the balance they need to best handle the situation at hand.

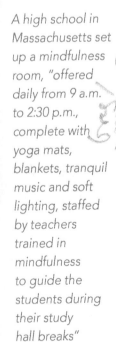

A high school in Massachusetts set up a mindfulness room, "offered daily from 9 a.m. to 2:30 p.m., complete with yoga mats, blankets, tranquil music and soft lighting, staffed by teachers trained in mindfulness to guide the students during their study hall breaks" (Wallace, 2016).

What Supporting Mindfulness Looks Like in the Classroom

BE AWARE OF THE PART YOU PLAY IN SETTING THE PACE AND TONE OF YOUR CLASSROOM

Students feed off of the energy of the teacher and the room. Whenever possible, start the day alone in your classroom with no distractions. Take a few minutes just to breathe deeply and focus on your purpose. Let go of the distractors—the tire that probably needs air in it or the colleague who just stepped on your last nerve—and be fully present for the students who will soon be right there, right now.

START EACH CLASS OFF WITH THE RIGHT ATMOSPHERE

As students enter the classroom, position yourself at the door or near the front to greet students and offer a sincere welcome. Calming music could usher them in, and taking a moment to start off with a focus activity can pay big dividends.

REMEMBER THAT MINDFULNESS IS NOT MANDATORY

When using mindfulness in the classroom, don't push students beyond their comfort level. Students can choose to participate or not. There is no judging. Some may wish to gaze out the window or put their heads down. The one requirement is that they do not disturb or distract others during the activities. Some may be open to describing feelings, and some might not be. Don't use the mindfulness area or any mindfulness activity as punishment. Students should see the act of being still and thinking as something that is positive and helpful.

BE A GOOD MARKETER

When teaching mindfulness (especially to middle school and high school students), it is helpful to sell it to your students and create a buy-in before you start your program. Explain to students why you are teaching the technique and what it can do for them. Start by having them discuss the stresses in their lives (see Activity 1.5, "Up in the Air," at the end of this chapter). You may want to share how these techniques have been used successfully in other schools. You might want to talk about how you use these techniques personally. You can always close with the question, "What have you got to lose?" Encourage your students to try just a few short techniques and see how they work.

KEEP IT SIMPLE

For younger students, don't overwhelm them with lots of complex terms for mindfulness. Keep it simple. Concentrate on breathing and focus. Present ideas in relation to the senses. "What do you hear, smell, feel?" In the beginning for all ages of students, plan to spend a lot of time debriefing to ensure they understand the purpose of the practice.

PRACTICE, PRACTICE, PRACTICE

Students need to have consistent, ongoing opportunities to practice training in focus and mindfulness. This is not a stand-alone activity you can do at the beginning of the year and forget. Early ed teachers can use an activity called "Breathing Buddies" (described on the *Thrive* website at www.teachingkidstothrive.com). Teachers of middle and high school students can regularly conduct three- or five-minute breathing exercises. As they gain confidence in the procedures, students can take an active role in leading mindfulness activities.

USE MINDFULNESS YOURSELF

Practice mindfulness activities both with your students and when you are alone. Try to find a mindfulness buddy or buddies at school to share ideas and support.

SET UP A MINDFULNESS AREA OR STATION IN OR NEAR YOUR CLASSROOM

Create a place that students can visit when they feel the need to regain their composure, their focus, and/or their sense of well-being. It can be as simple as a chair, headphones, a blanket, and items that act to soothe (a squishy ball, a density column, Wooly Willy, worry beads, a stuffed animal). Talk with students ahead of time about suitable times to use the station and appropriate behavior choices while there.

START EACH CLASS WITH AT LEAST A COUPLE OF MOMENTS OF GUIDED MINDFULNESS

Routinely remind students to put all other concerns on hold and prepare to focus on what is happening here and now. Offer them a moment to breathe deeply, relax, and choose how they will respond to today's class.

1. **Isn't having educators teach mindfulness training rather like asking us to become therapists?**

   Teachers have always served many roles including nurse, counselor, surrogate parent, coach, and others. We teach many things that are therapeutic to help with self-management as well as classroom management. That doesn't make us therapists; it makes us good teachers.

2. **What do you do with a child who doesn't want to participate and disrupts the others?**

   In the movie *Room to Breathe*, the more disruptive students are removed from the classroom during the initial phase of training. Many of them later choose to return when they hear how much the other students like the program. It might be helpful to meet with the disrupting student(s) individually and say something like, "I can see that you are uncomfortable. What can I do to support you?" You can also offer the option of sitting quietly, reading, or just putting their heads down during the practice session. Don't be surprised if some troubled students are reluctant to even close their eyes. Don't push. The purpose of mindfulness is not to elicit compliance but rather to help kids learn a new way to self-manage. It will take more time for some than others.

3. **How much class time can I afford to spend on this add-on activity?**

   First, it is our hope that teachers will not see this as an add-on activity but rather as an aid to help students learn an important lifelong skill. Anecdotal data from prekindergarten to twelfth-grade teachers suggest overwhelming support from those who have integrated mindfulness practices into their class time. They say that they more than gained the time invested in mindfulness back with the added attentiveness of students and the decrease in referrals and discipline problems. Hopefully, it will be your prerogative to establish the amount of time you want to spend. With younger students, you will want to spend less time at each session. With beginners, you will want to spend less time in focusing but probably more time in debriefing. Some teachers say that after initially introducing students to the practice they spend only two or three minutes at the beginning of class to give students a chance to pause, breathe, and focus. After an upsetting event or particularly stressful day, you may want to give yourself and your students a few more minutes to calm yourselves.

4. **What do you say to parents who think we are trying to inject Buddhism or other religious practices into the curriculum?**

We think it is imperative that in introducing mindfulness into classroom practice you also introduce it to the parents and the community as a secular, research-based, neuroscientifically sound practice that has shown extraordinarily positive results in helping students reduce stress, improve self-regulation, and heighten learning. Many schools offer mindfulness training to parents at the same time they are teaching it to students. Once parents experience the nonreligious, medically supported practices, they usually are quite excited about the concept. Know your parents and be cautious about using vocabulary that may trigger hot buttons for them (*Buddhism, Transcendental Meditation, Universal Mind*, etc.).

5. **How are schools paying for extra trainers in the school and/or for teachers to go to training?**

Most of the programs we are familiar with are paid for with grants. Funding possibilities are available from several of the resources listed in the Taking Mindfulness to the Next Level section on the *Thrive* website (www.teachingkidstothrive.com) as well as the usual grant-awarding agencies that support innovative programs. There is a wealth of empirical data supporting these types of programs, so you should have no trouble backing up your proposal with facts.

Also, several of the major corporations and colleges studying the effects of mindfulness training on students are willing to help support your program if you offer them the opportunity to collect data at your school. One way of keeping the cost of your program low is by offering professional development in mindfulness to your teachers through your regular professional development service provider as part of your ongoing teacher training. Be creative. Ask for help. Let your community know what you want to do and why. Share pictures and stories locally to keep support high. Encourage your students to spread the word about what they like about the program.

6. **I'm interested in trying this, but I don't know where to start. What do you suggest?**

Undoubtedly, the best way to start is to begin practicing mindfulness yourself. Familiarize yourself with the exercises and just start practicing. You don't need a trainer or a coach, but it might help to talk with someone who is experienced in mindfulness. Get comfortable with doing it yourself first. Second, make a plan on how you would like to integrate this into your classroom and/or school. Third, meet with your administrators to discuss your plan and make sure they are on board with your ideas. They may ask you to head up an exploratory team for your department or school. Be sure to inform all involved parties about your ideas and your plans. As we suggested earlier, talk to parents about your new program. Communicate your reasons for wanting to implement the new practice and be prepared to back up your plan with research. Next, talk with your students; advise them about procedures and protocols. Then begin. It won't be perfect, you'll make some missteps, and you'll have some naysayers. Just stick with it, learn, grow, and be mindful. We would love to hear from you about how you are doing or with any questions you may have. You can reach us at debbie@debbiesilver.com and dedra@dedrastafford.com, or on Twitter at @tchkids2thrive.

Discussion Questions and Exercises

We encourage you to tweet your responses to @tchkids2thrive.

1. Do a *silent brainstorm* with members of your small group. Everyone takes a pad of sticky notes and begins writing one thought per note. As you write each thought, place it in the center of the table without talking. After about four minutes of writing, still without talking, try as a group to organize the words and concepts written about mindfulness into some kind of order. After about three minutes (or when the group has silently agreed with the organization), begin talking for the first time. Have a discussion on your prior knowledge, experiential background, and questions you still have about using mindfulness in the classroom.

2. Have you tried practicing mindfulness in your personal life? Why or why not?

3. What would be the benefits of having students take a couple of minutes at the beginning of each day or each class period to focus on their breathing and clear their minds?

4. What do you see as the major obstacles to implementing a mindfulness program in your classroom? How could you overcome them?

5. What support do you need to start a mindfulness program in your school or classroom? From administrators? From the community? From your colleagues?

Thrive Skills in Action

ACTIVITY 1.1

The Five-Minute Mini-Meditation

Relax in the classroom, in your bedroom, or just about anywhere with this five-minute mindfulness exercise.

1. Find a quiet spot to sit, lie, or stand. Pick a place where you won't be disturbed.

2. Get in a comfortable position.

3. Rest your hands on your legs or at your sides.

4. Either close your eyes or focus on a single point in front of you.

5. Listen to your breath as you inhale and exhale.

6. Try to focus on your breathing and not what is causing you stress or pain.

7. Breathe in slowly and exhale slowly. That is one count.

8. Continue until you complete about ten counts of breathing.

9. If your mind wanders and you lose count, start again.

10. Open your eyes or shift your focus.

11. Notice how you feel.

12. Were you able to calm yourself even a little?

ACTIVITY 1.2

Musical Drawing

This activity is designed to allow students to experience how outside forces can influence your mood, pace, and feelings. You will need either several songs that vary in tempo and mood or one song that changes tempo and mood throughout.

1. Ensure each student has a piece of paper and a pencil.

2. Ask students to draw anything they want, real or abstract. But they need to keep drawing throughout the activity.

3. Have the music start out slow and relaxing, then have the music change to a fast-paced beat for about thirty seconds, then back to slow and relaxing, then back to fast with high intensity, and then on to peaceful nature sounds.

4. Ask students, "Did your posture change?" "Did the pace of your drawing change?" "Did the strokes become faster or slower?" "Did you change the grip on your pencil?"

5. Ask students why they think you did this activity with them. What does this activity have to do with mindfulness? Guide students into discussions of how the music affected their emotions and body during the activity and even possibly the outcome of the drawing.

6. Ask them how the body, feelings, and emotions are connected.

ACTIVITY 1.3

Blowing Wishes

This is a great activity to practice focus and start out the day with positive thoughts.

The teacher leads the activity with these steps:

Teacher: "Everyone stand and close your eyes."

Teacher: "Think of someone special. It can be a family member, a classmate, or even a stranger you saw on the way to school."

Teacher: "Think of a good wish for that person."

Teacher: "Now picture that wish as a feather."

Have students hold out their hand in front of them as you pass by and put a feather in each student's hand for them to hold (eyes are still closed).

Teacher: "Think about how light the feather is and how easily it can float through the air."

Teacher: "Now see in your mind the special person, and see your wish as the feather. In your mind, blow the wish to the special person."

Teacher: "See the wish (feather) making its way through the clouds and down to the person."

Teacher: "Take a deep breath. How does this make you feel?"

Teacher: "Open your eyes and look at your feather. It is a wish from your teacher . . . a wish for a wonderful day."

ACTIVITY 1.4

It Bugs Me, but I Breathe for Three

This is a great activity to practice letting go of the frustrations we let control our emotions and our day. It combines two activities from *Sesame Street* with a classroom activity. We can help students to connect breathing and thinking to control emotions.

1. Students brainstorm a class list of things that "bug" them (e.g., your mom nagging you to do homework, your little brother getting into your stuff, not being able to do something that is hard like ride a bike or skateboard).

2. Teacher prompt: "What happens when we get upset?"

3. Teacher prompt: "How do we calm down?"

4. Play the "Belly Breathe" song with Elmo, Common, and Colbie Caillat to teach students how to breathe through emotions. Search for "Belly Breathe song" on YouTube or access a link on the *Thrive* website (www.teachingkidstothrive.com).

5. Use the "Breathe, Think, Do" app by *Sesame Street* that teaches children the technique of taking three deep breaths, then thinking of possible alternatives to solve a problem. If you don't have a smart device, there are videos on YouTube that walk through the same process as the app. Just look for "Breathe, Think, Do" on YouTube.

6. Use Activity Sheet 1.1, "It Bugs Me, but I Breathe for Three," found on the *Thrive* website, to walk students through their frustrations and the techniques to cope with them.

ACTIVITY 1.5

Up in the Air

Talk to students about all the things that fill their minds each day. What activities, responsibilities, and stresses do they have from family, from school, from work (older students), and from other areas?

1. Have students brainstorm a list of those daily, weekly, and future stresses.

2. Ask one student volunteer to come to the front of the room.

3. Take a balloon (blown up ahead of time) and write one of the things mentioned on the balloon (e.g., "Homework").

4. Toss the balloon in the air and tell the volunteer it is his job to keep the balloon in the air and under control by gently hitting it to make sure it doesn't touch the ground.

5. Take another balloon, write another thing on it (e.g., "Worry about GPA or college"), and toss it up for the volunteer to also keep going (now he is working with two balloons).

6. Keep adding until you have five or six balloons being bounced in the air, and the volunteer is struggling to keep up.

7. Explain to the students that this is what their minds are like on any given day.

8. Talk to them about the mind's need to be calm and to clear out all the "noise" to let the thoughts, worries, and stresses fall to the floor (cue volunteer to let the balloons drop one by one).

9. Now look at the volunteer and point out how *still* he has become. Tell the students, "Your mind is full of 'noise' daily. It is full of worry, anxiety, stress, and pressure. Your mind is often working on overload. Research in neuroscience suggests that mindfulness strengthens the systems of the brain that are responsible for concentration and decision making. We all need to take time and let the thought balloons of our life fall to the ground as we practice the art of mindfulness."

10. Hold one balloon still in your hand. Ask all students to watch that balloon and focus on that balloon for thirty seconds.

(Continued)

(Continued)

11. Ask students if they were able to focus for thirty seconds. Did their minds wander to other things?

12. Ask students to write their reflections in a journal. How did they identify with the volunteer as he tried to keep the thought balloons in the air? How much "noise" do they deal with on a weekly basis? Do they ever take time to be still with no distractions? Have they practiced? Do they want to learn more?

Access the website **www.teachingkidstothrive.com** to find more classroom-ready activities, author-recommended videos, websites, and other resources.

HELPING STUDENTS WITH THEIR COMMAND AND CONTROL FUNCTIONS

The first and best victory is to conquer self.

—Plato, Greek philosopher

Using mindfulness is one way to help students understand how they can influence the way their brains work. Neuroscientists have tapped into possibly helping all students become better learners through a concerted effort to develop their command and control or *executive function (EF)* skills. EF skills are generally broken down into several subskills, which interact and overlap and are hard to separate from other abilities, but they all act to support the social and emotional skills we examine in this book. Sometimes, it seems our students need work in several areas at once:

●●● WHAT'S WRONG WITH SEAN?

Sean is an enigma to his teacher. Sometimes, in class, he seems oblivious to the teacher's instruction and to the class discussion. He appears to go to "Sean Land" and tune out whatever lesson is being presented. However, he is apt to jump in and make an astute observation or ask the most intuitive question, but frequently, it will happen at an inopportune moment.

(Continued)

(Continued)

©iStockphoto.com/ShaneKato

Getting him to start an assignment he doesn't want to do is like trying to get a nonsleepy three-year-old to go to bed. He has hundreds of delaying tactics ("I can't find my pencil," "I don't know where to start," "I don't feel good," "I'll do it when I get home," "I need to go to the bathroom," "What are they doing out there on the playground?"). He can sit unconcerned and stare at a blank piece of paper for eons, but more likely, he will find a way to disturb or disrupt someone who is trying to work.

Occasionally, Sean does get excited about a particular activity and dives right in. He doesn't plan or think about the project. He starts at full speed and doesn't seem to have an off switch. He pouts when he's asked to pause or stop to do something else. He may sulk and return to "Sean Land" for the rest of the class.

When admonished, Sean always has a reason. "I didn't know you meant I had to do it now." "I promise I did my homework, but someone must have taken it out of my book bag." "I'm not the only one who wasn't paying attention."

The teacher knows that Sean has plenty of ability to do the work in her class, but she's frustrated that he only tries when he wants to, and he seems so uneven in his performance. Even his parents have noticed that he seems a bit immature for his age. They, too, are exasperated. They ask to meet with the teacher and ask her the obvious question, "What's wrong with Sean?"

Being the professional she is, the teacher refrains from answering, "I wish the heck I knew because he is driving me crazy!" ●

Students like Sean who consistently procrastinate, tune out, rationalize, or deny responsibility for their actions can certainly test the tolerance of even the most mindful educator. The story above came from a middle school teacher, but if a few minor details were tweaked, it could have been written by a teacher at any level. It is easy to become exasperated with a learner who appears to be poorly motivated, distracted, inattentive, stalling, not trying, apathetic, careless, or just plain lazy. Instead of labeling or losing patience with students over these common behaviors, learning more about how the brain works can help teachers begin to employ more constructive responses and to recognize opportunities to encourage the growth of our students' EF skills. None of us would expect a six-year-old to be able to write a comprehensive five-paragraph essay. These learners' brains are simply not developed enough. The same frame of mind can be applied to EF skills.

Executive functioning begins to develop in early childhood and continues to mature through early adulthood. We are all using, practicing, and strengthening our EF skills throughout life, but it is important to realize that the ideal time to shape those skills is in adolescence. Mark Bertin (2015) theorizes EF in some may not reach peak performance until around thirty years of age. (Just ask parents who still have their twentysomethings living at home about that.)

Children with delayed EF skills are internally unstructured. The more freedom and flexibility they have, the more likely they are to demonstrate uncontrolled behavior. They can struggle with hypersensitivity to transitions, hyperactivity, lethargy, inattentiveness, impulsivity, and overreaction to minor stressors and challenges. A great deal of current research points out that environmental factors such as poverty, trauma, violence, abnormal stress, drugs, alcohol, and parental neglect can greatly impede the brain's maturation and normal growth of EF. Development of EF skills can also be delayed by learning disabilities, autism, depression, and even poor nutrition. Students diagnosed with attention deficit disorder (ADD) or attention deficit/hyperactivity disorder (ADHD) have deficits in multiple areas of EF and can be as many as three years behind their peers in some aspects of EF maturity (Barkley, Murphy, & Fisher, 2008).

Executive functioning can be wildly disparate among learners who are the same age. When a child is lacking the EF development of others her own age, frustrated parents and teachers often resort to unproductive comments, such as "You are thirteen years old, so start acting like it!" "I don't know why you can't be responsible like

Current research points out that environmental factors such as poverty, trauma, violence, abnormal stress, drugs, alcohol, and parental neglect can greatly impede the brain's maturation and normal growth of executive function.

your classmates." "You are old enough to know better than that."
"Stop acting like a baby." "I don't understand how you can *not*
remember that!" "You obviously aren't trying." "Snap out of it!"

Individual learners can have one set of EF skills that are highly
developed and another set of skills that lag far behind their
classmates. This explains the student who seems incapable of staying
on task for everyday classroom activities but can lose herself into a
state of flow when working on a personally inviting video game or art
project. It sheds light on why a student can demonstrate remarkable
focused attention during customary class practices but has a complete
meltdown when the teacher asks students to get into cooperative
groups. It is why the most academically capable students are often
the ones who have the most difficulty actually getting started on an
assignment. The good news is that all the EF skills can be improved
through positive life experiences and purposeful adult guidance.
The skills can be taught, practiced, and increased for every learner,
especially during school age.

Executive Function: What Is It?

Neurobiologists tell us the brain is composed of three regions (see
Figure 2.1): (1) The **brain stem**, the oldest evolutionary part of the
brain, is responsible for our basic survival needs. When activated, it
sets up the primitive behaviors such as fight, flight, and freeze. This
part of the brain asks, "Am I safe?" (2) The middle part of the brain is
called the **limbic system**. It consists of several interconnected brain
structures including the amygdala and the hippocampus. This part
of the brain processes memories, activates emotions, and asks, "Am
I loved?" It also tells us what is worth remembering and whether or
not to go into self-defense mode. (3) At the top frontal part of the
brain (just behind the forehead) is the most recently evolved brain
region referred to as the **prefrontal cortex**. This region of the brain
controls the executive functions that regulate the other parts of the
brain. It controls self-regulation, working memory, task initiation,
organization and time management, flexibility, emotional regulation,
and focus. It is the "director" part of the brain and has many
responsibilities, such as prioritizing tasks, setting and achieving goals,
filtering distractions, and controlling impulses. This part of the brain
says, "Hmmm, let me think about that." Simply put, EF refers to a set
of brain-based skills required for humans to perform (execute) tasks
effectively and to solve problems.

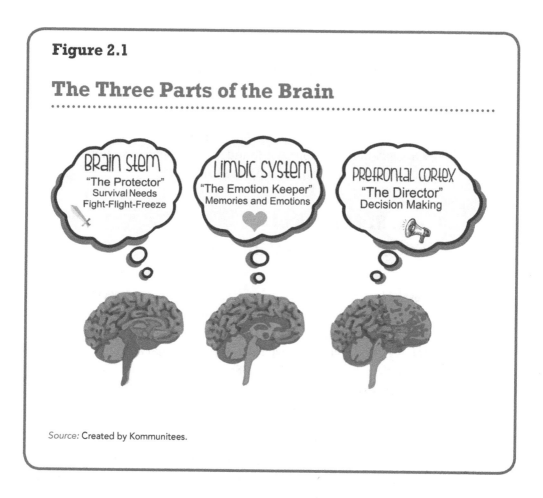

Figure 2.1

The Three Parts of the Brain

Brain Stem
"The Protector"
Survival Needs
Fight-Flight-Freeze

Limbic System
"The Emotion Keeper"
Memories and Emotions

Prefrontal Cortex
"The Director"
Decision Making

Source: Created by Kommunitees.

Siegel and Bryson (2012) refer to the brain as having an upstairs and a downstairs. The downstairs brain includes the brain stem and the limbic region. Instinctive reactions come from the downstairs part of the brain. The upstairs part of the brain is composed of the cerebral cortex and its various parts, and it performs much higher functions such as inhibiting impulse reactions and regulating strong emotions. EF takes place in the upstairs part of the brain.

When learners are operating in the upstairs part of their brains, they are in what is called *relaxed awareness*. They are able to focus on goal attainment, problem solving, knowing right from wrong, seeing other people's viewpoints, and generally overriding the "Am I safe?" and "Am I loved?" messages coming from the downstairs brain. It has proven beneficial for teachers to talk with students about the parts of their brains and how they work. Learners need to understand about causative instinctive behavior so that they are better prepared to control their actions. Asking students to reflect on the question, "Are you in your upstairs brain or your downstairs brain right now?" can often help them realize they have a choice about what they will do. Being aware and controlling their upstairs brain are important first steps to self-regulation (self-control).

You can test your own self-regulation quotient by taking the self-regulation questionnaire found in the Resources section on the *Thrive* website (www.teachingkidstothrive.com).

The Six Skills of Executive Functioning

Researchers vary broadly on the way they identify specific EF skills. While most basically agree on the context of the overall job of the prefrontal cortex, they categorize the skills in many different ways. For our purposes, we focus on the primary EF skill of self-regulation, but we also discuss five other important functions teachers can help build in students. All six EF skills are represented in Figure 2.2.

1. **Self-regulation or self-control.** The terms *self-regulation*, *self-control*, and *executive functioning* are sometimes used interchangeably when researchers/authors describe the ability we have to manage emotions, control impulses, and act in ways to help us counteract adverse instinctive behaviors. For clarity in this book, we address *self-control* and *self-regulation* as basically the same concept of conscious decision making with the caveat that self-regulation generally refers to a more automated response. Self-regulation is a major component of executive function.

2. **Working memory.** From around the age of six months, children's brains accumulate and store experiences. They become able to recall a past event and apply it to a present situation. As they gain more information, children's brains are able to triage and organize it. This skill involves the brain's ability to temporarily hold information while it is being used, organized, or sorted.

3. **Task initiation, organization, and time management.** Learners with this ability are able to (a) initiate action on a task in a timely manner without chronic or excessive

Figure 2.2

The Six Skills of Executive Functioning

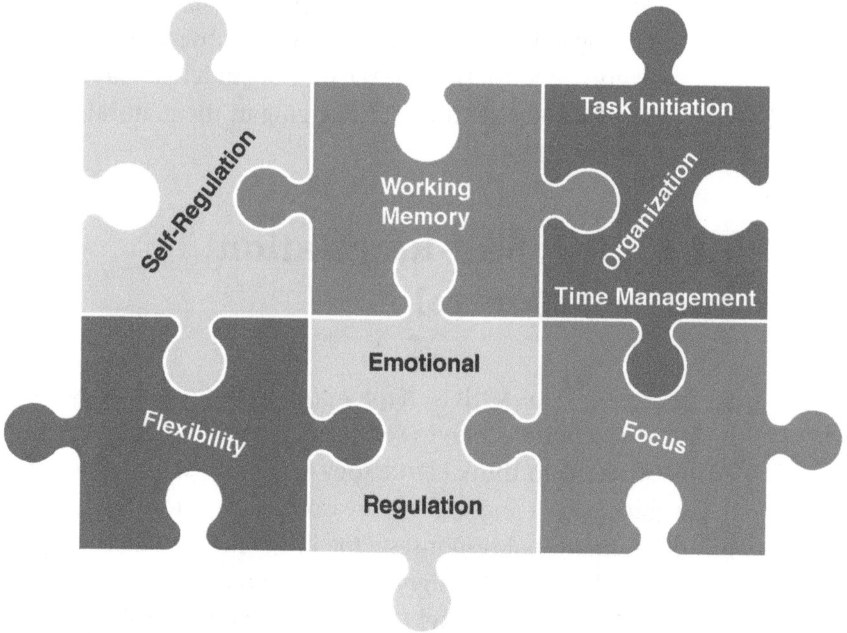

Source: Created by Kommunitees.

procrastination, (b) organize materials and multiple steps, (c) plan by prioritizing tasks, securing materials needed, and putting appropriate systems in place, and (d) manage time by estimating how long something will take and figuring out how to work within time limits.

4. **Flexibility.** Being able to change plans without a major meltdown and being able to make another selection when first choices are not available are evidence of flexibility. Students with this skill are able to alter their plans in face of obstacles, setbacks, new information, or mistakes. They can appropriately adapt to the situation.

5. **Emotional regulation.** Beyond just being consciously aware of their emotions (as in mindfulness), students who have emotional regulation are also able to override their instinctive reactions that may be harmful or disadvantageous to their

purpose. They demonstrate the ability to delay action as well as to monitor, filter, and reassign emotions as needed in the present situation.

6. **Focus.** This skill is also sometimes referred to as *sustained attention*. It allows learners to keep on track despite losing interest and to stay on task despite distractions, boredom, or fatigue. Easy distractibility is often observed in students diagnosed with ADD or ADHD, but students who manifest this difficulty are often just lagging in the maturation of this particular EF skill.

EF Skill 1: Self-Regulation and Self-Control

We began our book with a chapter on mindfulness because we believe it can be a stepping-stone to self-regulation. Self-regulation skills enable students to think before they act. These skills allow them to delay gratification and use their reasoning skills to overpower more primitive emotional responses. One of the most influential researchers on self-regulation and designer of the famous marshmallow experiment, Walter Mischel (2014), talks about "thinking hot and cool" (p. 43). He postulates that when we react with our primitive brain functions from the brain stem and the limbic system, we are using systems that trigger instantaneous action, thus utilizing the "hot" part of our brains (e.g., a fire alarm goes off; students panic and run toward the door).

The prefrontal cortex, however, is the "cool" controlled system that is crucial for future-oriented decisions and self-control (e.g., a fire alarm goes off; students are alert but wait for their teacher to direct them to walk calmly and quietly out of the building). Mischel believes the cool system can be developed and advanced from early childhood through adolescence. He also contends that the development of cool systems is dependent on age, gender, and other factors such as stress.

Most educators are familiar with Mischel's experiment whereby four-year-olds were offered a choice of one marshmallow on the spot or two marshmallows in ten to fifteen minutes if they were able to resist eating the first marshmallow while awaiting the return of the researcher. Students had varying degrees of success, and the researchers studied the strategies used by those who were able to resist

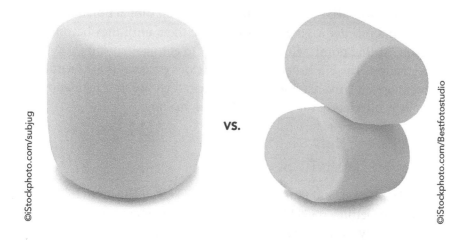

VS.

temptation in order to gain the bonus treat. Countless papers, articles, TED Talks, and YouTube videos are available offering guidance on how to help students move from their hot system of temptation to their cool system of rational thought.

SELF-CONTROL VS. SELF-REGULATION

Mischel believes that self-control requires an individual to make a conscious decision to override the body's hot system and remain in the cool cognitive system. He agrees with Baumeister and Tierney, authors of the *New York Times* best seller *Willpower* (2012), that constantly having to resist temptation can cause a depletion of resources in an individual.

Baumeister and Tierney coined the term *ego depletion* to describe the condition in which an individual no longer has the willpower to consciously remain in the cognitive part of the brain and is, therefore, likely to give in to the reactive demands of his hot system. An example of this would be a dieter who is able to deflect offers of delicious junk food all day long but around 10:00 p.m. gives in and eats a handful of stale tasteless cookies. The dieter's energy level for conscious decision making is depleted from all the day's temptations. This concept also explains why students can make rational decisions for long periods at a time and then suddenly give in to irrational thinking. Stress, fatigue, hunger, and other factors can deplete the body of the resources it needs to operate in the cool part of the brain and avoid judgment errors. Life in general and school in particular offer many hot triggers for students during any given day. Teachers can seek to remove or minimize triggers, but they also need to help students set up plans for action ahead of time and practice saying and performing them until they become a habit. At that point, self-control moves to automaticity and self-regulation. The effort-demanding conscious decision (self-control) becomes a relatively effortless subconscious choice (self-regulation), thereby alleviating the strain of decision making.

USING IF–THEN STATEMENTS AS A HELPFUL TOOL

Shoda, Mischel, and Peak (1990), and later Peter Gollwitzer (1999) and Gabriele Oettingen (2014), determined that in order to help students consistently use the cognitive part of their brains, teachers need to help them automate their conscious choices. When individuals have an automatic self-regulatory implementation plan in place, they are less likely to suffer ego depletion and far more likely to be able to maintain good choices coming from the cool part of the brain. They identify simple but powerful *if–then* plans for helping people deal more effectively with self-control problems—even under difficult circumstances and hot conditions. For the dieter, an *if–then* plan might be "*If* I start to feel hungry between meals, *then* I will drink a glass of water before looking for a snack." The term for these plans is widely referred to as *implementation intentions*.

Mischel (2014) believes that teachers need to show students that they do not have to be the victims of their social and biological histories: "Self-control can help us overcome our vulnerabilities. We cannot always change the things in our lives, but we can always change the way we handle them. Self-control involves more than determination; it requires strategies and insights as well as goals and motivation to make willpower easier to develop and persistence (often called grit) rewarding in its own right" (p. 230). According to Mischel, students need to be aware of their personal triggers so they can develop strategies to inhibit them.

IDENTIFY-PLAN-REHEARSE-ACT ACTIVITY (IMPLEMENTATION INTENTIONS)

Help groups of students or individual students *identify* what their hot-button trigger issues are likely to be and make contingency *plans* ahead of time. They can draw them or write them down. They can *rehearse* them aloud or role-play them with a friend. When learners take *action* to substitute the desired behavior for the instinctive behavior, they can pat themselves on the back.

Examples

If I get bored, **then** I will sit up in my chair straighter, take three deep breaths, and try to think of a question about the presentation.

If I feel myself getting mad, **then** I will pick a Self-Calming Card and do what it says until I feel in control.

If they hand me that first marshmallow, **then** I will push it as far away from me as I can and try to say the alphabet backward to distract myself.

If I get picked last for the team, **then** I will do my very best to make my teammates glad they picked me. ●

Helping students understand how the brain works and how our reactions to triggers can be controlled is an important step in developing and strengthening EF skills. For an easy *if–then* plan, we have created Activity Sheet 2.1, "My If . . . Then Plan," available on the *Thrive* website at www.teachingkidstothrive.com. (You can also visit the *Thrive* website for more on the Self-Calming Card strategy introduced in the examples above.)

Teachers of students with ADHD, ADD, and other challenges have found this identify-plan-rehearse-act activity is extremely helpful in strengthening learners' self-regulation skills. Likewise, some teachers are creating implementation plans for themselves to help them deal with student disruptions, negative colleagues, and other adverse issues.

My If . . . Then Plan

BUILDING SELF-REGULATORY SKILLS WITH STUDENTS

Amy Wang (2015) describes an Oregon State study in which researchers found that children who were guided in self-regulating activities for twenty to thirty minutes twice a week showed improved gains over the school year in their ability to pay attention, follow directions, remember instruction, and regulate their emotions. The biggest gains were among disadvantaged students.

Teachers need to talk regularly with students about executive functions and self-regulation. They can explain these concepts with metaphors,

diagrams, videos, and the like. Students should be encouraged to use the neuroscience terms when offering possible explanations for historical figures and their actions, for choices made by fictional characters in literature, and even with regard to their own actions.

Preschool teachers often help students internalize self-regulation with visual prompts such as handing a student a picture of an ear when it is her turn to listen. For students of any age, teachers can help them exercise self-control by agreeing on private signals that can indicate a need for assistance. The goal is to help learners move toward self-control and, ultimately, self-regulation. It takes time and patience, but frequent practice reinforces the idea of self-regulation.

Educators can utilize games to help students improve their skills. Young children learn better self-control by playing basic games that involve taking turns, strategizing, or learning new things such as reversing the rules to Red Light, Green Light so that red means "go" and green means "stop." Most games are designed to have the participants show at least some degree of self-control, but some specifically target self-regulatory skills.

EF Skill 2: Working Memory

Working memory is like a mental sticky note that keeps essential information in their brains while students attend to tasks. If a teacher reads aloud a math word problem, students have to listen for clues about which operations to perform as well as hold key numbers in memory until they figure out what to do with them. Knowing how working memory operates in conjunction with long-term memory gives teachers the ability to put activities and systems in place that make the most of what we know and understand about the brain. Marilee Sprenger (2015) cites three important areas to consider about working memory:

1. It helps students hold on to information long enough to use it.
2. It plays an important role in concentration and in following directions.
3. Weak memory skills can affect learning at all grade levels and in all content areas.

In this age of easy access to information, many children are not getting a chance to practice developing their working memory. Working memory can be defined as holding and processing new and stored information (Sprenger, 2015). This involves a combination of skills including reading comprehension, retention, drawing on prior knowledge, and synthesizing new information with recalled information in order to determine a correct answer on a test, often within time constraints. Sprenger reminds teachers that we often make the mistake of believing that students who suffer from poor working memory (performing mental math, taking notes during lecture, demonstrating inability to follow directions given verbally) are not listening or paying attention. However, it is more likely that their brains have not practiced using and developing their working memory. Thankfully, this is something teachers can help them with so that they will enjoy greater success with working memory tasks in the future (Sprenger, 2015).

William Klemm, a Texas A&M University professor of neuroscience and author of *Memory Power 101* (2012), thinks this generation's dependency on the Internet for information has made students lazy. He says that when students rely on the Internet for knowledge, they are programming themselves to look for information outside of their heads. When asked to recall information, they just look it up, and they don't remember it as well. Without memorizing some information, it's harder for the brain to acquire new knowledge and skills. It takes longer for the brain to process new information, and students are less likely and slower to ask informed and perceptive questions. He argues the more you know, the more you can make conclusions, and even be creative. All these things have to be done by thinking, and thinking has to be done from what's in your working memory.

Klemm believes in order for working memory to be strengthened, teachers need to help remove distractions including those just before and just after the learning experience so that the brain has a chance to use the newly acquired knowledge for reflection and build new knowledge. For example, using a mindfulness activity prior to learning will minimize distractions and set up optimum learning. Creating a partner "turn and talk" or reflection activity at the end of a lesson will help students process and store information before a distraction causes the learning to be lost. Klemm contends that distractions prohibit the brain from forming long-term memories. He also thinks that multitasking violates everything we know about good memory practices.

Working memory has its limits, but it can be stretched. Since working memory is stored in sounds *and* pictures, we can use both to practice and build this system. Students who play memory games have shown improvement in their attention and working memory skills.

CLASSROOM TIPS

Working Memory

- Work with individual students to help them find the best way to remember things (visual cues, music, mnemonics, etc.).
- Make eye contact with learners when giving them information you want them to remember.
- Keep distractions to a minimum.
- Chunk information (visually or verbally) into logical pieces.
- Use written and graphic reminders whenever possible.
- Have students pause to paraphrase what they read or hear.
- Teach students specific strategies like note-taking, test brain dumps, and use of memory checklists.
- Encourage students to play games that test their memory skills.
- Challenge students to memorize lists of things (states and their capitals, spelling words, countries on a given continent, elements of the periodic table, etc.).
- Visit the Thrive Skills in Action section at the end of this chapter and the *Thrive* website (www.teachingkidstothrive.com) for specific ideas to strengthen working memory.

EF Skill 3: Task Initiation, Organization, and Time Management

TASK INITIATION

Along with a majority of students who struggle in school, many students with high potential suffer an inability to start a task. They seem unable to follow logical steps to complete it. In young children, it manifests as an inability to start the chore or assignment soon after instructions are given. In older students, it is demonstrated by a failure to begin a task in a timely manner and not wait until the last minute. Students with a deficit in task initiation skills are repeatedly unsuccessful in getting started or meeting goals. They often feel overwhelmed by complex problems.

Several factors can contribute to a learner's task initiation challenges. Those pointed out by Dawson and Guare (2009) include the following:

- Students are daunted by the size of the task and fail to recognize that each individual step required is within their ability.

- Having failed in the past, they assume they will fail at new tasks as well.

- Having met criticism in the past, they are averse to risking criticism in the future. This is particularly true of perfectionists.

- Because others have swooped in to help in the past when they encountered an obstacle, they have never learned to overcome obstacles on their own.

HELPING STUDENTS DEVELOP THEIR TASK INITIATION SKILLS

Gollwitzer (1999) postulates that task initiation is often linked to the way a goal is framed. He recommends that goals include "when, where, and in what way" they will be implemented. Much like the *if–then* implementation strategies recommended for self-regulation, determining plans of action for possible goals ahead of time can be of great benefit to students who are challenged by task initiation. Teachers can model and reinforce these concepts for students.

Another way to help students deal with this EF limitation is to pay particular attention to them as they begin the task. If they lack a sense of self-efficacy, we can alter the task in some small way to help them experience competence quickly. It is important to make sure the required task is within the students' grasp and that they just need to put forth the effort to make it happen. Effective teachers ensure that students know that failure is merely temporary and is a logical step toward success. We discuss this concept in depth in Chapters 3, 4, and 5.

Examples of Task Initiation Plans

If I am given a long-term project, **then** I will immediately make a calendar and plan my steps. I will actually do at least one of the steps on the first day of the assignment.

If I have homework, **then** I will start on it at school or on the bus.

If I don't understand the assignment, **then** I will ask for help immediately. ●

CLASSROOM TIPS

Task Initiation

- Help students see the value in the task as it applies to learning and the larger goal.
- Help students break the larger goal into several smaller tasks with due dates.
- Provide visual cues to remind students how and when to get started.
- Work with learners to determine deadlines and cues that are reasonable for them and require realistic effort on their part.
- Encourage students to block out time and purposefully avoid other distractions when beginning a task.

ORGANIZATION

Students who lack organizational skills have difficulty keeping up with where things are (their books, their homework, their phones, etc.), and they generally lack the ability to set a beginning, middle, and end to projects. They forget to bring a pencil to class, to take their assignment notebooks home, and to return signed permission slips to school the next day. An important part of task completion involves the ability to create and maintain systems to keep track of information and materials. Even with young children, it is important to encourage students to think through and plan their actions before they begin a task. Students do not automatically understand the benefit of slowing down and thinking through assignments before they begin. Teachers of all grades need to allocate time for students to ponder about and work out a plan before beginning a task. Appropriate stops can be made in class to provide this opportunity and give feedback on how the students are making headway. In addition, students need to see their teachers model the process of formulating goals, organizing their thoughts, and arranging the setting to promote success before they proceed with a task.

Younger learners fare much better when they are reminded of the rules or protocols before performing a task. Experienced elementary teachers often take a few minutes before moving into

CLASSROOM TIPS

Organization Skills

- Take a picture of the desired finished product and ask students to compare their work with the picture.

- Model rather than just explain expectations.

- At the end of class, instruct students to sort and organize their thoughts.

- Teach students to use graphic organizers to group ideas, plans, and information.

- Have students share their personal organizing techniques and allow individuals to choose the one they like best.

- Encourage students to keep a growth chart to show how their organizing system improves their accountability.

- Focus on one area at a time (e.g., meeting deadlines). Once that system is working smoothly, move on to another trouble spot.

- Help students to visualize the end product.

groups or starting an assignment to go over the expectations. As a result, students are more diligent about following those protocols. Intermediate and secondary teachers who want to encourage EF skills should consider extending those reminders to their students as well. Focus on prioritizing steps by asking students what needs to get done first. Students who are weak in this skill area need more specific and short-term tasks with regular monitoring and feedback. Simply stopping by a student's desk to monitor progress and ask, "So what's your next step?" can help foster these skills.

TIME MANAGEMENT

"Quite frankly, many students have little to no concept of allotted or elapsed time. It's simply too abstract for them, especially when surrounded by digital clocks and devices that constantly remind them of the time or upcoming events with no thought required" (Petlak, 2013). Silver (2005) makes the case

©iStockphoto.com/Sezeryadigar

that 50 percent of learners have an inherent predisposition to be random rather than sequential. Random learners struggle with time management because they lack the so-called internal clock that others have. They consistently underestimate how long it takes to do tasks, and they sometimes get lost in the moment and lose conscious awareness of time.

But all students can improve their time management skills. Petlak (2013) recommends that teachers make time management fun by setting time-based goals, beating past times (or those of competing classrooms), and earning time-related activity rewards for being "time masters." She also offers these suggestions:

- **Countdown Timers:** Timers provide a visual display showing the time remaining for an activity.
- **Marker Clock:** Buy an inexpensive wall clock and use an erasable marker to shade in the chunk of time between the start and finish of an activity.
- **Stopwatch:** With a stopwatch, time students prepping for and cleaning up after activities.
- **Kitchen Timers:** Place inexpensive kitchen timers on each student table to serve as reminders for time remaining on activities.

CLASSROOM TIPS

Time Management

- Have students prioritize their tasks by importance.
- Put the due date on the top of all directions given to students.
- Remove as much clutter as possible from the work area.
- When working in groups, assign one student to be the timekeeper to ensure that tasks are completed on time.
- Before starting an assignment or activity, ask students to estimate how much time will be needed for the task.

EF Skill 4: Flexibility

Some students do not respond well to changes in routine, unexpected events, deviation of plans, or unanticipated results. Any departure from their perceived norms throws them for a loop, sometimes even leading to a major meltdown. They are completely derailed by unforeseen circumstances. The ability to revise plans in the face of obstacles, setbacks, mistakes, or new information is the EF skill called *flexibility*. It relates to having an adaptability to changing conditions. Students with this skill are able to adjust to unexpected changes in routines, deal with disappointments, and manage frustration with a minimum amount of fuss.

Playing children's games with reverse rules as described earlier in this chapter is helpful for building a capacity for flexibility in students. Providing students with a three- or four-minute prewarning cue that an activity is changing is often helpful. For younger children, it is beneficial to show a visual schedule of routines and activities so they can see what is coming next.

EF Skill 5: Emotional Regulation

Emotional regulation (or control) is the ability to manage emotions in order to achieve goals, complete tasks, and choose appropriate behavior. Students sometimes demonstrate an inappropriate lack of emotion, an exaggerated emotion, or a contradictory emotion. For example, the student who explodes when the teacher asks him to put his book bag on the floor is obviously not that angry over a simple request. The reaction is coming from pent-up frustration or rage stemming from something else. This is referred to as *displaced aggression*. The emotional part of the brain seems to hijack the thinking brain. Most of us have experienced the situation of angrily scolding another person while our upstairs brain is whispering, "Stop it. This isn't the right thing to say right now," in the back of our minds. But we are so mad that we temporarily override the thinking brain and do it anyway. This lack of emotional regulation can cause a lot of problems in children as well as adults.

Dawson and Guare (2009) report that in elementary school, children whose ability to manage their emotions is underdeveloped frequently encounter social problems. They have difficulties with sharing, losing games, and not getting their way. Conversely, kids who have good emotional control are the ones who can make compromises, accept winning and losing with grace, and often act as peacemakers.

These authors go on to state that in older students, lack of emotional regulation can bring new challenges including being more susceptible to breakdowns and an inability to handle stress. Because middle-level and high school students work so hard in trying to use their prefrontal cortex to tell the rest of the brain how to behave, they often overload their frontal lobe with demands that interfere with other EF functions such as decision making and working memory. Dawson and Guare (2009) recommend that teachers pay particular attention to ways to minimize stress for students as well as act as emotional coaches for them.

Rather than dismiss or reproach a student's emotional reaction (e.g., "Oh, come on, it's not the end of the world," "You can't possibly feel that way," or "What is wrong with you?"), it is important for educators to hear what students are saying and help them initiate ways to cope. Experts suggest that teachers be active listeners who focus on what the student is trying to communicate. We need to remember that behavior is communication, and the student is trying to let us know something. It is the job of the adult to understand what is behind the emotions and help the learner learn to cope with them in an acceptable way.

Behavior is communication.

Chris Bergstrom (2016) agrees that without techniques to help them cope, emotions can run wild in students, and they end up feeling sad, miserable, and defeated. He recommends utilizing mindfulness as a means to help regulate emotions. Mindfulness strategies can help achieve a state of calm that helps regulate the emotions we feel. "The point is not to totally take away the situations your child is experiencing trouble with, but instead help them learn how to cope, which is a valuable lifelong skill" (Bergstrom, 2016).

It is interesting to note that negative emotions have very little biological reason to persist. Shaina Cavazos (2016) interviewed Lori Desautels, who teaches about brain science to teachers and students in Indianapolis. Desautels says that our bodies rinse and clear negative emotions within ninety seconds. The reason people stay irritated so long is that we keep thinking about it, replaying it, and generating more negative emotions (Cavazos, 2016). Perhaps armed with this knowledge of physiology, students (and their teachers) can learn to take active steps to diminish harmful reactions that deplete them of their positivity.

When students exhibit meltdown behavior with any of the EF skills, the adult must become the surrogate frontal lobe and do the thinking for the children that they are unable to do for themselves in the midst of their frustration. Calmly say to the student, "I see you are upset. Let's see if we can work this out." State the problem and ask the student to help generate solutions. By acting as children's temporary cool zone and working with them to solve the problem, teachers model the strategies students need to internalize for themselves. With practice, they can learn to calm themselves without the intervention of an adult.

EF Skill 6: Focus

Professor of pediatrics at the University of Washington Dimitri Christakis refers to the ability to delay gratification as well as manage time and attention to stay on a task as one's "attentional capacity." He states that it can and should be taught by adults to children (Kamenetz, 2016). Others refer to this same capacity as "sustained attention" or *focus*. Teachers often take notice of this EF skill primarily when it is lacking in students. Learners who seem inattentive, jump from activity to activity, frequently forget things, are easily distracted, and fail to complete assignments or tasks are highly recognizable in a classroom. Too often, these learners are dismissed with the diagnosis of ADD or ADHD, but the jury is still out on whether or not ADD and ADHD are actual hardwiring problems in students' brains or an indicator of weakness in an EF skill that needs to be developed. Either way, there are steps that effective teachers can take to help students who demonstrate difficulty with staying focused.

Getting students to focus is only a problem when they are asked to pay attention to tasks they consider uninteresting or difficult. Sometimes, teachers can alternate preferred tasks with nonpreferred tasks in order to help students maintain concentration on the unappealing ones. In their 2012 book *Willpower*, Baumeister and Tierney argue that employing self-control uses a certain amount of energy. They contend that if students are asked to use too much self-control for too long without a break, they are more likely to falter or fail. An idea for teachers is to create lessons with shorter segments and separate them with some downtime. One teaching method that supports focus is the "Chunk and Chew" strategy (described on the *Thrive* website at www.teachingkidstothrive.com). Chunk and Chew uses ten minutes of teaching followed by two minutes of processing time (either in reflection or in a partner discussion). Another method would be to incorporate brain breaks (described in the Resources section on the *Thrive* website, www.teachingkidstothrive.com) on a regular basis.

Other tips include using a device that shows elapsed time, providing close supervision, and offering incentives for task completion. Reward those with appropriate sustained attention with opportunities for spontaneous, creative play and learning. Siegel and Bryson (2012) maintain that practicing focused attention can actually reshape the brain. They believe that helping learners repeat focusing skills can enhance their long-term ability to control their attention.

Gollwitzer (1999) studied how to enhance students' ability to focus by presenting distractions while they were working. Students who had previously stated their general intention of just ignoring any distractions that came up were not as successful in the experiment as those who had to state exactly how they planned to avoid the distractions, such as "*If* other kids finish early and start talking, *then* I will put in my earplugs and really think about what I am reading." As we discussed earlier, these implementation intention strategies work for an array of EF skills.

What Supporting Executive Function Looks Like in the Classroom

TEACH MNEMONICS

Help students see that using a variety of mnemonic devices is a powerful way to help strengthen memory. Mnemonics can be acronyms, acrostics, or visuals. Most of us have heard of "Please Excuse My Dear Aunt Sally" as a way to remember the order of operations (parentheses, exponents, multiplication, division, addition, subtraction). Allow students to practice this strategy by creating their own mnemonics.

TEACH NOTE-TAKING WITH SKETCHNOTES AND CORNELL NOTES

Sketchnotes is the term that represents purposeful doodling. Students use shapes, crude drawings, connector lines, and text to summarize the lesson as they listen. The visual and creative action makes powerful connections in the brain for some learners. For other learners, the Cornell method can provide a more structured note-taking format. The student divides the paper into two columns

CLASSROOM TIPS

Student Focus

- Make increasing sustained attention a gradual process. Start where learners are comfortable and purposefully raise the limit in incremental steps.

- Make the task interesting. Whenever possible, turn the task into a challenge or game.

- Offer positive feedback for staying on task.

- Periodically poll your students for their attentiveness. In Cando District in Regina, Saskatchewan, Canada, students in Grades 10–12 use a five-point scale where 1 means *hyper,* 5 means *lethargic and not alert,* and 3 means *just right.* In one primary classroom, the teacher asks students to point to pictures of *Winnie-the-Pooh* characters to show how attentive they are: Tigger means they are too distracted to listen. Eeyore means they are lethargic or uninterested. Pooh means they are just right for learning.

- Allow students to choose to stand during instructional time, sit on a large balance ball, make use of bouncy bands on the legs of their desks, or roll a foam cylinder such as a piece of a swim noodle back and forth with their feet.

- Tie pieces of yarn to chair legs so that students can braid the yarn instead of tapping pencils, drumming fingers, or wriggling in their seats.

- Keep impulsive, reactive students apart from one another.

- Be very quick to redirect inappropriate behavior for the benefit of both the transgressor and others in the room.

- Allow students to chew gum (silently) or sip water to stay focused.

- Keep a stock of fidget toys to hand to students who need to drain off some energy so they can better focus on listening or reading.

- When students are sluggish, take them on a walk outside, let them run around the gym, or have them do jumping jacks in the classroom.

and essentially creates notes used to refresh, study, and process information. See the Resources section on the *Thrive* website, www.teachingkidstothrive.com, for more information.

PROVIDE HIGHLIGHTERS TO HELP

Allow students who are struggling with EF skills to use a highlighter to highlight the directions to an assignment or the symbols in a math problem before working the problem.

USE RUBRICS AS A SELF-EVALUATION
TOOL FOR STUDENTS

Using rubrics, students can see where they might have lost focus or prioritized incorrectly. Figure 2.3 is an example that second-grade teacher Sara Lambert uses to help students in a weekly writing assignment. She creates a rubric in the form of an anchor chart with a visual representation as well as "I" statements. As students finish their assignment, they come up and compare their work with the anchor chart to see if they have missed important elements.

HELP STUDENTS MONITOR THEIR ATTENTION

Teachers use self-monitoring checks to help students realize when they are paying attention. Teachers can set timers or use audio from

Figure 2.3

Star of the Week Letter

Source: Created by Sara Lambert.

A.D.D. WareHouse. This audio sounds electronic tones at random intervals. When they hear the tones, the students ask themselves, "Was I paying attention?"

GIVE BRAIN BREAKS IN THE CLASSROOM

Brain breaks are not just for elementary students. There are several easy short activities that can be used in any classroom. Executive functioning is a taxing skill. Students who are still growing EF skills need brain breaks to reset their focus and help with working memory. See the Resources section on the *Thrive* website (www.teachingkidstothrive.com) for great brain breaks for elementary, middle, and high school classrooms.

Frequently Asked Questions ?

1. **Why are we hearing and reading so much about neuroscience these days?**

   New discoveries in neuroscience made possible by evolving technology that allows scientists to see more about what actually happens in the brain have fueled a flurry of interest in brain science. Educators are excited to have an explanation about certain behaviors in students as well as to be given scientifically based information about things they have intuitively felt for years. Expect this current interest to continue as it catches the attention of policy makers, curriculum planners, administrators, counselors, teachers, and parents. Education has trended toward choosing scientifically based programs and interventions for students, and neuroscience has offered a new platform for tools and strategies.

2. **I hear people use the terms *executive functioning* and *self-control* interchangeably. Is that not correct?**

   Self-control is a large part of the job of the prefrontal cortex where executive functioning takes place. However, there are other skills controlled by the same part of the brain and grouped with EF skills. Students can demonstrate an acceptable level of self-control and still lack flexibility, time management skills, and other EF capacities. Students develop differently, and so do their EF skills. Moreover, self-control is a precursor to self-regulation, which is more of an automated response that requires less thinking and effort. Researchers and theorists classify and prioritize EF skills in varying ways, but some of them overlap, and that may be what is causing the confusion.

3. **Are ADD and ADHD actually just EF weaknesses?**

As we mentioned in the chapter, there is an active debate going on about not only the nature of ADD and ADHD but also their very existence. Several states have removed those classifications from their special education screenings, which has frustrated both parents and teachers. Certainly, there are common characteristics between those students labeled with ADD or ADHD and students who exhibit immaturity in the executive functions mentioned in this book. While scientists try to figure out if ADD/ADHD is a chemical imbalance, a genetic predisposition, a hardwiring brain issue, or a delay in EF maturity, we think it is important to focus on what teachers and parents can do to help the students we have with all the resources we have available. EF research has given us hope that all students can grow the skills they need to succeed. It has also helped us reframe what some previously thought of as students who just didn't try hard enough or care enough to do what was asked of them.

4. **How do I find the extra time to work on EF skills along with all the curriculum and other issues I already deal with in my classroom?**

Like all of the chapters in this book, the tips, tools, and strategies we offer about EF skills are intended not to be add-ons, but rather to be ideas about improving good practices. Our belief is that if we can address some of the student challenges up front, we will ultimately free up more class time for both ourselves and our learners. Sometimes, a simple twist on an old idea, a shift in a classroom routine, or a discrete focus on a particular part of an assignment can make all the difference for a learner. We hope you will select some of the ideas in this book to try and let us know about any questions, concerns, or improvements you have.

Discussion Questions and Exercises

We encourage you to tweet your responses to @tchkids2thrive.

1. Whether you believe ADD/ADHD is a genetic condition or simply a sign of delayed EF development, how do you address the challenges of students who exhibit ADD/ADHD-like behaviors in your classroom?

2. Which of the six EF skills are you consciously aware of when planning for your classroom? How does your knowledge of EF skills affect the choices you make for your students?

3. What are your favorite memory boosters to use with students? Are there specific strategies for the age group and the subject(s) you teach that work particularly well? Discuss the benefits you have seen from using the strategies you choose.

4. List your favorite organizational tools for students. Describe the elements of your classroom that help students get and stay organized. Do you intentionally talk with and model organization skills with your learners? Why or why not?

5. Sometimes, teachers complain that students just won't communicate with them. The authors state, "Behavior *is* communication." What does that statement mean to you?

Thrive Skills in Action

ACTIVITY 2.1

Brain Guide for Kids

This activity involves researching the brain and its functions. Students are challenged to work in pairs to discover the parts of the brain, label them, and describe what each part does.

Hook

Neuropsychologists (people who study the brain and its functions) across the United States are struggling to teach kids what the brain does. They have challenged our class to come up with a "Brain Guide for Kids"

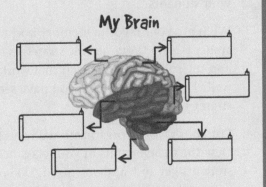

My Brain

that teaches the parts of the brain and what each part does, as well as providing a kid-friendly example of each. We will submit our brain guides for review by the top neuropsychologists in the country. Good luck!

1. Give students Activity Sheet 2.2, "My Brain," found on the *Thrive* website (www.teachingkidstothrive.com).

2. Ask students to first talk about what they know (or think they know) about the brain.

3. Have students work in pairs to research the parts of the brain and label them with the name and the function (citing how they know this to be true).

4. Once they have the brain labeled, have the teams each come up with a method of developing a kid-friendly guide to the brain (e.g., Glogster, PowerPoint, poster, children's book).

5. Ensure each guide has the six major parts of the brain, the functions of each, and a kid-friendly example of the function along with the sources.

6. Invite each team of students to submit their product along with a persuasive letter to the Department of Neuropsychology for review.

ACTIVITY 2.2

Be Your Own Time Manager

Learners often get frustrated when they are told what to do and when. This activity allows the learner to practice prioritizing tasks and planning time to complete tasks.

1. Introduce time management by telling a personal story about how you didn't manage your time well and ran short of time. Ask leading questions about students' own experiences that relate.

Source: Created by Kommunitees.

2. Explain that sometimes we have to plan enough time to get things done or we may run out of time.

3. Discuss how students spend their day once they go home from school: Do they have chores? Homework? Sports practice? What do they like to do? Play video games? Play outside?

4. Point out that there are things we *have* to do and things we *want* to do. We may not like it, but we all have to make time for the have-tos! What if we did the want-tos before the have-tos? What might happen to our time?

5. Ask students, "What are some have-tos? What are some want-tos? How will we ever get them all done if we don't set goals and manage our time?"

6. Say, "Let's see if we are good time managers!" Give students Activity Sheet 2.3, "Time Manager," found on the *Thrive* website (www.teachingkidstothrive.com).

7. Ask students to complete Activity Sheet 2.3 based on things they want and have to do after school.

8. Encourage students to estimate the time each task will take.

9. When they go home, have students do as many tasks as they have time for and record the actual time spent on each task.

(Continued)

(Continued)

10. In the following class period, discuss as a class how the students did at estimating and have them report if they got everything done.

11. Have students complete the reflection section of the chart.

TIME MANAGER

Have to or Want to?

Task	Have to or Want to	Estimated Time	Actual Time

Reflection:
Was my time/estimation correct?

Was it easier to prioritize once I labeled activities "Have to or Want to"?

How can I use this strategy in the future?

ACTIVITY 2.3

What Will You Take With You?

Work with your class to practice organization, planning, and flexible thinking with a simple activity called *What Will You Take With You?* Bring in a suitcase. Tell your students that you are going on a trip to the lake or to your grandma's house. Brainstorm possible activities to do on the trip and then tell them that you have to make a plan for what to take. Students will write down or tell you possible items to pack. Some children will add details to other students' items.

Source: **Created by Kommunitees.**

To extend this activity, say, "Now, if we changed our mind and decided to go to Iceland or Egypt instead, what would we need to take out of the suitcase, and what would we need to add?" You can easily extend this activity into a class story starter or math work problem.

ACTIVITY 2.4

What Is This?

This activity is an exercise focused on flexible thinking and writing.

Source: Created by Kommunitees.

- Set out three to five ordinary objects.

- Ask students to study the items and then select one object.

- Place students in small groups of three to five based on the items they selected.

- Have students brainstorm different things that this item could be (silly, imaginative, or real). This allows students to see everyday items in different ways.

- Send students back to their desks and have them use the item and one or more of the brainstorm uses for this item to create one of the following:

  o A story where one day they found a ___ from another planet

  o A cartoon showing how this item can be used differently

  o A persuasive story or commercial on how this item can be used

ACTIVITY 2.5

My Name Is, and I Like to _____

There are several variations on the name game. But each allows students to use their working memory while having fun. We have included one version here:

- The first person says, "My name is, and I like to _____ (insert hobby and act out a motion from that hobby)."

Working Memory

Source: Created by Kommunitees.

- The rest of the group then says, "(Person's name) likes to (hobby)" and acts out the motion. For example, "My name is Tyler, and I like to fish (acts out casting a reel)."

- The next person repeats the process. For example, "My name is Tanner, and I like to play guitar (acts out air guitar motion)."

- The rest of the group then says that person's name, hobby, and motion and then moves on to the first person's information. For example, "Tanner likes to play guitar (air guitar motion). Tyler likes to fish (casting reel)."

- This continues until the last person goes, at which point the entire group calls out the last person's info and moves along through the whole group and repeats everyone's information.

ACTIVITY 2.6

Bandleader

This game practices self-control and flexible thinking. Kids play musical instruments (like maracas and bells or even pretend instruments). When the bandleader waves her hands fast, students increase their tempo; when her hands move slowly, students reduce their tempo. Then reverse the cues: Kids play faster when the bandleader moves her hands slowly and play slowly when she moves her hands quickly. Students can take turns being the bandleader.

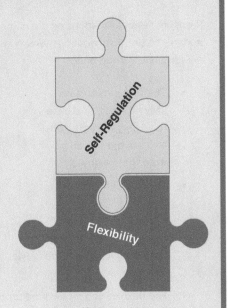

Source: **Created by Kommunitees.**

Access the website **www.teachingkidstothrive.com** to find more classroom-ready activities, author-recommended videos, websites, and other resources.

CREATING STUDENT AGENCY THROUGH SELF-EFFICACY AND GROWTH MINDSET

All of old. Nothing else ever. Ever tried. Ever failed. No matter. Try again. Fail again. Fail better.

—Samuel Beckett

●●● "I THINK I CAN. I THINK I CAN" AND AGENCY

When recalling the familiar children's story *The Little Engine That Could* (Piper, 1930), most people remember the famous line "I think I can. I think I can." Some use that phrase as a model for positive thinking. And while it is true that the little engine needed positive thinking, something deeper was going on. The little engine had a resolute belief that she really could pull those heavily loaded cars of toys over the mountain. She had a profound conviction that if she exerted enough effort, she could accomplish this major feat. If she had not first believed

(Continued)

(Continued)

©iStockphoto.com/Balakleypb

she could actually do it, it is doubtful she ever would have been able to summon the amount of effort it took to accomplish her task. The little engine had *self-efficacy* (the learner's belief that she has the skills it takes to reach a goal).

It should also be noted that the little engine had a plan of action. She assessed the problem, thought about what skills she possessed, and devised a means to achieve her goal (putting her self-efficacy into action).

On the way down the other side of the mountain, the little engine fortified her assuredness with the self-message "I thought I could. I thought I could" (buttressing her self-efficacy by reflecting on what worked and what did not).

The little engine also evidenced a *growth mindset* (a frame of mind that values effort and learning from mistakes). The little engine did not succeed on her first try, but she was willing to keep working and make incremental progress.

Having self-efficacy, planning and taking action, reflecting on learning, and having a growth mindset are all instrumental to long-term student success. Researchers refer to this composite set of essential skills as *agency*.

While uplifting message posters, T-shirts, cheers, and mantras in the classroom can certainly reinforce positive belief systems, they need to be undergirded with an intrinsically held confidence of the learner and a plan of action—*student agency*. Not only did the little engine "think she could," she acted with what we might refer to as "little engine agency." ●

Agency is what allows students to take an active role in shaping their future, rather than being solely influenced by their circumstances (Bandura, 2006). Student agency includes a capacity for self-efficacy but also requires the intentional forethought to set a course of action and adjust it as needed to fulfill one's goal (Bandura, 2001). In writing about this very important concept, educators and researchers at the University of Chicago stated, "This definition of agency acknowledges that external factors form very real constraints, and also that people have the will and the power to influence external factors and can make choices about how to respond to constraints" (Nagaoka, Farrington, Ehrlich, & Heath, 2015, p. 14). In other words, students can be empowered to Thrive through guidance on how to control those aspects of their lives they can change.

A Harvard study, sponsored by the Raikes Foundation, suggests that *student agency* may be as critical to outcomes of schooling as basic academic skills (Vander Ark, 2015). In this chapter, we explore two dynamic components of student agency: self-efficacy and growth mindset. A student's value system is also associated with his sense of agency, and we examine that proficiency in Chapter 7.

Self-Efficacy: What Is It?

"Efficacy beliefs influence how people feel, think, motivate themselves, and behave" (Bandura, 1993, p. 118). Students with a strong sense of self-efficacy will work harder, try longer, overcome greater obstacles, and bounce back more quickly from setbacks than their less self-efficacious peers. Students with self-efficacy are more likely to engage in tasks they feel confident in completing successfully and tend to withdraw from tasks for which they lack such confidence.

Self-efficacy affects

- The choices we make
- The effort we put forth (how hard we try)
- Our perseverance (how long we persist when we confront obstacles)
- Our resilience (how quickly we recover from failure or setbacks) (Silver, 2012)●

HOW CAN STUDENTS
EXPAND SELF-EFFICACY?

Bandura (1985) describes four chief ways he thinks students gain self-efficacy:

1. **Mastery of learning experiences.** Providing opportunities for genuine competency and a sense of earned accomplishment is a strong way to boost students' self-efficacy. Using carefully designed lesson strategies that stretch students' abilities is also an excellent way to structure and reinforce it.

2. **Vicarious experiences.** Observing or reading about more accomplished peers or role models with whom they can relate is a secondary way for students to add to feelings of self-efficacy.

3. **Verbal persuasion.** Though generally not as effective as the first two methods, providing guidance and feedback can boost students' sense of control.

4. **Physical and emotional states.** Each of these can influence perceptions both positively and negatively. Emotions are formidable and can have a spiraling effect. In maintaining a stress-free classroom, a teacher can help students learn to regulate their moods (e.g., mindfulness). Teachers can also encourage good health habits in their students.

Annie Murphy Paul (2013) contends that a feeling of hopefulness can lead students to try harder and persist longer if it is paired with practical plans for achieving their goals. Together with a teacher, they formulate a plan ahead of time for how they will proceed when (and if) their original plans don't work out as expected. This implementation planning (as discussed in Chapter 2) is a valuable strategy for students who are easily discouraged or hesitant to try new things.

Self-Efficacy: What Is It Not?
(Learned Helplessness)

A learner with little or no self-efficacy often manifests *learned helplessness*. We sometimes think of these students as Eeyore, the gloomy little donkey from the *Winnie-the-Pooh* stories. Students with Eeyore-like characteristics are generally passive pessimists who consistently evidence a victim mentality. They believe they have no power over what goes on around them, and nothing they do contributes to their success or lack of it. In 1965, Martin Seligman and Steven Maier (see Seligman, 1990) did experiments at the University of Pennsylvania, which led them to originate the term *learned helplessness*. In experiments with dogs, they showed that they could influence dogs to behave in a powerless manner and, therefore, proved the dogs' helplessness was learned. They went on to conclude that helplessness in students is generally learned behavior and can be *un*learned under the purposeful intentional attention of educators (Seligman, 1975).

In her book *Fall Down 7 Times, Get Up 8*, Silver (2012) identifies several intentional ways teachers and parents can help students *un*learn their helpless dispositions:

> Self-efficacy is bolstered when a student achieves something previously thought unattainable. Overcoming initial failure is a powerful incentive for further pursuits. We should provide students with numerous examples of ordinary people who have become extraordinary by overcoming failure repeatedly. We ought to model for them how to learn from missteps and how to stay true to their goals. We have to help students understand that their efforts and their choices make a tremendous difference in outcomes. (pp. 4–5)

On the next page are some suggestions for working with students who lack self-efficacy.

In addition to implementing these tips to enhance self-efficacy, try to avoid certain traditional practices that tend to diminish self-efficacy such as placing too much emphasis on direct instruction or comparing students with each other. Instead, try using instructional approaches like the workshop model, project-based learning, and inquiry-based instruction. These styles are focused on direct experience and lend themselves to a responsive teaching model that is more student centered.

Aim for the Zone of Proximal Development (ZPD)

Silver (2012), Tomlinson (2001), Weiner (1980), and others advise that self-efficacy is optimized when students are asked to work

CLASSROOM TIPS

Enhancing Self-Efficacy

....

1. Help students understand that everyone has problems, fears, failures, and self-doubt. Share stories about people like those who have overcome similar or even harsher circumstances.

2. Help learners attribute their success or lack of it to internal rather than external causes and show them how they have power over the results.

3. Treat students' successes as though they are normal, not an isolated example or a fluke.

4. Help learners seek alternate paths to success when they encounter a roadblock or setback.

5. Help students learn the difference between hard work and strategic effort.

6. Continually reinforce the idea that the students can work on things within their control, like effort and choices, and they can always control those parts of their lives.

7. Concentrate on improvement rather than on a finite goal. Give frequent feedback on progress towards the goal.

8. Keep the learner operating in the zone of proximal development (ZPD). Tasks that are too easy or too difficult will squash motivation.

9. Help students understand that intelligence and talent are not permanent entities. They can be incrementally improved in everyone.

10. Use feedback that is specific, constructive, and task specific. (Silver, 2012, pp. 61–64)

within their *zone of proximal development* (ZPD; see Figure 3.1). Lev Vygotsky (1980) developed his theory that students Thrive in the sweet spot of engagement between what they can do easily without help and what challenges their present capabilities. It is important for teachers to regulate tasks and offer needed assistance (when necessary) so that an activity is not so difficult the student will lose interest or confidence.

Working within a student's ZPD (where she is pushed but not overwhelmed) is a major key to building self-efficacy and—eventually—student agency. By understanding what students are able to achieve alone as well as what they are able to achieve with assistance from an adult, educators can develop plans to teach skills in the most effective manner, gradually encouraging students to perform tasks independently. This process is referred to as *scaffolding*, which is the way in which an adult helps the child

Figure 3.1

Zone of Proximal Development

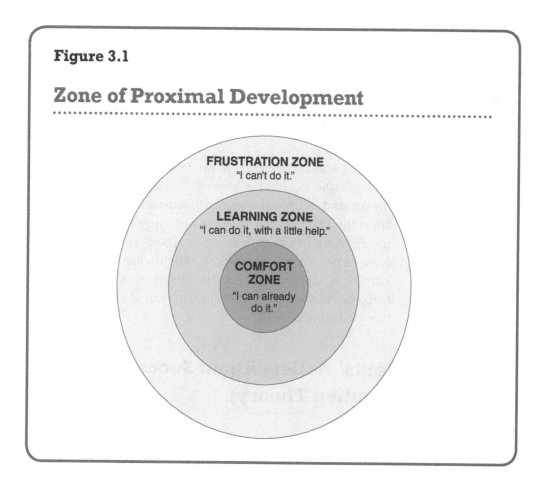

learner move incrementally from not yet being able to perform a task to being able to do so without help.

As teachers, we have all seen each of these children in our classrooms:

- Learners who are operating in the **Comfort Zone** are students who complete the independent assignment while the teacher is still introducing the lesson. They are unmotivated and often bored in class. Children who are always operating in this zone never learn what challenge feels like. When they reach the inevitable place where learning is no longer comfortable or easy, they often experience diminished self-efficacy and an inability to move forward.

- Learners who are operating in the **Learning Zone (Vygotsky's ZPD)** are students who have that lightbulb moment in class. They struggle, but it is a good struggle. The teacher is there to act as a facilitator and help them *right the course* as they learn. They are engaged, on task, and after a little success eager to try the next problem or challenge on their own. The new information is resonating, and they are applying it in ways that are meaningful while gaining confidence with each new step. All children, despite their ability level, deserve to be working in their Learning Zone. This experience is what fuels the fire of learning and propels them to the next challenge.

- Learners who are operating in the **Frustration Zone** are students who feel like the pace of the classroom is too fast or the demands are too stringent. Students around them seem to know the answers while they are still struggling to understand the question. In a classroom setting, these children are often *carried along* by teachers or other students, and no real learning is happening. These students often exhibit learned helplessness and simply stop engaging out of frustration or fear of looking dumb.

Students' Beliefs About Success (Attribution Theory)

One of the major considerations in determining student self-efficacy and student agency is how learners view their success or their lack of it. Do they attribute the result to external factors such as the difficulty of the task, an innate ability, talent, or luck? Or do they attribute the result to the amount of effort they did or did not put in? When people attribute their task success or failure to factors that are external, they are essentially giving away their power. They say things like this:

"Oh, I aced that test because it was easy."

"Well, if I had a better teacher, I would not have missed all those problems."

"Of course I didn't do well on that project. I'm not an artist!"

"That tryout was a piece of cake. I've always been good at this."

"Well, yeah, if my mom helped me with my homework, I might make good grades, too."

"I did well in the game because I'm lucky enough to have athletics in my genes."

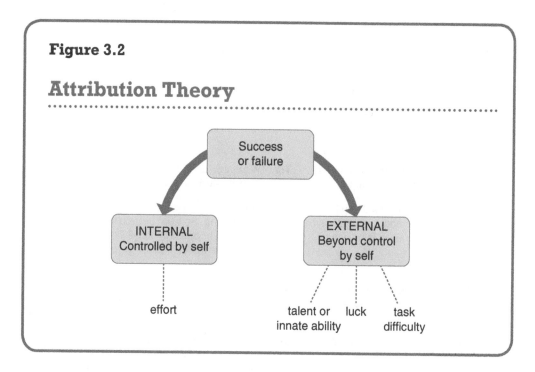

Figure 3.2

Attribution Theory

Success or failure

INTERNAL
Controlled by self

EXTERNAL
Beyond control
by self

effort

talent or   luck   task
innate ability   difficulty

As long as students can point to external causes for their success or lack of it, they can deny their own responsibility for making good choices and putting in the amount of required effort. They can remain in a state of learned helplessness. If, however, students are taught to ascribe results (positive or negative) largely to their effort and their choices, they assume control over their destiny and develop self-efficacy. Attribution theory (see Figure 3.2) has been significant in shaping its successor, growth mindset.

USING ATTRIBUTION THEORY
TO BUILD STUDENT AGENCY

In order to reinforce self-efficacy, teachers who are attentive to attribution theory make changes in the way they give feedback. Figure 3.3 shows some examples of small but very significant changes in wording that put the learner back in control.

Growth vs. Fixed Mindsets

Growth Mindset (Incremental Theory): A set of beliefs that suggest one can grow and develop intelligence and skills needed for success. People with a growth mindset focus on how they can get better.

Figure 3.3

Build Self-Efficacy With Words

FROM "Wow, you aced the test! You are so smart!" **TO** "Wow, you aced the test! All your extra effort to study certainly paid off!"

FROM "I don't want you to feel bad about losing. Maybe this sport is not your thing." **TO** "Nobody likes to lose. That's not a good feeling. So what did you learn from what happened today? What can you do to get the results you want next time?"

FROM "Count yourself lucky to be so talented. You are so blessed." **TO** "It is obvious that you care a great deal about your craft. Tell me how you have managed to make such progress."

FROM "Don't worry about your grade on the project. That was a hard assignment." **TO** "It looks like you are disappointed in your score on that project. Let's talk about some of the choices you made that left you in this position."

FROM "Oh, look how fast you finished. I guess this task was too easy for you." **TO** "You are already through? You must have been really prepared and focused."

Fixed Mindset (Entity Theory): A set of beliefs that suggest a person has a predetermined amount of intelligence, talents, or skills. People with a fixed mindset focus on how they look compared to others.

Carol Dweck, who began her career as an attribution theorist, took her research one step further to develop one of the most influential theories in current education, *mindset theory*. Mindsets are a group of beliefs and attitudes about oneself, the external world, and the interaction between the two. They are the filters through which individuals process everyday experiences. Mindsets are an outgrowth of self-efficacy and a subset of student agency. Though mindsets are malleable, they tend to persist until they are disrupted and replaced with a different attitude or belief.

Growth Mindset/Fixed Mindset Preassessment

This is an activity to get a quick overview of students' beliefs regarding growth mindset. The teacher stands in front of a line of students who face her standing one behind the other. As she reads each statement, students can do one of the following:

- Step to their right to indicate "I agree"

- Step to their left to indicate "I disagree"

- Stay in the line to indicate "I am not sure"

The teacher notes the choices and asks the students to step back in line (or remain in line) to listen to the next statement.

Sample Statements:

1. It is actually possible to get smarter.

2. Once a failure, always a failure.

3. Some kids are born smarter than others.

4. If you can't sing by now, you will never be able to.

5. Some people have all the luck.

6. Working hard is for people who are not gifted or talented.

7. If I set my mind to something, I can usually make it happen.

8. The smartest kids make the best grades.

9. Making a mistake means you do not know what you are doing.

10. Real pros are those who no longer make mistakes.

A student's mindset about whether she can or cannot learn has a direct effect on her academic perseverance. Our learners need a growth mindset in order to have agency. Students also need to understand that struggle is part of learning and that it is ultimately a worthwhile endeavor. When students hold a fixed mindset, they try to circumvent challenge and struggle as a way to avoid failure, and too often they are overly concerned with others seeing them struggle or fail (Farrington et al., 2012). Students with a strong growth mindset can struggle, fail, and face challenges while working toward a long-term goal more successfully than students who have a fixed mindset (Dweck, Walton, & Cohen, 2011).

We have observed both struggling and highly accomplished students deny the fact that they tried hard or put in a lot of effort. They seem to believe that trying hard is evidence that they are not as talented or as gifted as others. This belief is one indication of a fixed mindset. They need "plausible deniability" for coming up short, so they tell everyone (including themselves) that the task was unworthy of their effort. However, students with a growth mindset understand that even geniuses have to work very hard for their achievements, and they feel gratification in striving for their goals.

Classrooms that focus on productive effort more than on finished products help students feel they have more agency. Teachers who value valiant attempts, risk taking, and perseverance more than perfection also provide a place for students to feel safe about taking control of their learning. In such classrooms, failure is seen as an event, not an outcome. Failure can even be celebrated! For a fun example of this, see the *Meet the Robinsons* video clip in the Resources section on the *Thrive* website (www.teachingkidstothrive.com).

Effective teachers create a classroom environment that values learning as a journey and requires effort, choice, and reflection. They promote and grow learners who have control over their own experiences. We suggest making it possible for students to "fail forward." If students fail a quiz or a test, consider allowing them the option of completing a reflection sheet and attaching it to the failed assessment to gain a chance to retake the test (or a similar version) to raise the grade. Reflection question possibilities include (1) When you finished the test, how did you think you did? (2) Explain how you prepared for the test. Be specific. (3) If you got another chance to take this test, what would you do differently? Why? (4) What have you learned from this experience? See Activity Sheet 3.1, "Redo Request," on the *Thrive* website (www.teachingkidstothrive.com).

How Do We Help Students Develop Growth Mindsets?

Mindsets are hard to shift and shape, and like all new habits, shifting to a growth-oriented mindset takes practice and rehearsal. As discussed in Chapter 2, a good starting point is for teachers to make the time to teach students about the basic physiology of the brain and explain how it works. Students can understand that exercising the brain will help them become better learners. Offering challenges that stretch students in a safe environment is one way to reinforce how people learn differently and at varying rates. We offer several ideas for teaching about the brain in the Resources section on the *Thrive* website (www.teachingkidstothrive.com) and in the Thrive Skills in Action section at the end of Chapter 2.

It bears noting that teaching growth mindsets is a relatively new concept in education. Currently, educators are trying new ideas, many are writing about it, and a few are trying to find ways to assess it (we hope they proceed very carefully with that). There are some problems in schools that profess to be focused on growth mindset but still maintain routines and policies that are extremely fixed. There are teachers who claim to be committed to growth mindset but conduct their classrooms like autocrats and still praise kids for being smart and talented and compliant. As with all unfamiliar territories, there is always room for—pardon the pun—growth. Teacher and author of the blog *The Accidental English Teacher* Cheryl Mizerny (2015) writes about some of these problems, but she sums it up with what she likes about growth mindset:

What Is Good About Growth Mindset Instruction

1. **It is not summed up by a grade.** Teachers tell students they should grow from their mistakes. Rather than mark an *F* on an assignment and dismiss the student, the teacher uses something like "Not there yet" and helps the learner work to complete the task.

2. **It is not a now-or-never experience.** Teachers revisit ideas and concepts to make sure that students are making progress toward their goals.

3. **It is not a race to the finish.** Teachers encourage collaboration and inquiry rather than speed and competition. The goal is for growth rather than perfection.

4. **It is not about intimidation.** Teachers create safe classrooms where students are encouraged to try new things, test new ideas, and understand that everyone's journey is important.

5. **It does not foster lazy assessment practices.** Teachers do not just grade a myriad of assignments, then average the scores for an end-of-the-period mark. They give regular constructive feedback throughout the learning process as they guide students to mastery toward the end. ●

●●● TEACHERS AT LENOX ACADEMY FOR GIFTED MIDDLE SCHOOL STUDENTS DON'T USE THE TERM *GIFTED*

Lenox Academy, located in the heart of Brooklyn, New York, offers an academically accelerated program for middle school students in Grades 6–8. While the overwhelming majority of the school's students exceed New York state standards in English language arts and mathematics, a deeper analysis reveals a disturbing trend. In 2011, the school discovered that as the curriculum became more challenging over the course of middle school, many of its high-achieving students retreated from putting forth the effort needed to Thrive. The result was that academic performance actually declined in sixth, seventh, and eighth grades for a large number of students.

In 2011, the school embarked on a growth mindset program, *Brainology*, in the hopes of changing the culture of the school to one that focuses on growth mindset. "Kids no longer hear 'You're so smart!' or 'Brilliant!' Rather, teachers praise students for their focus and determination. 'You must have worked really hard!' or 'To have performed this well, you must have put out a lot of effort'" (Smith, 2014).

Teachers even shy away from using the term *gifted* to describe their students or their school, even though it is part of their official name, Lenox Academy for Gifted Middle School Students. They want to focus instead on the effort and strategies students use to make progress. From 2011 to 2014, not only did Lenox Academy change its general focus to one that values process over product, but its students also raised their test scores by ten to fifteen points (Smith, 2014). ●

While self-efficacy, growth mindset, and student agency do not provide a panacea of solutions for every academic and social-emotional challenge in our schools, they do provide promising avenues for improving the way we can help learners master habits and skills that will serve them in whatever future paths they choose. The ideas behind them are based on strong empirical data, and so far, the anecdotal evidence of their success has been overwhelming.

What Supporting Self-Efficacy and Growth Mindset Looks Like in the Classroom

Teachers emphasize *how to think* and how to learn over *what to think* and what to learn. Instead of always questioning to see if students know the "right" answer, the teacher uses probing to push students to think about their learning. Questions like "How did you reach that conclusion?" "What is another possible answer?" and "Walk me through your process" help to deepen student learning and build growth mindset.

Real learning is messy and not easy. A supportive learning classroom emphasizes effort, practice, and determination. By witnessing how their classroom community honors and appreciates learning, students will start to realize learning is not *just* about getting the right answer; it is about understanding *how to get* the right answer.

TEACHERS MAKE SURE ALL LEARNERS GET A CHANCE TO THINK

Teachers do not readily give away "the answer." They provide students with time and support to grapple with the problems. They encourage learners to use the problem-solving techniques they already know and are cautious about jumping in too quickly with an unneeded assist. They maximize wait time for every learner.

TEACHERS MAXIMIZE FORMATIVE ASSESSMENT

The classroom culture makes it acceptable to struggle and to fail as one strives for mastery. Teachers don't grade every single assignment. They rely on mostly formative assessment, and they teach students to take risks in their learning.

TEACHERS VALUE AND MODEL RISK TAKING

Teachers model risk taking by attempting things that are new to them in front of students. Instead of saying, "Oh, I can't do this," they say, "Okay, that didn't work. I see now where my mistake was. Let me try something else."

Learning is not just about getting the right answer; it is about understanding how to get the right answer.

TEACHERS INCORPORATE THE POWER OF *YET* WITH STUDENTS

The teacher makes it a habit to answer every student "I can't" statement with the word *yet*. For example, a student says he can't do a math problem. The teacher responds, "You can't do the math *yet*. You've got lots of time to figure this out."

TEACHERS TURN MISTAKES INTO LEARNING OPPORTUNITIES

Whenever students stumble, teachers ask them, "So what did you learn from what just happened?" "What will you do differently next time?" Teachers help their students see the inherent value in making mistakes as long as they learn from them.

TEACHERS NORMALIZE THE STRUGGLE

Students are taught the value of the struggle. Praise isn't heaped on them for being the first, the fastest, or even the best. The focus of the class is on learning and for every learner to get a little better than she was the time before. Teachers focus feedback on things learners can control and refrain from making judgment calls that serve to excuse or rationalize failure or reinforce feelings of entitlement.

 Frequently Asked Questions

1. **I like the idea of not overly praising kids, but I have some students who expect it, and I'm talking about my high fliers. What do I do with these overachievers who are used to praise?**

   It is true that we as a collective society have been guilty of praising kids so much that many have become dependent on it for their sense of well-being. We know that long term this does nothing to help them become self-fulfilled independent thinkers. It will not happen overnight, but we can begin by tapering off the praise and substituting it with feedback that genuinely helps learners get better. We can turn their need for attention into personal reflection by asking them how they feel about their work. For students who have easy success and want us to brag on them for finishing work early with almost no effort, we need to sincerely apologize to them for wasting their time and direct their attention to something more challenging.

2. **My school requires me to give grades. How can I promote a growth mindset in my classroom and then turn around and do something with a fixed mindset like giving scores?**

Even if you are required to turn in a final grade, it may be that you can use more alternative assessments, in which you give students a choice about the way they are assessed (an oral presentation, a PowerPoint presentation, a written exam, a demonstration, a debate, a letter written to the editor, etc.). As long as you make sure that each assessment choice clearly demonstrates mastery of the curriculum content, there should be no problem with differentiating assessments. On a daily basis, you probably want to do a lot more formative assessment and give the students feedback rather than giving a grade or score. It is all about growth. So when you are teaching a new skill rather than grading their first effort, it is far better to let your students learn from their mistakes and try the task again (and again, and again, if necessary). Formative assessment takes the pressure off your praise-oriented how-can-I-make-a-perfect-score obsessives as well as your oh-no-I-can't-ever-pass-a-test strugglers. In life, everyone has to pass tests of some kind or another, but life is usually a little more forgiving of first attempts than classrooms. We need to turn that around.

3. **Can you have a growth mindset about some things and a fixed mindset about others?**

Definitely yes. Much like self-efficacy, a growth mindset is specific to certain tasks or areas of one's life. It is not unusual to have a growth mindset about school work and a fixed mindset about participating in sports. A student can have a growth mindset about math and science and a fixed mindset about reading and language. Even people we know with growth mindset in most areas of their lives sometimes surprise us with a sudden attack of fixed mindset thinking. It is the same with our students. Sometimes they manifest what appears to be an irrational fear or worry over a particular task or situation. Following the incremental steps for ZPD, helping students focus on the things they can control and offering support and guidance work well to help students move from a fixed mindset to a growth mindset in almost any situation.

4. **Are researchers saying that helping all students develop agency will help close the achievement gap?**

Helping students develop personal efficacy as well as a growth mindset is a huge step toward empowering all students to be lifelong learners and self-advocates, but there are other factors involved. Something we do not address in this book is the concept of *integrated identity* because it generally does not fall within the scope of a classroom teacher's control. An integrated identity means that students are able rather smoothly to transfer their agency from school to the other facets of their lives. While having agency equips students to make good choices and take positive action, their ability to successfully pursue a desired path can be limited by financial resources, parental support, community norms, and any number of external factors outside of school that differ from student to student. For some kids, the support and encouragement they get at school are the opposite of what they face when they get home. While researchers routinely agree that helping students have agency is an excellent idea, they understand that inequitable factors outside the school setting still influence the achievement gap. As educators, we have to do the things we can do in the classroom to help our students have a fighting chance to have successful lives. In our many years in education, we have not seen an educational strategy as promising as targeting social and emotional learning (SEL) skills in general (and bolstering student agency in particular) to help close the achievement gap.

Discussion Questions and Exercises

We encourage you to tweet your responses to @tchkids2thrive.

1. Describe a scenario in which you were asked to perform a task far beyond your existing ability level and no scaffolding was provided. How did you respond to the challenge? What happened to your self-efficacy?

2. What is the difference between scaffolding for learners and "dumbing down the curriculum"? Do you think parents and the general population understand the difference? Explain.

3. What kind of praise do you typically give students who are extremely bright or talented? Has new research on mindsets persuaded you to alter your praise statements? Explain why or why not.

4. Do you teach any students who have to act differently outside of your classroom? (For example, in his neighborhood, a boy cannot let people know he's intelligent and interested in learning, or he will be ridiculed.) How do you help the learner who has to maintain two separate identities—a school persona and an "everywhere else" persona?

5. Name three to five areas of your life where you exhibit a growth mindset. Name two or three areas in your life where you are trapped in a fixed mindset. How might you go about changing from a fixed mindset to a growth mindset in those areas?

6. The authors assert that it is beneficial to students to experience hard-earned success. How is that any different from success that is easily achieved? Which of these is appropriate for the classroom? Why?

Thrive Skills in Action

ACTIVITY 3.1

Attribution Theory Assessment

Questions can be modified to best suit the developmental level of your students. In the classroom or hallway, tape evenly spaced large printed numerals (1–5) on the wall above student height. There should be enough room for a line of students to stand in front of each number. Tell the students you are going to read some statements about something that might happen, and you would like for them to think about what would be the most likely cause if it happened to them.

Number 1 stands for "It has nothing to do with me," and number 5 stands for "It has everything do with me." Ask students to stand in front of the number that best represents how the event would relate to them. They can stand in front of 1 or 5 or one of the numbers in between. If multiple students pick a number, they should make a line in an orderly fashion one behind the other so that they are all facing the number. For each question, record the number of students who selected each number so that you can create a graph for later discussion. Alternatively, you can take digital photos after each question to capture the representative bar graph students have created with their lines.

Sample Statements

1. The teacher passes back a set of tests. More than half the class has really low scores. You made a failing grade.

2. You tried out for a team. You didn't make it.

3. Your best friend made a better grade than you did on an assignment.

4. One of the honors (GT/TAG) students outperformed you on an assignment.

5. You are struggling in math class.

6. Students are choosing sides for team play. You are the last to be chosen.

7. You did your homework, but now you can't find it.

8. A lot of kids are off task. The teacher calls you out for talking.

9. You can't do your homework because you don't understand the assignment.

10. You just got selected for the Honor Society.

Feel free to change the statements to personalize them for your own class. This activity is an excellent introduction to a discussion on attribution theory. It is interesting to use this as a pre- and postassessment.

ACTIVITY 3.2

Me Me Me

Students create a life-size outline of themselves using butcher paper or cardboard.

Students label each part:

Top of body: All the things I can do well.

Bottom of body: All the things I need to work on.

Arms: Ways I got good at the things I can do.

Legs: Things I can do to improve on the things I need to work on.

Head: Positive thoughts that will help me work hard.

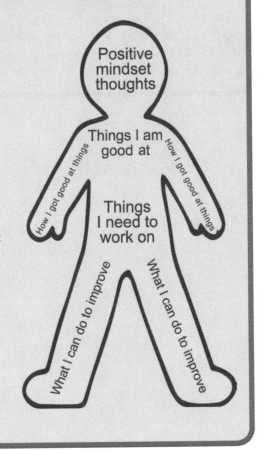

Positive mindset thoughts

Things I am good at

How I got good at things

How I got good at things

Things I need to work on

What I can do to improve

What I can do to improve

ACTIVITY 3.3
Failing Isn't Final

Teach students that to succeed at something difficult, you must fail before you learn. Challenge students to practice one of the activities listed. All of these activities have an element of failure before success. Encourage your students as they take on one of these challenges. Give students plenty of time to practice and find success. Pick one of the activities and model as you learn each new step.

As students struggle, help them make the connections that will stay with them far beyond your classroom:

- **Acknowledge that learning new things is hard:** Don't get frustrated. Take a break and come back at it again and again. Think about the mistakes and how you can approach it in a different way.

- **Don't give up:** When you accomplish that first (knot, fold, stitch, or step), practice it over and over, note your improvement, and then move on to the next step.

- **Keep track of your efforts:** Journal what went well and what you are struggling with. Look back on past practice period journal entries and see the progression.

- **Acknowledge your feelings of frustration:** Talk about what you are feeling. Failure is frustrating. How you deal with frustration can help you or hold you back. How can you deal with frustration in a positive way? How can you deal with frustration in a negative way?

- **Celebrate with others:** As students around you have success, celebrate with them and encourage those who are struggling. We all need cheerleaders.

Possible Activities

Art of Knot Tying

Balloon Animals

Crochet or Knitting

Juggling

Origami

Rubik's Cube

ACTIVITY 3.4

Rolling From Fixed to Growth Mindset

After students learn about fixed and growth mindsets, this activity can reinforce the words we use in each type of mindset. Students work in groups of two, and each takes turns rolling a die. The number they roll determines the statement. (If the same number is rolled more than once, the student needs to roll again until a new number comes up.) They then reframe the statement from a fixed mindset to a growth mindset out loud to their partner. Each student records the statement and one other statement that could be used to promote a growth mindset. Visit the *Thrive* website (www.teachingkidstothrive.com) to access Activity Sheet 3.2, "Fixed to Growth."

FIXED TO GROWTH

	FIXED STATEMENT	GROWTH STATEMENT	MY EXAMPLE
•			
••			
•••			
••••			
•••••			
••••••			

Die Roll: Fixed Statement to Turn to a Growth Statement

1: "I have never been good at _____!"

2: "I have to win."

3: "This is too hard. I quit!"

4: "I am finished with my project; I can't do any better than this."

5: "My parents both sing, so it's easy for me."

6: "She's so good at sports. I wish I were."

A few other statements to use: "It's not my fault, she didn't explain it right." "I am no good at math." "I think I know the answer, but I am not saying it. I might be wrong." "I don't care what you think of my essay!"

ACTIVITY 3.5

Fabulous Fails

This activity looks closely at mistakes and how we can learn from them.

Model

Start the lesson by telling a personal story about a time you remember making a mistake—not a simple easy-to-fix mistake, but one that was big and had consequences. Talk about why you made it and what it felt like in the moment to realize you had made such a mistake. Then ask students if they think they learned anything from that mistake. Would it have been better not to have tried than to have tried and made the mistake?

Journal

Next, ask students to write a journal entry about a time they made a mistake and what they learned from the experience.

Task

Students become reporters who investigate learning.

- Ask several people of different ages (under 12, 12–20, 21–50, 51–99) to tell about a mistake they made and what they learned from it.

- Transcribe the interview in writing or record it with a voice recorder (first ask permission if you can record the information "for the record").

- Note the interviewee's name, age, and profession.

Reflect

Students reflect on the stories they heard trying to discern a central theme or common element.

Product

Student reporters use their collected data to write a newspaper article about learning from mistakes.

Access the website **www.teachingkidstothrive.com**
to find more classroom-ready activities,
author-recommended videos, websites, and other resources.

PERSEVERANCE
PUSHING THROUGH DESPITE THE SETBACKS

If you can't fly, run; if you can't run, walk; if you can't walk, crawl; but by all means keep moving.

—Martin Luther King, Jr. (1960)

●●● A TALE OF TWO STUDENTS

Sixteen-year-old Jessica is the oldest of five children born to a mother who was little more than a child herself when she had Jessica. They live in poverty without the economic or social status of many of Jessica's peers at school. Many times, her evenings are spent taking care of her younger siblings while her parents are out partying or in the next room fighting and causing chaos. Even when they are home, her parents are emotionally unavailable for their kids. No one in Jessica's family has ever graduated from high school. The emotional stress of Jessica's life has her feeling depressed and disconnected to the fun-filled high school world of football games and proms. She is a smart girl; she can do the classwork with ease, but due to the pressures at home, she is absent regularly, and when she does go to school, she is often unprepared and feels disconnected. It all just seems so pointless to her. Feeling isolated, overwhelmed, and useless, Jessica quits school to escape her situation and moves in with a guy who offers her a place to live and a way to have

(Continued)

(Continued)

"lots more fun." Before she knows it, Jessica is seventeen, unemployed, pregnant, and alone. How could such a smart girl end up in this situation? Why didn't she see that with a little hard work and determination she could have gotten that diploma and made it out of the cycle?

Fifteen-year-old Isabelle is the second of five children, and she, too, was born to teen parents who are trapped in the poverty cycle. Isabelle took on the role of pseudo-parent at a very early age because her parents are often drunk or high. She has always been the nurturing type. She cooks, cleans, and tries to provide as much as she can for her younger siblings. It is not easy to balance everything. Sometimes she is stuck doing her homework with a flashlight because the electric bill wasn't paid. Isabelle's mother thinks she should go to beauty school after high school so she can make a living as soon as possible. High school is Isabelle's refuge. She is not the smartest girl in class, but she manages. She enjoys the escape from the reality of her home life when she is in the classroom at school. She may not have the clothes or money other kids in her class have, but she does not care because she knows if she works hard, she will be able to graduate with honors, and then maybe she can get into a good college on a scholarship. She is on track to have a quality life with a lot more choices. ●

Quit Now or Finish?
What Makes the Difference?

Educators everywhere know the story all too well. Students come to us every day with the emotional baggage from a less than idyllic home life. The stories are alarming—poverty, domestic violence, drug and alcohol abuse, homelessness, sexual abuse; they are real distractions to learning for many students. The question is, What makes a girl like Jessica buckle at the pressure and just give up on herself by dropping out of high school while Isabelle (who also has a damaged environment and struggles with self-image) pulls herself up by the proverbial bootstraps and graduates with honors? Is it an innate trait that one of these students was lucky enough to inherit? Or is it an attribute that can be developed and nurtured over time?

As it is with many learners, *perseverance*, or the lack thereof, is probably the deciding factor for these two students. Despite Isabelle's at-risk factors, she is able to marshal the resolve it takes to stay on track.

Carol Dweck describes perseverance as a kind of tenacity. She depicts tenacious students as those who believe they belong in school, are engaged in learning, can forego immediate pleasures for the sake of schoolwork, and are not derailed by intellectual or social problems. She describes such students as those who see setbacks as opportunities for learning or problems to be solved. "They know how to remain engaged over the long haul and how to deploy new strategies for moving forward effectively" (Dweck, Walton, & Cohen, 2011, p. 4).

The good news is research indicates that perseverance is a malleable quality and certainly worth the effort to help develop in students despite their academic success or risk factors. Every one of our students—affluent, middle class, and poverty stricken—will encounter adversity in his or her lifetime. How they handle that adversity can depend on learned techniques, practiced self-talk, and reflections about past challenges. If students do not learn how to set goals, overcome obstacles, and push forward, they can become averse to risk taking of any kind. They develop habits of avoiding challenges and quitting anytime things get too difficult.

How do we help our students recognize perseverance in themselves and others? How do we help them see the benefit of the struggle? How do we instill in them the ability to persist when things get rough? Research shows that high-achieving individuals draw upon "attributes, dispositions, social skills, attitudes, and intrapersonal resources—independent of intellectual ability" (U.S. Department of Education, 2013, p. 1).

For us as educators, this validates what we have known all along—there is more to success than learning content knowledge. Whether we teach first grade, middle school language arts, or high school government, the job of a teacher (*every* teacher) has always been to prepare our students for success in the real world. And in order to succeed in the real world, they will need perseverance.

Perseverance: What It Is and What It Is Not

Current educational researchers and writers refer to this particular skill set by a number of terms including *conscientiousness, tenacity, willpower, determination, industriousness,* and *perseverance.* Angela Duckworth has branded the term *grit* to describe what she calls "perseverance and passion for long-term goals" (Duckworth, Peterson, Matthews, & Kelly, 2007, p. 1087). In her new book *Grit: The Power and Passion of Perseverance* (2016), she encourages parents and educators to help build "grittiness" in learners. Students should be invited to persevere, and we believe some specific strategies and tools can help all students toward this endeavor.

Perseverance is not merely goal setting or problem solving. Nor is it just being willing to go the extra mile. Perseverance is the ability to see a long-range goal, set the goal, define the steps, work toward each step, and deal with obstacles and setbacks as they arise.

We often think of perseverance as the Energizer Bunny who just keeps going and going and going. However, there's a downside to being an Energizer Bunny. What if he continues to beat his drum all the while running into the same wall? That image brings to mind the familiar adage, "The definition of insanity is doing the same thing over and over and expecting different results." Merely butting one's head against an immovable object is not perseverance. Perseverance involves another significant aspect, *adaptability*, which means learning to work with the resources and circumstances within reach. So perseverance includes learning what does and doesn't work and adjusting actions and strategies as necessary to keep moving forward.

In Chapter 3, we discussed self-efficacy and its relationship to mindset. The belief that one has a certain amount of control over a

Simply put, perseverance comprises these six steps:

1. Determine your goal.

2. Figure out your next step.

3. Identify what (if anything) is going to be an obstacle.

4. Remove the obstacle.

5. Take the step.

6. Repeat as many times as necessary to achieve the goal. ●

situation is an intrinsic part of a growth mindset. It is also a vital part of perseverance. Until students believe they have some measure of influence over their future, they see no need to continue striving. In Chapter 2, we discussed self-regulation as an executive function (EF) skill. *Effortful control* is an extension of self-regulation. It refers to a situation where a task might be important for long-term goals, but it doesn't feel very desirable or intrinsically motivating at the time. Students have to use *controlled effort* to stay on course. Successful students regulate their attention during such tasks and in the face of distractions. They utilize effortful control along with a growth mindset to stay on track. As illustrated in Figure 4.1, perseverance, effortful control, and growth mindset work together and are necessary cogs in providing the learner with a mechanism for success.

What Educators Need to Know About Perseverance

It is not a simple matter of students either having perseverance or not having it because everyone has some measure of this quality. It can vary not only from individual to individual but also from activity to activity for the same person. Most importantly, though, as with all social and emotional learning (SEL) skills, it is flexible and can be strengthened through modeling, instruction, and practice. Perseverance training should incorporate the tools, strategies, and mindset skills that promote a drive toward success. It should be embedded in everyday classroom applications throughout the student's educational experience. The student, Jessica, who lacked the perseverance to finish school is hopefully not doomed to a life of running from challenges and obstacles. She is, in fact, quite

Figure 4.1

Perseverance Wheel

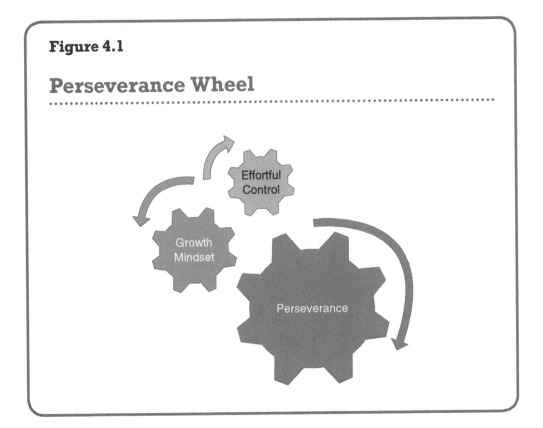

capable of learning appropriate coping techniques, adopting a growth mindset, and understanding that when faced with failure there is an opportunity not only to grow but to Thrive.

As educators, we are quite familiar with the concept that what gets measured gets funded. With the current emphasis on SEL in classrooms along with the national Every Student Succeeds Act (ESSA) mandate to include at least one measure of nonacademic learning in school accountability, there has been a rush to construct ways to measure growth in SEL skills. In 2017, the National Assessment of Educational Progress (the Nation's Report Card) will start surveying and collecting data in the areas of motivation, mindset, and grit (Sparks, 2015). Some of the popular Knowledge Is Power Program (KIPP) charter schools currently provide a Character Growth Card for students along with their academic report card.

Duckworth et al. (2007) have developed a self-report Grit Scale, and others are rushing to develop valid and reliable measures that can be used to identify and report the status of SEL in schools. Many of the first-generation measurement methods of the essential skills are plagued by the fact they rely mostly on surveys and self-reports.

However, there are researchers in psychology and education who reportedly have developed more evidence-based systems. We hope this is true, but we have a wait-and-see attitude.

While we understand the need for tests to detect problem areas for students as well as to document successful growth, for the present time we favor a more formative approach whereby teachers discuss student self-assessments and provide quality feedback. Hattie and Timperley (2007) note that effective feedback is most often oriented around a specific achievement that students are (or should be) working toward. They suggest that when receiving feedback, it should be clear to students how the information they are getting will help them progress toward their final goals.

"It's not that I'm so smart, it's just that I stay with problems longer" (Albert Einstein).

What Does Perseverance Look Like in the Classroom?

Most of our students are familiar with perseverance in one form or another, but they may not be aware of its impact on success. They may not recognize the skills and mental endurance that are a part of the process, but they can all relate to a time when they or someone they know demonstrated perseverance. Teachers can help students reflect on some of the processes, skills, and strategies used in reaching the desired outcome in order to help them draw on those skills when needed the next time. There are countless examples we can draw upon to help relate to the students' own experiences. Many of our middle and high school students can relate to the struggle and sense of accomplishment when they attained a personal best at a video game (without using a cheat code) or learned a new dance move or even used YouTube as a way to teach themselves to do something new.

Examples: It takes perseverance to learn to

- Tie a shoe
- Learn to skateboard
- Complete a complex craft project
- Open a combination lock
- Ride a bike without training wheels
- Learn to walk
- Figure out how to work a smartphone
- Learn to play a sport
- Play a musical instrument
- Learn to drive ●

Using these prior learning experiences, students can realize that when they attempt new things, it takes deliberate practice to see improvement. They can expect to fail numerous times, but that should not stop them from moving forward. Teachers can remind students about all of the incredible things they have already learned by (a) not giving up, (b) trying different strategies, (c) practicing deliberately, and (d) staying focused on the goal.

●●● THE POWER OF *YET*

In her book *Sharing the Blue Crayon*, Mary Ann Buckley (2015) teaches her kindergarten and first-grade students about perseverance by taking them to the playground. She shows her students the monkey bars and talks about how most five- to seven-year-olds have not mastered the skill to hoist themselves across the bars . . . yet. She tells her learners that she believes that each of them will build their muscles and successfully cross the bars, but it may be at different points in the year. She and the children talk about the need for daily practice and how those who learn early on can show others what they did to be successful. She goes back to the emphasis of daily practice and trying to cross more bars on every attempt. She explains how some days it will be harder to hold on than others and how the children may want to quit, but with effort and practice in crossing the monkey bars just once each day, they will get closer to their goal. Her students surmise that if they work hard and believe they can, they will each eventually become a monkey bar expert! Back in the classroom, she creates a chart where students record their personal advancements. Ms. Buckley then uses the monkey bar experience as an analogy of academic perseverance as the year's curriculum unfolds. ●

What Supporting Perseverance Looks Like in the Classroom

THE ENVIRONMENT IS EMOTIONALLY SAFE FOR LEARNING

From day one, teachers can set the classroom norms and send the message that they care and that *learning to learn* is important in this classroom. This message can happen in a variety of ways—with words, with visual reinforcement on the classroom walls, and, most importantly, with intentional actions. Make sure the environment for risk taking is safe. Don't belittle a student for a wrong answer or allow others to laugh or ridicule. Students will not embrace growth mindsets when the environment says it is not safe to take risks.

ALL STUDENTS ARE TREATED "AS IF . . ."

Teachers treat all students as if they are smart enough, strong enough, and dedicated enough. They believe in each child's ability to do the tasks that are presented. While questioning, they are mindful of providing enough wait time for students who struggle. The silence can be stressful, but they don't jump in too fast; some students need more time to process. It is educationally sound to help scaffold the response, but teachers need to avoid merely giving students an answer. There is a fine line between leaving a student hanging and moving on too quickly.

TEACHERS INSPECT WHAT THEY EXPECT

When they have students use a "turn and talk" or "show what you know" strategy, teachers peruse the room and ensure that students are indeed talking about the curriculum. They don't let students quit halfway through a task even when it is difficult.

TEACHERS HELP STUDENTS BREAK LARGE TASKS INTO SMALLER, MANAGEABLE ONES

They encourage learners to take a breath, give positive self-talk, and go back to the task at hand. Some students benefit from chunking an assignment. An easy way to chunk an assignment is to cut a file folder so that only certain parts of the assignment show at one time. Students generally feel less overwhelmed with the task they are facing when it is divided up into smaller sections.

THERE'S A NIKE SPIRIT IN THE CLASSROOM—JUST DO IT

Teachers give students kudos for trying new things and setting goals. After a winter or spring break, they start the morning by asking if anyone tried anything new or set a new goal. They know that sharing these stories can inspire other students to step out of their comfort zones.

STUDENTS ARE HELD ACCOUNTABLE
FOR THEIR WORK

For late and unfinished work, teachers do not focus on the reason or excuse. They require all students to finish the task and be accountable. They expect them to put in the extra effort to go back and finish the work and move forward. An idea for middle school and high school students is to provide a "finish and move forward" notice. When a student does not have the assignment, the focus is on the student finishing the task and not dwelling on excuses or rationalizations. See Activity Sheet 4.1, "So You Didn't Do Your Homework . . . ," on the *Thrive* website (www.teachingkidstothrive.com).

So You Didn't Do Your Homework...

Date: _____ TB: _____

Name: _____ Assignment I missed: _____

Completing your homework is *your responsibility as a student*. Homework is purposefully assigned and created to help you gain knowledge in my class. Please help me understand what happened and how will you solve this issue so it does not happen in the future.

I do not have homework today because: *(Please Check One)*

——I did the assigned homework, but I did not bring it to class

____I chose not to do my homework

____I forgot to do my homework

____I did not have the appropriate materials at home

—— Other_____

Please explain (in complete sentences) how you are going to sove this issue so it does not happen again:

_____

_____

_____

☐ I will bring this assignment in by the next class day because I want to succeed in this class.

_____

Student Signature

STUDENTS ARE TAUGHT TO SEE
THE VALUE OF OBSTACLES AND MISSTEPS

Teachers create a classroom environment that honors vulnerability, chance taking, and capitalizing on mistakes. They develop opportunities for classmates to encourage each other when errors happen. Some classes chant "Good try!" when a fellow student takes a chance and is wrong or *"Boom, you are one step closer!"* Teachers help students understand that failure does not define people, but what they *do with failure* does.

STUDENTS LEARN TO REROUTE

Students need to understand how to look at obstacles and reroute or overcome them. Use literature, teacher think-alouds, and modeling to help students understand that encountering obstacles is not necessarily the end of the road.

STUDENTS PRACTICE THE POWER OF *YET*

Reframe "I can't" with the word *yet*. "I can't _____ *yet*." A high school algebra teacher placed the word *yet* on the back wall of his classroom. When students said "I can't" (or a version of it), they had to get up, go to the back wall, and tap the poster, reciting "I can't _____ *yet*!" before returning to their seats to make a new attempt. Students soon become experts at helping their classmates remember the growth mindset power of *yet*.

THERE IS AN EMPHASIS ON PERSONALIZED LEARNING

Personalized learning is a path to passion, motivation, and agency. Designing time for students to participate in ongoing exploration in the classroom is an excellent way to encourage students to persevere toward goals. Consider incorporating one of the following methods:

- *Project-Based Learning* (PBL) is a method of teaching in which students learn knowledge and skills as they work on a project to answer a complex question, a problem, or a challenge (often called an essential or driving question). The components of PBL involve investigation, real-world context, collaboration, and authentic learning. PBL lessons are ideal for teaching students to practice their persistence skills.

- *Genius Hour*, based on a concept developed by Google to help workers stay motivated, is a movement that taps into student choice. It allows students to explore their passion for learning in any area during a set period of time during school. Students can choose to learn a language, to write code, or to learn basket weaving—the possibilities are endless.

- *Makerspaces* provide classroom space where hands-on activities encourage students to design, build, invent, and learn as they tinker and explore.

The *Thrive* website (www.teachingkidstothrive.com) has links to more information on these three methods in the Resources section.

1. **What do you do with the student who gives up easily and just won't try no matter what you do?**

   A student who refuses to try is probably one who has had very little success at anything or one who feels so overwhelmed that he would rather quit than fail. Maybe he's never been given a reason to persist toward a goal. It is important to find out what the student values and start with something that appeals to him. Design a task in incrementally harder steps that begins with something he can readily do. Offer positive feedback for each completed step and try to get him to reflect on the positive feelings of achievement. Be patient. Depending on the age of the student, you will be trying to undo any number of years of programmed learned helplessness. Cheer him on when he does not give up. Talk to him about his effort and his feelings along the way. Particularly get him to share what it feels like to accomplish things for which he has a passion. Help him learn to accept his stumbles along with his triumphs. It will probably take awhile to reset his "perseverance mode," but eventually you will see him become more and more independent and determined. Seek a balance of challenge, reflection, and joy.

2. **What do you say to those who criticize an emphasis on *grit* as just another way to "blame the victim"?**

   There are those who proclaim that the *grit phenomenon* is an attempt to justify inadequate schools and programs, particularly in poverty areas, for underserved children. First, our goal is not to blame but rather to empower. We do not see teaching children perseverance as pointing the finger of blame. While we believe in working tirelessly for better schools and resources for all students, we also seek ways to encourage the students in their current circumstances. Perseverance is a trait that supports students of all backgrounds and social status. If students can learn to focus on their goals, exercise care in their choices, and steadily put forth effort, statistics say they can improve their lives. We are not suggesting that they do this by themselves. The purpose of this book is to give teachers strategies, tools, and methods for helping students to help themselves.

3. **Some critics say that poor and other marginalized children already have plenty of *grit*. They say these kids have to have perseverance just to survive in their circumstances. Do you agree?**

   Ethan Ris (Strauss, 2016) writes that children reared in poverty (and other unbearable circumstances) already have plenty of *grit* because they had to develop it early on just to survive. He believes that lessons about grit are counterproductive for learners who may think that educators are romanticizing the challenges of overcoming poverty and neglect. We agree that students reared in hardship often have to learn to be tenacious at an early age, but we don't know anyone who romanticizes the situation. We think most teachers respond with empathy to their students' plights and encourage them to focus on the things they can control—their efforts and their choices. Even though these learners have demonstrated an uncanny ability to survive in the face of obstacles, they don't necessarily know how to use that same perseverance to Thrive. It is important for teachers to show students how they can use that same stick-to-it-iveness to reach goals that bring them joy.

4. **Should we tell our students to always try as hard as they can and be relentless no matter what?**

   We have always been told that "anything worth doing is worth doing well." That is simply not true. There are many things we do in life that have to be done, but they don't take a full-blown commitment to excellence. Sometimes, you may need to stop dusting the leaves on your potted plants and just take a walk, which also does not have to be perfect. Kohn (2014) mentions the term *nonproductive persistence* to refer to a state whereby the learner continues toward a goal that no longer makes any sense. Because of changes in circumstances, because all avenues have been exhausted, or even because the learner loses interest—all are good reasons to terminate perseverance toward a particular goal. Just as Don Quixote demonstrated the pointlessness of tilting at windmills, there are times when it is better to pause, recalculate, or just stop pursuing a goal altogether. We want to teach our students to put forth diligent effort toward goals that are important to them now or in the future, but we also want to teach them good judgment and how to determine when it is time to terminate or save that goal for another day. To plunge headfirst, full throttle toward a goal just because a person says to herself "I am not a quitter" is just as harmful as never trying at all. The goal is to help students develop persistence around things that really matter to them.

5. What is the role of the instructor in teaching perseverance?

As we have mentioned before, it is important to provide an environment for students that is safe, inviting, and challenging. Adults need to give learners a chance to wrestle with obstacles and challenges on their own and not be too quick to offer an assist or do it for them. There's a fine line between what Matthew Alexander (2016) calls being a "warm demander" and being overly tough. As warm demanders, teachers need to be able to communicate a shared desire with the student for meeting goals but also be able to keep the expectation just beyond the student's present reach. For example, "You must be really proud to have accomplished that, Max! Let's see if you can go a little further." It is not an exact science, and it is not always easy, but when teachers master their content and make every effort to connect with students, they have a much better chance of being effective warm demanders.

Discussion Questions and Exercises

We encourage you to tweet your responses to @tchkids2thrive.

1. Describe a student you know who demonstrates extraordinary perseverance. Explain what leads you to this conclusion and how you think this student mastered such high perseverance skills.

2. Describe a student you know who demonstrates extremely poor perseverance. Explain what leads you to this conclusion and why you think this student has not yet developed better perseverance skills. What might the student do to develop stronger perseverance skills?

3. List and describe the specific strategies you use in your classroom to foster perseverance skills.

4. What is your policy on failed assignments or tests? Do students have the option of trying to improve their scores? Describe the thinking behind the policy you have.

5. A student tells you she is thinking about quitting gymnastics. She says it is getting too hard, she's not any good at it anymore, and she just doesn't feel like continuing. Upon probing, you find that she just lost (for the first time ever) a major competition. She tells you she hates the new gymnastics coach who, she says, "always brags on her favorites, and I'm not one of them." Her parents told her it was her choice, but she wants to know what you think. What do you do?

ACTIVITY 4.1
Ladder to My Success

This activity is designed to help students see that to reach any goal there are steps that must be accomplished. By creating a ladder with rungs, students build the mental image of obtaining each small step to get to the big goal.

1. Model what your own ladder might look like for a goal you want to achieve (for example, running a marathon or learning to crochet). Begin the ladder with a starting point of today and model the steps it will take for you to reach your goal.

Source: **Created by Kommunitees.**

2. Model what a ladder might look like for a student who wants to learn to read or learn to write in cursive.

3. Brainstorm with open discussion things your students' age-mates would have an interest in learning to do.

4. Have students draw their own ladder or use Activity Sheet 4.2, "Ladder to My Success," found on the *Thrive* website (www.teachingkidstothrive.com).

5. After setting a personal goal, have each student create the rungs (or steps) it will take to achieve the goal.

6. Ask students to make weekly ladder reflection reports on the status of their efforts.

ACTIVITY 4.2

Perseverance Teach and Trade

This activity is designed to help students transfer the knowledge learned about the process of perseverance and make personal connections. The activity is meant to be used after teaching the lesson or as a closing activity on perseverance.

1. Give each student a card with one word from the list below.

2. Allow students three minutes to turn and talk to their neighbor, brainstorming how they think each of the words relates to perseverance.

3. Have students write down how the word on the card relates to perseverance, including an example or story they can explain to someone else.

4. To begin the Teach and Trade activity, ask students to stand up and find a partner.

5. Then have students take turns explaining how their word relates to perseverance.

6. Signal the students to high-five, trade cards, and find a new partner.

7. Now that they have a new card, invite them to use the story or example that is written on the card or make up their own example.

Words relating to perseverance (feel free to add others):

- Celebration
- Challenge
- Courage
- Determination
- Distraction

- Failure
- Goal
- Patience
- Persistence
- Planning

- Self-talk
- Stress
- Struggle
- Success

ACTIVITY 4.3

Keep Swimming (or Shaking)!

Materials

- Small baby food jars or small plastic condiment containers with lids (one for each student)

- Whipping cream

- Small plastic plates and plastic knives

- Bread or crackers

- Video clips of *Finding Dory* (optional)

Directions

1. Give each student a small jar, filled halfway with whipping cream, and a tightened lid.

2. Explain to students that each jar has ingredients to make butter and that they will just need to follow your directions.

3. Tell students to start shaking their jars. Discuss the Disney movie *Finding Dory* and how Dory is determined to find her family. (Optional: Show the *Finding Dory* trailer or other clips from the movie.) As the students listen and discuss as a class, the cream will become thick, like whipped cream. Say, "Don't stop . . . keep shaking."

4. Keep discussing the movie: "Dory is willing to go far to reach her goal, and she encounters many obstacles—can anyone name the obstacles she encounters?" After about five to ten minutes of persistent shaking, the cream will become very hard to shake. Again, say, "Keep shaking!" Ask students what would happen if they gave up now. Explain that when things get hard, we can quit or persevere, but if we quit, we will not get to enjoy our anticipated goal.

5. Keep discussing the movie: "No matter what, Dory doesn't give up. She even has a motto: 'Keep swimming!' What does her motto mean to her? How does a motto help when things get hard?" Students will start to see clumps in the jar, and their arms might get tired. Once more, say, "Keep shaking!"

6. Unexpectedly, the cream in the jar will become easy to shake! Now, say, "You did it! You made butter."

7. Have students take off the lid. They can use a knife to put the clump of butter on a plate, leaving the liquid that is left in the jar.

8. Pass out bread or crackers.

9. Invite students to spread the butter on their bread or cracker and enjoy the product of their hard work.

ACTIVITY 4.4

Everyone Has a Story: Personal Interviews

As a class, generate interview questions that focus on learning about perseverance, dealing with struggles, and learning lessons during the struggle. Each student will pick an adult to interview. It can be someone from the student's family, neighborhood, school, or community. Students can record or film the interview (this will be a family artifact treasured years later) and then show the interview to the class and report what life lessons they learned from talking to the individual.

Possible Question Stems

- Name something that you learned from your parents or an older relative.

- What is the most important thing you have learned so far in life? Who taught you that, or how did you learn it?

- Did you ever feel like giving up on something you were trying to do, but you kept going? Tell me about that time.

- Can you think of a time you learned a valuable lesson from a mistake or failure? What lesson did you learn?

- What accomplishment are you most proud of?

Modification of This Activity

Instead of interviewing individuals, invite a local community member in for a class talk and have students ask questions.

ACTIVITY 4.5

Dreaming and Planning the Road to Getting There

This activity is designed to help students see that the road to their dreams will take work, and they may encounter obstacles on the way.

1. Ask students to write down (or, for younger students, draw a picture of) something they want to become or do when they grow up.

2. *For older students*, have them write the possible road (steps) to get to their dream along with a list of potential potholes in the road (obstacles and actions that might prevent them from getting to their dream).

3. *For younger students*, as a class create a list of general steps needed to fulfill their dreams as well as obstacles that might get in the way.

4. As a class, brainstorm ways to deal with obstacles.

5. Arrange students into pairs and have them share their dreams, road, and potholes.

6. Reflect. Either as a class or in a journal entry, have students reflect on what they learned from this activity.

Access the website **www.teachingkidstothrive.com** to find more classroom-ready activities, author-recommended videos, websites, and other resources.

BOUNCING BACK
TEACHING KIDS ABOUT RESILIENCE

Resilience is all about being able to overcome the unexpected.
Sustainability is about survival. The goal of resilience is to thrive.

—Jamais Cascios (2009)

●●● A DIFFERENT KIND OF RESILIENCY

While teaching my middle-level science students about properties of matter, I asked them to do several quick activities to help clarify different concepts. To illustrate *elasticity*, I asked them to select a rubber band from their lab tray, measure the length, and record it. Next, I asked them to stretch the band very fast as they counted the number of pulls. They were to note changes that occurred. Students were quick to notice their bands grew warmer but tended to snap back to their original form each time. I asked them to measure the length of their bands again. The length for most was the same as before. No matter the size of their rubber band—short, long, or somewhere in between—the band had returned to its original form (even if the length had changed slightly). I went to the board and wrote, "*Resiliency* (elasticity) is the property of matter that enables it to resume its original shape or position after being bent, stretched, or compressed."

(Continued)

(Continued)

©iStockphoto.com/Pixel_Pig

A student who was normally very subdued suddenly blurted, "So that's like real life. Sometimes a person can go through all kinds of horrible things at home and still come out okay on the other end. That's being resilient, and that's a good thing, right?" Struck by the sincerity and plea in her voice, I answered, "Oh, of course, Shelly, that is exactly what resilience is when applied to humans." Noticing the knowing looks on the faces of her friends, I put the discussion of properties of matter on hold and pursued the topic of how people learn to move past all kinds of hardships without letting the events pull them apart. I told them about Viktor Frankl, the famous Holocaust survivor, who said, *"Everything can be taken from a man but one thing: the last of the human freedoms—to choose one's attitude in any given set of circumstances, to choose one's own way"* (Frankl, 2006, p. 66).

As the stories about resilience poured out of my students, I noticed that Shelly never took her eyes off me. When class was over, she walked up to me and said, "I need to show you something." She rolled up her sleeves. It was the first time I had ever seen the scars from dozens of tiny cuts made by a person trying to control her internal pain. (Debbie Silver) ●

Resilience: What Is It?

Souers and Hall (2016) remind us that "forever changed" does not have to mean "forever damaged." They warn that when we give students too much sympathy, we may be giving them permission to quit. Souers and Hall advise teachers to look beyond the parts in the lives of our students that we cannot change and focus on the time we do have with them in our class or during the school day. We can influence those intervals in a positive way by showing students what they are capable of, exposing them to different ways of being, teaching them healthy ways to Thrive, empowering them to learn and grow, and showing them we respect and care for them—both for now and for what they may become in the future.

For kids living in turmoil or chaos, the long-term goals of perseverance for future attainment (as discussed in Chapter 4) can have little or no meaning. The experiences and emotional baggage they shoulder daily can simply impede their ability to envision a different kind of life in the distant future. Teachers need to foster resilience to help students live with the here and now. No matter the background or status of students, they all have to face the fact that life is uncertain. There is a lot of fear and worry for everyone, but for some that uncertainty is compounded by the present havoc of their environments. The American Psychological Association (APA, 2016) defines *resilience* this way:

> Resilience is the process of adapting well in the face of adversity, trauma, tragedy, threats, or even significant sources of stress—such as family and relationship problems, serious health problems, or workplace and financial stressors. It means "bouncing back" from difficult experiences.

All students need to know how to pick up the pieces after they face adversity, disappointment, loss, or trauma and go on. They need guidance in how to find healthy ways to move past their emotional, and sometimes physical, pain. They need to believe they can persevere toward goals as they reframe the current negative aspects of their lives.

According to Allison-Napolitano (2014), resilience is not extraordinary; it is the means by which the human race survives, and is, therefore, far more common than uncommon. She believes the positive habits of self-regulation, mindfulness, student agency, and emotional regulation and a strong social network contribute to a stronger personal resilience. She strongly supports the idea that resilience can be fostered in all learners.

Perhaps it is surprising that most people actually do succeed despite their struggles and adverse conditions. Werner and Smith (2001) report that close to 70 percent of youth from high-risk environments overcome adversity and achieve acceptable outcomes. Perhaps we should change the labeling of our students from "at risk" to "at promise." Seeing students through a lens of promise makes it harder to write them off or to dismiss our role in helping them achieve their dreams.

Acknowledge the Struggle

"Together we will cry and face fear and grief. I will want to take away your pain, but instead I will sit with you and teach you how to feel it" (Brené Brown, 2012).

Students do not need adults to try and eliminate all their problems, but they do need us to be willing to listen, to validate their feelings, and to help them move to a more positive place. "Shelly, thank you for trusting me enough to show me what you've been doing to yourself. I can see that you are in a lot of pain right now. Tell me about what you are feeling when you make these cuts." (Shelly tells her story.) "The situation you describe is one that would cause anyone to feel afraid and to doubt herself. You have been very brave in managing to keep yourself together through this, but cutting yourself is not a healthy option, and we need to explore more suitable ways for you to deal with your pain. I am here to support you no matter what. You are safe here, and you have people who care about you. I'm going to bring the counselor in on this, and the three of us are going to see if we can figure out some options for you."

Of course, situations are sometimes way beyond the scope of what a teacher and a counselor can do. Shelly's case required the enlistment of child welfare services. She later agreed to a two-week stay at an adolescent psychiatric care facility for intense therapy. She returned to school a stronger and more hopeful young lady. Every time a child manages to get through a difficult experience, it teaches her a lesson about coping as well as confirms how strong she actually is. Later, Shelly can look at a current crisis and say, "Well, I got through something like this (or worse than this) before, so I figure I can handle this, too."

Thankfully, most student struggles are not so dramatic as Shelly's. Nevertheless, the teacher's response needs to be the same one of listening and supporting without trying singlehandedly to rescue the child. We need to move from sympathy and defeat ("You poor little thing, how will you ever be able to overcome this?") to a culture of empathy and optimism ("Wow, that's a difficult predicament for you. Let's put our heads together and see how to figure this out").

> **Student:** "My dog, Ranger, died last night. I've had him since I was little. My mom told me I didn't even have to come to school today because I cried all night. I told her I wanted to come and be with my friends, but now I'm thinking that was a mistake. I can't do anything. I just can't write that persuasive paragraph you want us to work on right now. I feel like I'm about to lose it."

Sympathy and Defeat Response	Empathy and Optimism Response
Teacher: "Oh no, I am so sorry to hear about your dog, Ranger. That is just horrible. They say that losing your dog is like losing a family member. It is a lot to handle. I hate that you are so upset. You poor thing. I totally understand that you can't think about anything else right now. Shall I call your mom and ask her to come get you?"	**Teacher:** "Oh, I am so sorry to hear about your Ranger. It really hurts to lose a family pet. Thank you for sharing about what you are feeling. I know when I lost my cat I thought the pain would never go away, but thankfully it eventually did, and now I have my memories of funny stuff she did and great times we had together. I'd like to hear more about your special dog. Why don't you take the time in class today to write about why Ranger was a dog who should be honored? It may be hard at first, but you can create something today that will affirm Ranger's memory and that you will always be able to treasure."

Wendy Mogel explains in her book *The Blessings of a B Minus* (2010) that letting our students wrestle with everyday disappointments helps them be better able to handle major disappointments that will arise later. Teachers need to listen to students' stories without constantly trying to fix everything. At the risk of sounding oversimplistic, a teacher's response sometimes is the determining factor of whether a student's emotional state is worsened or improved. Not every struggle has a quick or obvious solution, but the teacher's influence is real, and it is profound. Nationally recognized psychologist Julius Segal (1988) writes that children who overcome misfortune frequently have a charismatic adult in their lives: "In a surprising number of cases, that person turns out to be a teacher" (p. 2). Resiliency is best taught by an adult who mentors a student through caring, listening, offering nonjudgmental coaching, and providing authentic feedback (Markham, 2014).

"What does not kill me, makes me stronger" (Friedrich Nietzsche, 1888).

Normalize the Struggle

An effective way of reinforcing resilience is to help students understand that struggle is a normal part of living. Julie Lythcott-Haims addresses the topic of resilience in her 2015 best seller *How to Raise an Adult*. She feels we need to prepare students for the hard work they have ahead of them to move forward in school. She advises adults to be willing to give learners a reality check by sharing what we know about limitations and potential trials—not to derail them, but to prepare them for what they will need to do to reach their goals. We need to normalize the struggle to reduce the shame of having to battle in the first place. Let students know that everybody struggles.

Lythcott-Haims points out that when people cannot deal with the struggle, they sometimes turn to unhealthy choices such as drugs or alcohol. Addicts have little resiliency. They do not want to feel discomfort or loss because they have never learned to deal with those emotions. They substitute food, alcohol, drugs, gambling, thrill seeking, and other stimuli as a way to avoid the pain of the struggle. In his 2007 book *Thrilled to Death*, Archibald Hart explains his view that many young people use various addictions (e.g., preoccupation with video games, social media, or the Internet) to create an emotional numbness. Learning to work through unpleasant feelings is an important part of being educated.

It helps for students to hear about others, particularly kids like them, who have used resiliency to bounce back or Thrive. Teachers can share stories with students about literary figures, sports heroes, historically significant people, and even regular people who have faced adversity and prevailed. They can act as role models by discussing some of their genuine struggles in their personal journeys. It's important to help students differentiate between trying to be *their* best and trying to be *the* best.

Brené Brown is working to reduce the stigma of shame people feel over their personal struggles. She points out in her 2010 TEDxHouston talk (currently the fourth-most-watched TED Talk ever) that we need to teach learners to go to bed at night thinking, "Yes, I am imperfect and vulnerable and sometimes afraid, but that doesn't change the truth that I am also brave and worthy of love and belonging."

©iStockphoto.com/asiseeit

Researchers from Columbia University's Teachers College wanted to see if they could improve how ninth- and tenth-grade science students were able to dispel the notion that they would never be *real* scientists because they just didn't have what it takes. Students were divided into three groups who studied about accomplished scientists including Marie Curie, Albert Einstein, and Michael Faraday. One group read about the scientists' mistakes, setbacks, disappointments, and other intellectual struggles. The second group read about personal conflicts the scientists faced due to factors like poverty and a lack of family support. The third group read conventional stories that only mentioned the great achievements of the scientists without any discussion of the accompanying struggles they faced. Researchers found that students who read the stories about the scientists' struggles (either intellectual or personal) significantly improved their in-class performance over the students who either read just the conventional achievement stories or read no stories at all. The results were even more pronounced for low-performing students (Ahn, Lamnia, Nightingale, Novak, & Xiaodong Lin-Siegler, 2016). ●

The Classroom as the Tribe

In writing about how agents with the Federal Bureau of Investigation (FBI) increase their resilience, LaRae Quy (2016) mentions how important it is for agents to maintain a close relationship with people who have their back. Her point is that a supportive community can make all the difference in the world in helping a person climb back up after he is down. Helping students understand the difference between a clique and a group of trustworthy people who regularly demonstrate having your best interest at heart is a valuable lesson. Tribes can be family members or not, multigenerational, and made up of any combination of people who respect and care about you.

Our classrooms should act as surrogate tribes to students who have no community elsewhere to support them. Creating safe and caring classrooms is done with intention and by design. First and foremost, the teacher models the behaviors of acceptance, respect, and courtesy. But it is also the teacher's responsibility to help students internalize and act with those same behaviors.

Cooperative learning activities don't work unless rules, procedures, and expectations are clearly communicated, modeled, and reinforced. Taking the time to build collaboration skills among class members is time well spent. Many times, teachers engage the students in constructing the guidelines for positive interactions among themselves. James Nottingham (2017) gave the task of generating the rules for small-group dialogue to nine- and ten-year-olds. The following is the list they produced:

1. Everyone should have a turn to speak.
2. Don't interrupt when someone else is speaking.
3. Try to answer what other people say.
4. Accept advice and suggestions.
5. Don't make others feel bad about what they say. (pp. 24–25)

He recommends that once rules for group work are established, the teacher and group members keep referring to them. He believes regularly revisiting the rules greatly enhances their influence.

Some teachers routinely assign students to small groups and encourage them to interact with one another. Some rarely assign students to groups at all and generally opt for whole-group or individual activities. Whatever the choice of teaching style, it is vital that teachers make the time to help students get to know each other, get comfortable with each other, and support one another. Icebreakers and team-building activities are readily available and can be grounded in curriculum standards to also reinforce content. Providing opportunities for classmates to have friendly competitions between teams goes a long way toward promoting collegiality and shared goals. Teams should often be changed so that students have an opportunity to get to know everyone in the class.

••• TEAM-BUILDING DAY

To foster a sense of tribes in our middle school, our seventh-grade class created a team-building day shortly after school started. We divided students into small pods (ten to twelve students) that were hand-selected by teachers to get students interacting with others they normally would not choose. Throughout the day, the pods moved from activity to activity. The activities were centered on team building, communication, and relationship building. Teachers, counselors, principals, and others led the activities. We encouraged students to see themselves as a large family. We let the students pick the name of their team for the year, create a logo and mantra, and choose several other identity acts. At the close of the day, we brought the pods together for a final talk about what it means to be a team. We closed the day with a giant lap-sit of 140 seventh graders! You could feel the energy and camaraderie in the room as the students did what they thought could not be done. Students still come back to us and talk about that day. (Dedra Stafford) ●

Resiliency in Boys

Many times, boys have an unspoken agreement among themselves about what it means to be a man (i.e., dominant, unemotional, detached, unrepentant). Because of culture, media, or allegiance to men who model this kind of stereotype, boys sometimes feel compelled to exhibit the same kind of behavior so they can fit in and belong. Participating in team games and talking about feelings can go against the *Boy Code*. In their book *Helping Boys Succeed in School* (2007), educators Terry Neu and Rich Weinfeld paraphrase researcher William Pollack's Boy Code:

1. Do not cry (no sissy stuff).

2. Do not cower, tremble, or shrink from danger.

3. Do not ask for help when you are unsure of yourself (observe the code of silence).

4. Do not reach for comfort or reassurance.

5. Do not sing or cry for joy.

6. Do not hug your dearest friends.

7. Do not use words to show tenderness and love. (p. 24)

In her book *Teaching Boys Who Struggle in School* (2011), Kathleen Cleveland explains that boys often feel the pressure to refrain from expressing or even acknowledging emotions because of the fear of being labeled "a sissy," "not a man," or other exclusionary terms. She says boys' need for belonging can be so strong that it often sparks self-protective or deflective behaviors that squash their social skills and diminish their emotional resiliency. This does not mean that boys are incapable of building their resiliency, but it does heighten the importance of creating heterogeneous groups, designing activities that alternate leadership roles, and modeling respectful interactions with everyone. Males and females alike Thrive in environments that allow them to feel safe to be themselves and in groups of peers who support them.

Developing Resiliency Through Competency

According to the Edward Deci model (Deci & Flaste, 1996), students Thrive when they (1) feel a sense of belonging and connection, (2) have a sense of autonomy, and (3) feel competent. Sometimes students' feelings of incompetence lead them to a sense of futility rather than one of success. They have trouble mustering the initiative to overcome even small setbacks because they believe that basically they are incapable of making substantial improvement. School ought to be a place where students can discover their distinctive and individual strengths. Having a skilled adult highlight their areas of expertise and success can give students a reason to hope and the motivation they need to keep trying.

Resiliency expert Nan Henderson (2013) writes about her childhood history of abuse, alcoholism, and violence in a home that could have doomed her to the predictable downward spiral of defeat. She believes it was the "resilience-building power of schools" (p. 22) that saved her. Among other things her teachers did for her,

> they [gave me] the opportunity to express my human uniqueness [in ways] that were all so different from what I was experiencing at home that I began to believe I was a valuable, capable human being. (p. 23)

Henderson goes on speak about how important it is for adults to provide a mirror for students to see their strengths and realize just how significant they are: "In the process, a student's self-concept shifts from 'I am a problem' to 'I have strengths and talents and capabilities in spite of my problems'" (p. 24).

TEACH STUDENTS TO BE WARY OF "THOUGHT HOLES"

We discussed the power of competency (self-efficacy and perseverance) building in Chapters 3 and 4, but we want to go further here and talk about the power of reality-oriented thinking when it comes to competence. It's normal for kids to blow things out of proportion ("I'll never have friends again") and jump to conclusions ("Oh, look what I made on this test! I'm going to fail this course for sure"), but sometimes this distortion of reality can lead to *thought holes*. According to Renee Jain (2013), adversity is often perpetuated by misguided thinking:

> Studies show that thought holes can provoke self-defeating ideas (i.e., "I'm a loser") that trigger self-defeating emotions (i.e., pain, anxiety, malaise) that, in turn, cause self-defeating actions (i.e., acting out, skipping school). Left unchecked, inaccurate thoughts can also lead to more severe conditions, such as depression.

Mayla has never been a strong math student. She sometimes gets so anxious on tests that she accidentally makes careless mistakes. Her teacher last year used to give her extra time to check her work, and that helped a great deal. She heard that her teacher this year is very strict and does not allow students to have extra time. Mayla just got her first test back. She just missed passing by two points. She is embarrassed, upset, disappointed, and angry. She blames herself for thinking she could pass math this year. She knows this teacher doesn't care about her, and she will never be able to pass with someone like him for a teacher. Now she's going to have to go to summer school to take this course again. She slumps down in her chair, folds her arms across her chest, and decides just to stop trying altogether. ●

Mayla's reaction results from several illogical assumptions (or thought holes) that are outlined by Jain. Based on the work of Aaron Beck (1976) and David Burns (1980), she identifies what she calls "eight common thought holes." Below is a brief description of each thought hole along with how it pertains to Mayla's situation.

1. **Jumping to conclusions:** Judging a situation based on assumptions as opposed to definitive facts. Without even talking to her teacher, Mayla assumes he will not understand her anxiety and her need for extra time.

2. **Mental filtering:** Paying attention to the negative details in a situation while ignoring the positive. Mayla was very close to passing and could probably get her score up with a little effort.

3. **Magnifying:** Magnifying negative aspects in a situation. Mayla immediately determines that she can't do the work and will fail the entire semester.

4. **Minimizing:** Minimizing positive aspects in a situation. Mayla has made failing grades in math before, but she has always been able to buckle down and pass. More than once she has made a C for the semester.

5. **Personalizing:** Assuming the blame for problems even when you are not primarily responsible. Mayla blames herself for her positive thinking in the first place. She thinks her disappointment came because she allowed herself to have hope.

6. **Externalizing:** Pushing the blame for problems onto others even when you are primarily responsible. Mayla wants to shift the blame to her teacher.

7. **Overgeneralizing:** Concluding that one bad incident will lead to a repeated pattern of defeat. Mayla decides that she will never be able to pass a math test in this class simply because she didn't pass the first one. She is assuming she will have to go to summer school based on only one piece of evidence.

8. **Emotional reasoning:** Assuming your negative emotions translate into reality, or confusing feelings with facts. Mayla allows her insecurity about her math ability to cloud her view of this single incident. Her past feelings of embarrassment and disappointment are causing her to predict a very discouraging view about the future.

The incident with Mayla illustrates common thought patterns of students who lack competency. It is helpful for teachers to talk with students about common thought holes and even help them practice identifying the patterns when they emerge in classroom discussions. Students learn to point out distorted thinking in their small-group interactions and to identify them in their own perceptions. Even more helpful is showing students how to negate them. Collecting evidence and challenging our perceptions are effective ways to fight thought holes. We can encourage students to gather as much information as possible before deciding to act on or react to a thought. We can also show them how to view their assumption(s) from a different angle.

Building Hope

Mayla decides she is just going to quit trying. If she stays in that frame of mind, she may eventually decide that showing up for school is just not worth the effort. Absenteeism is a mark of hopelessness. Having hope also leads to better education outcomes. Students need something to look forward to and to hope for; it can be big or small. Receiving encouraging feedback, experiencing a small celebration, or accomplishing a goal can fuel their hope and help them learn to think about future things rather than always looking over their shoulder for the next threat.

Travis Wright (2013) works with educators in helping them understand how students reared with severe challenges often resist help from teachers. Their refusal to accept help can be viewed as a resilient act of self-preservation. Wright maintains that a child whose life is consumed

by trials often doesn't know when to stop struggling. Many times, these children have no idea how to embrace joy or even hope. "Unfortunately, if all one ever has known in her short life is stress and struggle, the seeds of hope may never have been planted. Growing without hope is a recipe for disaster, for the child and the world" (Wright, 2013, p. 40).

Jacobs (2015) finds that mindfulness breeds resilience. He cites research from India that confirms individuals who demonstrate greater mindfulness habits exhibit greater resiliency. It seems that mindfulness helps people stop obsessing and replaying negative self-messages in their heads. Thus, mindfulness can provide a practical means of enhancing resilience.

Research tells us students who remain resilient in the midst of adversity tend to enjoy school, even when their grades don't show it. The classroom often offers them the only structure they have in the midst of their otherwise chaotic lives. Their relationships with positive adults at school give them a sense of worth, self-control, and hope. Wright feels that teaching resilience requires an emphasis on teaching students to hope rather than just to wish.

Wishing and hoping both bring satisfaction to the learner in terms of a temporary step into a possibly better circumstance, but wishing is generally short-lived and not attached to any specific goal (e.g., "I wish I could be smart," "I wish I could look like a supermodel," "I wish I played baseball like Adrián Beltré"). It is actually hope that puts dreams into action (e.g., "I hope I can pass this test," "I hope I can lose weight by eating healthy," "I hope I can improve my fielding skills at third base"). Hope helps students get moving. Hopes are generally sustainable, and wishes are not (Lopez, 2013).

Clearly, resilience and hope go together; they fortify each other as students move forward to a future they envision. Getting to know our students and being aware of their visions for their future selves is a valuable way to make sure that what we teach in our classrooms is relevant to them. We can help them see the connections between what they are currently doing and what they hope to be doing in the future. Students learn best when they feel safe and respected and are challenged by a curriculum that matters to them. A class environment that offers a place to belong and feel connected helps students Thrive with resiliency and hope.

What Supporting Resilience Looks Like in the Classroom

RESILIENCY IS MODELED

The teacher encourages and validates survivor mentality over victim mentality. While demonstrating empathy, the teacher maintains high expectations for every student and works with individual students to help them find hope for improvement both in the classroom and beyond. Teachers have to model not only survival but also the ability to Thrive. We need to tell our students about times we wanted to quit or felt overwhelmed. They actually enjoy hearing us tell our stories about being embarrassed and making incredibly dumb decisions. Our journey back to Thriving is an important one that students need to hear. Watching us deal with our own frustrations and disappointments teaches them effective ways to handle loss, disenchantment, and any number of life occurrences. For some students, the adults at school are the only appropriate role models they encounter.

TEACHERS PURPOSEFULLY ESTABLISH POSITIVE CONNECTIONS WITH STUDENTS

Again and again, the research is clear that resiliency in students is best fostered in classes where they feel they are cared about. Students want to be noticed, recognized, nurtured, and valued. Resilience-friendly classrooms are those in which teachers make the time to find out about who their students are, what their immediate and distant hopes are, and what strengths they have. Operating from the vantage point of knowing what is important to their learners, these teachers are able to connect curriculum to student interest and build relationships of trust and respect with every learner. Personal interest surveys, journal writing, and personalized assignments yield important information about who learners are. Teachers can use these and other means to let students know, "You matter to me, and you are worth the effort it takes for me to discover what you care about."

STUDENTS FEEL CONNECTED TO THEIR PEERS

As we discussed earlier in this chapter, positive peer interactions are vital to establishing a secure and compassionate classroom that strengthens resiliency. Teachers need to thoughtfully plan ways to build a sense of community among all members of the class. Offering opportunities for students to help one another is a positive step toward building a kinship. In resilience-friendly classrooms, the teacher creates chances for students to build relationships, share common experiences, and work together toward mutual goals.

THE CLASS HONORS, ENCOURAGES, AND REINFORCES FEELINGS

Depending on the age, gender, and prior experience of students, as well as the dynamics of the social culture of the school, it may be difficult for students to express their emotions. (Generally, a high

Remember the eight Ws: "Work will win when wishy washy wishing won't" (Thomas S. Monson).

school boy does not want to admit fear of rejection in front of his teammates.) However, the heart of building resilience is genuinely acknowledging what one is feeling and dealing with those emotions in effective ways. Teachers can use their personal intuitiveness and experience with students to find a way to help them admit their true feelings (at least to themselves) and can use nonthreatening means to help students learn how to deal with them. Stories, videos, role play, games, journal writing, and small-group discussions are good places to start. In resilience-friendly classes, no one disparages, disrespects, or disregards another person's feelings. Everyone has a right to his personal feelings, and hearing them out is part of the class code.

RESILIENCY IS A PART OF THE CURRICULUM AS WELL AS THE CLASSROOM CULTURE

There are so many ways to bring the topic of resilience into every classroom. It is a science term, it has application to sports, plots in literature revolve around the fictional characters' resilience or lack of it, history is full of stories about how major events were shaped by an army's or even a person's resilience, health and exercise are directly related to resilience, and artists, musicians, and mathematicians have to demonstrate resilience to pursue their focuses. Resilience is a part of living and should be introduced into all aspects of education so students are constantly building the skills they need to respond to the unexpected in strategic ways.

STUDENTS ARE ENCOURAGED TO RECOGNIZE AND CHANGE NEGATIVE, DEFEATING SELF-TALK

A powerful way to teach students how to monitor their negative thoughts and trips down thought holes is to have a candid discussion with them about how our thoughts affect the choices we make and the actions we take. A teacher can ask her students to call her out when she makes a negative assumption or engages in disdainful self-talk. Likewise, the teacher and students can help redirect a class member who uses faulty logic to draw an erroneous conclusion or make a poor decision. Students quickly get adept at spotting these incorrect inferences and enjoy reporting those they hear outside the classroom. Students who learn to identify erroneous assumptions in others are much more likely to be able to see them and clarify them in their own thinking.

HEALTHY CHOICES (BODY AND MIND) ARE PROMOTED

With a strong body and mind, students are not as vulnerable to disease, to anxiety, or to despair. Good health is generally associated with more positive thinking. Students who learn how to deal effectively with stress are more likely to develop stronger resilience. Through both designed instruction and informal coaching, teachers in resilience-friendly classrooms repeatedly focus on the importance of healthy minds and healthy bodies. Students are encouraged to make nutritious food choices, to get plenty of rest, to stay hydrated, to practice good hygiene, and to make decisions that maximize their body's potential.

Frequently Asked Questions

1. **How do you know if a student is resilient or not?**

   Observing how students recover from disappointments and embarrassments is one way to get a general idea about their resiliency. Other things you can look at are these:

   - Do they dwell on things they cannot do anything about?

   - Do they get derailed the moment something unexpected happens?

   - Do they have trouble finishing things or seeing things through?

   - Do they worry excessively about being liked?

   - Is their energy level generally low?

   - Do they have difficulty multitasking?

   - Do they have a lot of self-doubts?

   - Are they unreliable?

   - Do they have trouble laughing or seeing the humor in things?

   - Are they overly concerned with future events?

If your answer is yes to most of the questions, it is probable that your student is not very resilient at this point. Keep in mind that resiliency can be cultivated in students by helping them appreciate their unique gifts, structuring tasks so they can earn success, and making sure they feel safe in your classroom.

2. **What is the difference between sympathy and empathy? Don't teachers need to have both to promote resilience in students?**

Souers and Hall (2016) use the term *forever damaged* in describing the way teachers may look at students when they sympathize too much with them. When sympathy turns to pity, it often limits our expectations for our students and fogs our view of their strengths. The problem with sympathy (pity) is that it draws our attention to what has happened (or is happening) rather than to what can be done about it. Time spent wringing our hands over poor decisions by parents (or others), unfortunate accidents or circumstances, and other realities that draw our attention away from solutions is unproductive. When we (the authors) talk about empathy, we are referring to the process of trying to understand from a student's perspective. Empathy is what allows us to change our presumptive feelings and focus on the root cause of a student's behavior rather than on just the behavior itself. Empathy gives us a student-centered lens through which to view what *could be* rather than merely *what is*, and thus help our students build their resiliency. We talk more about empathy in Chapter 8.

3. **As a teacher, I have a problem with the young men in my class who think it's not cool to be kind to kids outside their crew. What do I do about all their posturing and eye rolling when I'm trying to get other kids to open up?**

Many young men have an underlying fear of being vulnerable. They believe that expressing or even tolerating authentic emotions will lead to being labeled unmanly in some way. It is important that we tell them that they may not be able to be kind (yet), but they can definitely be respectful. Almost every student behaves respectfully in a class where he feels respected. As teachers, it is vital that we let our students know they matter and help them save face while still adhering to classroom protocols. Power struggles with these students never end well. Wise teachers enforce the rules but keep their reprimands as private as possible and work with students individually to help them find a way to behave appropriately and still maintain their sense of security. Students' resilience is strengthened when they believe they are valued for their authentic selves more than their macho selves.

4. **I once had a teacher whose standard answer was "Suck it up, Buttercup" to every complaint we students had. Do you think that's a good way to help students build resiliency?**

It's hard to respond to that without knowing more about the overall demeanor of that teacher's response. We have known several teachers who might say this with a wry smile and a wink conveying that they are listening and understand but they want the students to handle things themselves. Those teachers would have already led extensive discussions about resiliency and would be indicating they wanted the student to draw on the skills they already knew. The teachers would follow up to see how the students were doing and let them know they have their backs if the students seriously need help. However, if the response was a stock answer said with a tone that indicated disinterest and if there was no follow-up with the student, that definitely would not promote resilience. When teachers sigh, drop their shoulders, roll their eyes/heads upwards, or otherwise communicate to students what a bother they are, it only adds to the students' feelings of helplessness and further diminishes their resilience. Students need to be heard, and we teachers need to remind ourselves that what we may think is relatively unimportant is very important to them (at least for the present time). We hope your teachers fell into the former and not the latter description.

Discussion Questions and Exercises

We encourage you to tweet your responses to @tchkids2thrive.

1. What is the difference between perseverance and resiliency? Give three examples of each. How are they connected?

2. How do you help foster your students' resiliency skills? Talk about what you do in general, but also cite specific strategies you use. What things have you thought about trying that you've not yet implemented?

3. Describe the most resilient students you know. Where do you think their resiliency strength comes from? What do they do that tells you they are resilient?

4. A student confides in you that she is having trouble at home. Her parents drink a lot and start yelling and cursing. Her mother frequently gets mad at her and calls her horrible names. She grounds her for minor infractions, and when she's not grounded, she can't invite friends over because she never knows how her parents are going to behave. What are your responsibilities here—legally, ethically, morally? How do you help this child develop her resilience?

5. Do most of your interactions with students model sympathy and defeat or empathy and optimism? Give examples of when you have used each kind of reaction. Which of those methods was most helpful (long term) to the learner? Why?

6. Why is it important to normalize the struggle for students?

7. Describe thought holes in your own words. Are these leaps of assumption typical for your students? How can you deflect this kind of negative thinking?

8. Do you think there is a Boy Code among your male students? What evidence makes you think that way? What can teachers do to overcome the Boy Code when they are trying to get boys to open up about their social and emotional learning?

ACTIVITY 5.1

Eggsample of Optimism

This is a science experiment that teaches center of gravity, but can also demonstrate optimism with kids. Eggs naturally lie on their long axis parallel to the surface. But with the right additions (positive self-talk), a raw egg can stand up vertically! This is an easy task, but you should practice a few times before you do the demonstration with the class.

Materials

- A raw egg
- Salt
- Pepper
- A hard surface
- Precut paper speech bubbles

Directions

1. Talk to students about the ability of an egg to stand upright. Can it happen?

2. Say, "Sometimes, when negative things happen to us, we want to just give up like the egg *[demonstrate the egg lying down]* and be sad or negative. But by adding in just a little positive thinking and positive self-talk, we can do what we once thought we could not."

3. Continue: "People can be a little like the egg on the table. When things happen, like we fail a spelling test, we want to lie down and think, 'I can't spell no matter what I do! *[add pepper to the table]*. There is no sense in even trying; I just can't' *[add more pepper]*."

4. Try to stand the egg upright on the pepper pile (it won't work). Say, "Negative talk does not help us feel better or bounce back."

5. Then say, "But sometimes, with a little added self-talk, the impossible gets easier."

(Continued)

(Continued)

6. Move the pepper and pour a small pile of salt on a flat surface. Say, "The salt is positive talk: 'If I study my spelling words a little each night, I can get better.' 'Maybe I can find online games to practice spelling.' 'I know if I work hard, I can do better than last week.'"

7. Place the egg on top of the salt vertically (long axis pointed up).

8. Gently shift the egg back and forth until it feels stable in its upright position and then let go! The egg should remain standing.

9. Ask students to share situations where they had positive or negative self-talk. Did it help or hurt?

10. Give students precut speech bubbles and ask them to go back and write positive self-talk statements they can use when they get discouraged. See Activity Sheet 5.1, "Speech Bubbles," on the *Thrive* website (www.teachingkidstothrive.com).

ACTIVITY 5.2

Dear Me, Erase the Negative and Replace It With the Positive

Step 1: Create a Class Word Cloud

On a whiteboard, write a negative statement (e.g., "I can't do this," "I never win") in the middle of the board. Later in the day, have students add other negative thoughts, traits, and self-talk all over the board. It should look like a giant word cloud when finished. Leave the board for the rest of the day. Before the next day, erase the original statement in the middle of the board and replace it with a positive statement that is opposite (e.g., "I can learn to do a backflip; I just need to practice more," "I am organized, and that helps me in school"). When students come in the next day, see how long it takes for someone to notice the one positive statement among all the negatives. Once someone notices, ask her if the positive statement feels better than all that negative self-talk. Challenge the students to look for a statement, trait, or thought that they could erase and replace with a positive one. As the day goes on, students can find moments to go to the board and erase and replace quietly. Once the board is complete, discuss how seeing all the positive talk feels so much better.

Step 2: Top-Ten List—My Ideas

Students create a top-ten list of their positive traits such as well-organized, good sense of humor, and so on. Students should also write at least four positive thinking strategies (pick-me-ups) they can use during difficult times. Create symbols or pictures to go with the four pick-me-ups.

Step 3: Dear Me Letter—Summarize

Students should then use the top-ten list to help them compose a letter to themselves about the power of erasing negative thoughts and replacing them with positive ones.

ACTIVITY 5.3

Building Tribes

This activity is a compliment-building activity where class members give each other compliments.

1. Have students decorate a large envelope or piece of construction paper with their name on it.

2. Pass out strips of paper to each student. If there are twenty-five students in the class, then each student should receive twenty-five strips of paper.

3. Have students work throughout the week to write a compliment for each student on the slips of paper. *Be sure to talk to students about compliments—what they look like and sound like.*

4. You will probably want to read through the contributions to make sure that they are all kind and appropriate for class.

5. At the end of the week, have students place the compliment strips in each person's envelope.

6. Then invite students to pick up their personal envelope and read all the nice things the class has to say about them.

7. Finally, have students write a journal entry telling how reading their personal compliments felt. Students can draw on these positive statements when they are feeling discouraged.

ACTIVITY 5.4

Resiliency Reminders

Resilience is not a trait that people either have or do not have. It involves behaviors, thoughts, and actions that can be learned and developed in anyone.

To reinforce this idea, have students jointly create a list of adverse things that occur in almost everyone's life:

Examples

- Being late for something important
- Not being invited to a party
- Coming in last at something
- Thinking you did a great job and getting a failing grade
- Finding out someone you trust lied to you
- Having an event canceled because somebody else misbehaved
- Getting blamed for something that wasn't your fault
- Breaking something valuable
- Discovering you are the only one in your group who can't do something

Invite students to share their experiences and feelings in these situations. Brainstorm methods they (or those they have observed) use to deal with adversity in a positive way. Students can individually select the ideas most appealing to them and create their own resiliency reinforcement reminders to keep for when they need to get past a difficult situation. See Activity Sheet 5.2, "Resiliency Reminders," on the *Thrive* website (www.teachingkidstothrive.com). Encourage students to remember times they overcame the odds and carry those memories to reinforce their resilience when the time calls for it.

ACTIVITY 5.5

The Path to Overcoming Challenges

In order to get students to reflect on their tribes, it can be helpful to think about the following questions either by talking about them (primary and elementary) or by writing their responses (middle and high school).

1. Name a person who supported you during a particularly stressful or traumatic time. How did the person help you overcome the challenge(s) you faced? What did you learn about yourself? What did you learn about the person?

2. Name a friend whom you supported as he went through a stressful event. What did you do that most helped your friend? What did you learn about yourself?

Access the website **www.teachingkidstothrive.com** to find more classroom-ready activities, author-recommended videos, websites, and other resources.

BUILDING A CULTURE OF RESPONSIBILITY IN THE CLASSROOM

The moment you are old enough to take the wheel, responsibility lies with you.

—J. K. Rowling (2008)

●●● TEACHING RESPONSIBILITY?

Teacher: "It's your turn to clean out the hamster cage."

Student: "I don't know how."

Teacher: "Yes, you do. The steps are listed on the information sheet posted on the wall behind her cage."

Student: "I don't want to clean the cage. I want to go to recess."

Teacher: "As a class family, we all work together, remember? Today it's your turn to clean the cage. This is your responsibility."

Student: "I don't even like the hamster. I don't know how to clean stupid hamster cages."

(Continued)

(Continued)

©iStockphoto.com/Kingarion

Teacher: "Here, let me remind you how I like it done. First, I take the hamster out and put her over here while I clean her cage. Next, I empty the dirty shavings into this container like this. . . . Hey, you're not even watching me!"

Student: "I was watching them play soccer outside. They really, really need me out there to help."

Teacher: "Well, not until you clean this cage. Next, I take the disinfectant soap and scrub the bottom tray like this. . . . Here, you try it."

Student: [Makes a feeble attempt, then spills soapy water on the floor.] "Oops, the soap got all over the floor."

Teacher: "Oh my stars! Look at the mess you've made. What were you thinking? This is not how you are supposed to do it. [Sighs.] Now I'll have to mop this entire area."

Student: "I didn't mean to. I just want to go play."

Teacher: "Well, just go play then. I need to get this hamster back in a clean cage and have this mess cleaned up before the bell rings. Just go on. I can do this quicker without you standing here complaining." ●

Give Kids a Chance
to Act Responsibly

Many times, when we advise teachers to turn over more class jobs and assignment obligations to students, the protest we hear is, "But I do not have time to stop and teach them how to do every little thing. Honestly, it is just easier to do it myself." No question about it, working with a beginner is usually a long arduous process. But isn't that a rather important part of our job as teachers?

Part of the challenge of teaching 21st century students is the same as it has been for every previous generation—how do we transform children into adults capable of meeting the challenges of life head-on? How do we help them become responsible? Do we do it by succumbing to the temptation of getting it done faster and exactly how we script it, or do we slow down and take the time to engage, model, question, observe, and give feedback only as needed? Many teachers who employ the learner-centered approach tell us that if their daily lessons had an attached GPS, it would mostly say, "Re-cal-cu-la-ting. . . ." It's hard to be ready for all the teachable moments, but those are the times when teaching seems so "lifelike."

Teaching Responsibility
in an Entitled Society

Entitlement is one of the fastest-growing obstacles for prekindergarten through twelfth-grade educators, college boards, and the workforce. In this everyone-gets-a-trophy, don't-feel-sad, show-me-the-money, keeping-up-with-the-Kardashians society, it is hard to find a way to reset the entitlement button on our students in just nine short months. We think at least part of the answer lies in embedding the essential Thrive skills into our curriculum and our instruction. These basic foundational skills support helping students develop into balanced, productive citizens.

Using Accountability to
Promote Responsibility

Teachers often complain about the enabling "lawn-mower parents" who run along in front of their child mowing down the obstructions

CLASSROOM TIPS

Lessening the Feeling of Entitlement

1. Help students experience delayed gratification.

2. Promote gratitude in the classroom.

3. Encourage students to own the outcome of their conduct.

4. Help students see they are no more (or less) deserving than anyone else. (Elmore, 2014)

and pushing the hurdles out of the way. With a little self-reflection, educators might have to acknowledge that sometimes we act a bit like "lawn-mower teachers." There are times we rush in too quickly to "save" a child struggling with an assignment or we boost grades because we don't want students to feel discouraged.

Lippmann, Bulanda, and Wagenaar (2009) believe that teachers sometimes perpetuate the entitlement issue with the use of grade inflation: "Grade inflation has important implications for student entitlement, primarily by fostering inflated expectations among students about the quality of their work and about the amount of work expected of students" (p. 199). Perhaps the best way we can foster success beyond the classroom is to teach students to be accountable for their learning as we hold them to reasonable (and high) expectations.

Building a Culture of Responsibility

BUILDING A CULTURE OF RESPONSIBILITY
BY PUTTING STUDENTS IN
CHARGE OF THEIR LEARNING

As a former dean of freshmen and undergraduate advising at Stanford University, Julie Lythcott-Haims witnessed firsthand what happened to top-tier students from across the country who were unable to perform even simple tasks when they were separated from their parents (e.g., clean their rooms, work out problems with a roommate, get a flat tire repaired, navigate in a new city, or even make a scheduling decision without calling home).

Lythcott-Haims provides guidance for parents, but like most good parenting advice, many of her observations hold true for educators as well. Traditionally, teachers have acted not only as role models for responsibility but also as guides. Some of our styles are better suited than others for developing conscientiousness in students.

Researchers agree that students learn responsibility best from adults acting in ways that are *authoritative* rather than *authoritarian*. Lythcott-Haims (2015) defines *authoritarian* as "demanding and unresponsive" (p. 147). Adults who are authoritarian do not give reasons for their actions. Their standard response is along the lines of "Because I said so." Students of authoritarian teachers have a lot of rules to follow and very little freedom to make choices. These teachers value order, compliance, and strict discipline. Figure 6.1 illustrates the difference between authoritarian and authoritative modes of management.

In the hamster cage scenario, the teacher is extremely authoritarian. She has an exact way she wants things done, and when the process doesn't go the way she has planned, she gives up on the student and

Figure 6.1

Authoritarian and Authoritative

AUTHORITARIAN	AUTHORITATIVE
Leader of the classroom	Guide of the classroom
Gets obedience	Gets respect
Order and compliance	High standards and firm limits
Disciplined	Responsive to learners
Rule based	Encouraging
Little choice	Accountability with choice
"Because I said so!"	"Here's why we do it this way."

takes over. Having the hamster cage cleaned to her specifications with little or no mess is what she values. What her student learns from this encounter is that whining and doing a poor job can get you what you want. He learns nothing about being a responsible classroom member.

Authoritative teachers set high standards and limits, which they uphold with logical consequences. Unlike authoritarians, they are warm and responsive to the needs of learners. They encourage students to explore, to take risks, and to make their own decisions about how to deal with their mistakes. They treat students as independent, rational beings, and they are willing to discuss the reasons behind the rules.

An authoritative teacher would have listened attentively to the student not wanting to clean the hamster cage and perhaps even empathized with his feelings. However, she would have gently insisted that he take care of the business at hand. When he made the mess, she would have calmly asked him how he intended to clean it up. She would have supported him in his efforts, even if they weren't quite perfect, and applauded his finished accomplishment while thanking him for doing his part.

Lythcott-Haims (2015) recommends that for every activity, job, event, project, and assignment teachers ask themselves, "How can I give my students more responsibility here? I don't want them to stand around while I do all the work." The person who is doing all the work becomes invested in the process and is the one actively learning.

Robyn Jackson, the author of *Never Work Harder Than Your Students* (2009), agrees. She is concerned about the diminished capacity of student responsibility in teacher-centered classrooms. She reasons that when teachers control every aspect of learning—planning what will be taught, how it will be taught, how the students will learn, and how the students will demonstrate their learning—there is not that much that students are asked to do. She asks the question, "How will students learn to take more responsibility unless we first relinquish some of the control?" (p. 173). She makes an excellent point that one of the greatest ways to instill responsibility is to make sure that students are accountable for their own learning.

Jackson encourages teachers to resist the temptation to give students every detail of the lesson up front, and instead provide them with only the information they need to discover things for

"There is a big difference between teachers who are controlling and teachers who are in control" (Debbie Silver).

One teacher uses glue sticks as an opportunity for students to gain responsibility and power in their classroom. Elementary teachers collectively lament about all the glue sticks that have gone dry well before their time. Yet getting students to simply place the lids on the glue sticks after use is a never-ending battle. One day, the teacher decided to stop telling the students what to do with the glue sticks by putting the students in charge. Right before the art lesson, she handed out glue sticks to everyone, and it didn't take long before the group of seven-year-olds who were to do their art turned to her in frustration, "These glue sticks are dried up!" With concern and compassion, the teacher listened to the children as they vented their irritation over trying to get their art to stick. She allowed the students to come to the natural conclusion she had been trying to teach for years—glue sticks have to be treated with care if they are going to last. The students were inspired to create a new class procedure for caring and storing the sticks after each use. Voilà! Students took ownership and looked beyond their immediate needs to ensure the glue sticks would be in good shape for the next student to use (while the teacher stood back and watched in amazement). ●

themselves. Like many reform-minded educators, she implores teachers to ask more open-ended questions of students and answer fewer of the questions they can find out for themselves. Curriculum and management issues are key ways teachers can teach and reinforce responsibility. For tasks requiring subtle deductions or inviting personal inquiry, teachers need to use more coaching, facilitating, discussions, and problem-based learning and less direct instruction.

BUILDING A CULTURE OF RESPONSIBILITY
WITH CURRICULUM

One of the greatest gifts we can give our students is building a culture that supports their growth and development as responsible members of society. Students Thrive on being responsible and doing what needs to be done. Sarah Fine (2015) sums up the importance of weaving opportunities for student responsibility into the curriculum in her statement, "Pedagogy enacts culture."

"Conscientious students understand they have a responsibility to learn and to reach their fullest potential" (Stamps, 2006).

The one-size-fits-all instructional model, where teachers focus on the "I do, we do, you do" method of instruction, is being used less and less in the classroom. Districts are rethinking traditional structuring as personalized learning models gain momentum. Although there is an array of names for the new design, the method centers on truly meeting the needs of every learner in the most efficient way via diverse learning experiences and instructional approaches. This student-centered approach combines online learning, face-to-face instruction, collaboration opportunities, and other support strategies with the learner's needs as a focus. The key element of success for personalized learning is responsibility. Students are no longer able to passively "sit and get" instruction.

If the student-focused model is to be successful, students must take the initiative, solve issues that arise, be accountable, and actively seek clarification when needed. Sherry Crofut, a Milken Educator and a learning specialist at TIE (Technology and Innovation in Education), believes that the skills students master in a customized learning environment go far beyond the academic skills taught. "Students who learn in a customized learning environment have more ownership in the process than the traditional student. They are aware of their personal learning styles and learn to work at their own pace in a way that pushes them to balance, prioritize, and make responsible choices" (personal communication, July 24, 2016).

BUILDING A CULTURE OF RESPONSIBILITY
THROUGH CLASSROOM MANAGEMENT

Another important aspect of creating a culture of responsibility involves classroom management. Proactive teachers think ahead about all of the routines, procedures, and protocols they will need to help the class run smoothly and which ones they can delegate to students (all but those that absolutely have to be done by the teacher). Students can be responsible for collecting papers, passing out materials, taking attendance, beginning and ending class, and any number of tasks that teachers have traditionally done. On the *Thrive* website (www.teachingkidstothrive.com), we have a suggested list of classroom tasks that elementary and secondary teachers may consider turning over to students.

Responsible teachers make the time to instruct students on appropriate ways to handle common issues such as turning in late homework, making up for absent work, forgetting a book

©iStockphoto.com/asiseeit

Mary Ann Taylor set up a Cafeteria Council to tackle a problem that involved a chaotic school cafeteria situation, including aides yelling at students, students yelling at each other, food fights, and the general appearance of a "war zone." Each classroom elected student delegates who were charged with representing their constituency's ideas as expressed in class meetings. Delegates carried their classrooms' views to the weekly meetings where they worked with Taylor and the school principal to set up action proposals. The council conducted surveys, set up suggestion boxes, and even published a monthly newsletter reporting progress. Over time, the student cafeteria behavior showed marked improvement. Students, as well as their parents, showed enthusiastic support for the changes. A recycling program was begun. Most importantly, though, the school decided to keep its new delegate system of democratic student government as a way to deal with other issues. Students were able to experience the kind of opportunities for real-life decision making that build responsibility (Lickona, 2004). ●

(or iPad), and other predictable circumstances. They explain the logical consequences of student choices and unilaterally enforce them. (It is fine to make accommodations for individual student needs, but those should be discussed up front with as much disclosure as prudently possible.)

Many teachers create codes of conduct with their students in order to give them a sense of shared responsibility for what goes on in class. Whether student generated, teacher generated, or school mandated, expectations must be clearly communicated to students. Students need to be made aware of logical consequences that are a result of less-than-desirable choices.

Barbara Coloroso (2008) maintains that holding students accountable is not judgmental, arbitrary, confusing, or coercive: "It is a process that gives life to learning; it is restorative and invites reconciliation. Its goal is to instruct, teach, guide, and help children develop self-discipline—an ordering of the self from the inside, not imposition from the outside" (p. 106).

Teachers need to give learners the chance to prove their trustworthiness, their competency, and their ability to answer for their behavior. With opportunities to self-evaluate and accept responsibility for mistakes, students gain confidence and feel more capable. As teachers, we can promote responsibility by creating "responsibility forms" for students to use in reflecting on situations in which they demonstrated poor judgment (e.g., didn't turn in an assignment, let their group down, didn't do their personal best).

BUILDING A CULTURE OF RESPONSIBILITY
BASED ON RELATIONSHIPS

Finally, the culture of responsibility is underpinned by positive relationships and close connections with students. Teacher–student relationships affect everything in the classroom, including responsibility. Teachers who find ways to connect with students within the classroom realize that influence through relationships is a powerful tool. Students work harder and behave more responsibly for teachers they like and respect. This relationship can be further expanded by finding creative ways to connect with students outside the classroom (e.g., attending their extracurricular events, conversing with them in the halls or at lunch, inviting them to participate in activities outside of school).

One of my favorite ways to create an avenue for building relationships with my students is to have a "Who Is Mrs. Stafford?" bulletin board. I put all kinds of things up on the board (e.g., pictures of my family including my pets, my favorite sports teams, my dream car, places I want to visit, my favorite TV shows). Students love to start conversations about things we share in common. It's a great way to build relationships! (Dedra Stafford)●

Teachers as Models of Responsibility

We teachers realize that students watch everything we do (and don't do) and listen to everything we say (and don't say). They are extremely savvy about measuring our words against our actions. And whether we like it or not, we are role models for just about everything to learners including shaping their views on responsibility. So first and foremost, it is our obligation to behave in responsible ways. Lumpkin (2008) states, "Teachers demonstrate responsibility by being morally accountable for their actions and fulfilling their duties. When teachers create and sustain a positive learning environment and focus on providing educational services to students and society, they are acting responsibly" (p. 48).

Teachers can demonstrate personal responsibility by

1. Showing up on time and being where we are supposed to be

2. Following district, school, and class rules

3. Being prepared for every class

4. Grading assignments in a timely manner

5. Attending important school events as well as extracurricular activities valued by students

6. Being collegial with other staff members and supporting all adults on campus

7. Helping out where needed no matter what our assigned duties are

8. Taking opportunities to grow professionally and letting our students know it

9. Being fully present with students and not distracted by electronic devices, colleagues, or personal agendas

10. Setting up a classroom that invites and supports students to behave responsibly ●

We believe that intuitively most teachers understand the importance of their function as role models. Perhaps it will be reassuring to review the list on page 151 and see how many of these activities you do as a matter of routine.

How Do We Reinforce Responsibility?

●●● A TEACHER CHANGES HER MIND ABOUT REWARDING "RESPONSIBLE" BEHAVIOR

Teacher and blogger Amber Chandler (2016) writes about her recent realization of how cautious teachers need to be when grading student responsibility, especially when it involves factors a student cannot influence. She examines the popular practice of awarding points or grades for students who bring in all their supplies the first week of school. Until she had children of her own to buy supplies for, she did not realize how unfair this policy was to children from low-income families who cannot afford the very expensive long list of teacher-requested items. She mentions her own struggle in trying to find a yellow, three-prong plastic folder, with pockets, requested by one of her children's teachers. The search required visits to several stores. She wondered what happened in families who did not have the opportunity or the transportation to go folder chasing. She vowed to stop withholding rewards from students who had little or no control over the situation and to stop assuming they are just being irresponsible. ●

Researchers agree that arbitrary punishment for students behaving irresponsibly is counterproductive. It is much more effective to have them experience a logical consequence for their choices. Evenly and rationally, the teacher can help the students focus on what they can control and assist them in finding ways to improve their decisions.

Responsibility is an important, beneficial life trait needed for success. Because we believe its value should be intrinsic and associated with a certain gratification and dignity of its own, we think teachers should generally refrain from using extrinsic rewards (candy, stickers, and other prizes that have nothing to do with being responsible) to reward students for their conscientious behavior. It is far more beneficial to acknowledge responsible behavior with affirmations, more privileges, and even more responsibility (because that is what students really want).

On the other hand, some educators expertly use meaningful symbols of accomplishment to supplement their focus on integrity and responsibility:

Jim Triplett inspires his all-male class of fifth graders with a promise that when they demonstrate extraordinary integrity and responsibility, they will receive a solid red tie from him to wear proudly with their uniforms. The ties are hard earned, and in this situation, they serve less like a reward and more as a symbol of achievement. His students are inspired to display the behavior needed to earn their ties (Crouch, 2014). ●

Brent Vasicek honors his students with either silicon or woven integrity bracelets he has made just for them. Students wear them as a symbol of honor and report their bracelets help keep them inspired (Vasicek, 2010). Money and toys have nowhere near the power or positive impact of these deep, meaningful worked-for treasures. Our hope is that these students' strongly held personal sense of responsibility will lead to a feeling of integrity (described in Chapter 7). ●

It needs to be reiterated that student responsibility does not just happen. To develop responsibility, students have to draw on some of their executive function skills including organization, task orientation, self-regulation, and focus. Other key dispositions that go along with responsibility are self-efficacy and perseverance. For teachers to maximize opportunities to teach student responsibility, it helps if the following practices are in place.

What Supporting Responsibility Looks Like in the Classroom

Acknowledge responsible behavior with affirmations, more privileges, and even more responsibility (because that is what students really want).

THE TEACHER MODELS RESPONSIBILITY

As discussed previously, the teacher is instrumental in helping students visualize what being a conscientious community member means.

The best way to get students to respect and value the teacher is for the teacher to respect and value the students first.

RULES, ROUTINES, AND PROCEDURES ARE COMMUNICATED

Rules, routines, and procedures are clearly communicated and maintained. The classroom is set up in a manner that increases the likelihood that students will remain engaged. Previously agreed-upon logical consequences are dispensed for violations of class codes.

CONSEQUENCES ARE GIVEN CALMLY WITHOUT JUDGMENT OR LABELS

The teacher focuses on the negative behavior, not the student's character. Students are given a chance to make up for inappropriate behavior and held accountable. The behavior choice by the student is often not a reflection of the classroom or the teacher; it is simply a poor choice. Teachers who respond with understanding but hold students accountable to right the wrong create a better chance for students to learn from the experience instead of feeling as though they were mistreated.

THE TEACHER IS NOT WORKING HARDER THAN THE STUDENTS

Students do the majority of the work in the classroom. The teacher acts as a facilitator. The teacher is available for assistance but does *not* do the work for the student. Teachers offer the least amount of help required to help students move forward and are comfortable with waiting for learners to sort things out. Teachers realize that new learning takes practice and are willing to help students transition into the role of self-managers. They give them authentic feedback and gradually raise the bar of expectation so that students are stretched to new levels of capability.

STUDENT-CENTERED LEARNING IS ENCOURAGED

As much as possible, assignments are student centered and learner directed. Not all instruction can be project based or learned in discovery, but whenever it is appropriate, the teacher gets the students involved in finding their own solutions.

RESPONSIBILITY IS VALUED YEAR ROUND

Responsibility is not a stand-alone lesson of the week. Discussions about what is responsible and what is not responsible behavior are woven throughout the curriculum through characters in fictional stories, historical anecdotes, current events, sports, and other appropriate moments. Teachers regularly point out responsible acts and help students discern what acts are not responsible and why.

PARENTS ARE INCLUDED

Include parents in the vision by giving them information on how to help students learn appropriate responsibility for their grade level. Let them know you are focused on helping their child develop responsibility during the year. Make it clear that you would rather have a student show up without the homework or assignment and learn how to make it right than receive homework that parents have virtually done for the child. You will find a sample parent letter in the Resources section on the *Thrive* website (www.teachingkidstothrive.com).

STUDENTS ARE HELD ACCOUNTABLE FOR THEIR CHOICES

Teachers do not rely on giving zeros for late or missing work to promote responsibility. Students should be required to explain why the work was not completed and what they will do to remedy the situation. Hold them accountable for making up the work.

> Grades by themselves are terrible teachers of self-discipline or builders of responsibility. Receiving an unrecoverable F or zero on a final project or a test for which they did not prepare doesn't teach students how to get their act together and meet deadlines or how to study better for tests. If Fs taught students to be responsible, we'd have a lot more responsible students. (Wormeli, 2016a)

1. **I was told that I should keep ample supplies like pencils for students in my classroom so that they are not academically penalized for forgetting to bring their materials to class. How is that teaching responsibility?**

This perennial question is a hard one. It is tough to know when we are helping students to have what they need to have a reasonable chance at success and when we are enabling students to be irresponsible. It's important to have a policy that is reasonable but does not reward the student for irresponsible choices.

We suggest having a stash of stub pencils (like those used at miniature golf courses) on hand for emergencies. Students do not like them, and that serves as motivation to bring their own. One teacher we know keeps new pencils available. When a student doesn't have a pencil, she asks the class for volunteers to trade their old pencil for a new one. She chooses the shabbiest pencil to exchange and hands it to the student who did not bring one.

One more idea that fits with our idea of teaching responsibility while keeping the learning process going is this from one of our teaching buddies: Keep a small stockpile of books, materials, and supplies students are required to bring with them to class. If a student forgets an article and needs to borrow one from the reserve, he must exchange something of value for it (e.g., his phone, a piece of jewelry, a shoe). At the end of class, the student returns the borrowed item and is given a way to earn back his possession (e.g., straighten desks, pick up trash from the floor, clean the board). This strategy serves the dual purpose of making sure all students have what they need and ensuring there is a consequence for not being prepared.

The bottom line is that you have to thoughtfully consider your long-term goals for students when you make decisions about procedures like dealing with missing items. We advise teachers to be true to their belief systems and work with students to find a reasonable solution.

Don't be afraid to modify or switch any policy that is not working for you, and don't hesitate to get your students involved with both creating and enforcing the plan.

2. **I understand the concept behind providing logical consequences, but what happens when logical consequences don't work?**

There will always be times when students choose the consequence over a behavior change. That is why it is called a *choice*. Hopefully, over the long term, students will internalize the relationship between their choices and adverse results from those choices, but sometimes that takes awhile. As teachers, we try very hard to make sure any consequences we dispense are logical and as close as possible to what would happen in life outside the classroom. Sometimes, a private chat with the student will provide insight or suggest another means to solve the problem. However, it is important never to compromise your standards or give up on the student. Let students know you support them as people even when you cannot accept their behavior. It is essential that teachers enforce consequences in a consistent manner and that they are careful to refrain from making this a power struggle. Be firm and empathetic and resolute and open. Try not to paint students into a corner; help provide a way for them to fulfill their obligation and still save face.

3. **Doesn't having consequences for your actions mean giving zeros for missing work? If I always give kids second and third chances at doing an assignment, aren't I just teaching them the opposite of responsibility? I don't see how letting students make up five assignments right before the semester is over will teach them anything.**

One of our guiding principles for any decision about classroom procedures is to ask ourselves, "What is my ultimate goal for my students when they leave my class?" We want students who are responsible and believe they can succeed. We want to instill a certain sense of urgency in our learners so that they don't fall behind, but we want to make sure they are not disproportionately penalized for a poor decision error. Giving students a zero makes it almost mathematically impossible for them to make up that deficit in a grading period, and it sometimes leads to their reaction, "Then why bother trying? I'm already going to fail."

A zero in the grade book does not really teach responsibility because it lets students off the hook for something they didn't want to do in the first place. Wouldn't a better idea be to give them an incomplete and require they make up the work (maybe during lunch, during a fun school event, or whenever it is inconvenient for the student)? Many teachers accept do-overs, but they take a penalty (e.g., 10 percent or a letter grade off) from the score. That usually limits your do-overs because students think, "Well, if she's going to make me do it anyway, I might as well do it now and get full credit for it."

You have to decide what works best in your situation. You could ask the students for help in setting your policy. That would not only give them more responsibility up front but would also ensure more of a buy-in from them once the policy is in place.

4. **I have always given grades or at least bonus points for a student who brought back signed permission slips or supplies to class by the required date. If I don't do that, what is the motivation for students to be responsible?**

We have had to rethink that issue ourselves. As we mentioned in the chapter, you may want to question a policy that offers bonus points to students over things they cannot control. If parents are not available for signatures or if families have no way to buy the supplies you request by a certain time, is it fair to withhold points from that student? Even though the points are for a bonus, does that still put some students at a disadvantage?

The motivation needs to be the intrinsic value of a responsible action, but we know you are asking for something a little more tangible than that. You could hand students a form asking them to estimate when they will be able to have the requested item back to you. Tell them just to fill out the form as honestly as they can and let them know that if there's a problem, you will work with them. Ask them to write down a specific plan for how they will get the job done. For example, "Tonight I will give my mom my supply list. I will ask her to take me to the store to get the things I need. When she can take me to the store, we will go and buy the items on the list. When I get home, I will write my name on my materials and pack them in my book bag so that I will remember to take them to school the next day. I plan to have all my supplies by Monday."

Just the act of generating a written plan will make it more likely that students will remember to do their part. You could plan a small celebration for when all signed slips are back or when all supplies have been brought, but don't let the students know whom you are still waiting on. Privately talk to students who seem to be having a problem with your request. If you suspect the problem is the students' forgetfulness, have them write another plan of action.

Discussion Questions and Exercises

We encourage you to tweet your responses to @tchkids2thrive.

1. Think back over the best teachers you ever had or presently know. Were (are) their teaching styles more authoritative or authoritarian? How did (do) they help their students become more responsible?

2. Would you rate yourself as having more of an authoritative or an authoritarian teaching style? On what do you base your assessment of your personal style?

3. Make a list of routine and procedural activities you now do in your classroom that could be delegated to students. What is your reason for not asking students to do these tasks?

4. What is your policy about makeup work and do-overs? How does your policy fit with your belief system about responsible student behavior?

5. Are your classroom management policies designed to help foster student responsibility? In what ways do the strategies you use in class help cultivate student responsibility?

6. Looking at the list for how teachers can demonstrate personal responsibility (see page 151), can you think of others that should be added? Do you disagree with any items on the list? How would you rate yourself on the ten items listed?

Thrive Skills in Action

ACTIVITY 6.1

A Responsibility Challenge: One Pencil

Create a challenge to see how many students can keep track of a single pencil for a set amount of time (a day, a week, a month).

1. Establish the timeline and the prize if the goal is reached. Is it a responsibility medal? Lunch with the teacher? A decorated pencil?

2. Get a box of new pencils (preferably a good brand so there are not a lot of issues with breakage). Label each pencil with duct tape and a number (wrap it around the top so it forms a little flag).

3. Assign each student a number and explain that the class is practicing responsibility with a challenge. The challenge is to keep track of and use the numbered pencil for X number of days.

4. Explain what being responsible for the pencil looks like: Keep your pencil in your desk when you are not using it, don't chew your pencil, don't purposefully flick or break your pencil, and so on.

5. Collect the pencils at the end of each day and return them the next morning.

6. Disqualify any pencils found on the ground, and remove the number flag. Place those pencils in the pencil bucket for anyone who needs a pencil, and count the student out of the challenge.

7. At the end of the time period, examine the results as a class. What percentage of the class met the challenge? What skills and methods did individuals use to keep track of their pencils?

8. Follow up with a new challenge: maybe extend the period or, better yet, challenge a nearby class!

Thrive Skills in Action
Chapter 6 Activities

ACTIVITY 6.2

Four Types of Responsibility

Teach students the basics of what it means to be responsible in all aspects of their lives.

1. Give each student four sticky notes along with Activity Sheet 6.1, "Responsible Me," found on the *Thrive* website (www .teachingkidstothrive .com).

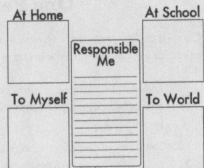

2. Ask students to come up with all the things they are responsible for in each of the four categories.

3. Make a list for each on a sticky note (responsibilities at home, at school, to myself, and to the world).

4. Look at each of the lists carefully. Ask students to consider if there is one thing they could do better or something they need to start being responsible for.

5. Have them create an improvement goal for each of the four categories and write it in the square on the activity sheet.

6. Have them place the corresponding sticky note on each square (covering the goal).

7. Ask them to write a summary paragraph, poem, or mantra in the middle square about what it means to be responsible in all areas of your life.

8. Revisit these goals later in the month to remind students to keep working hard.

ACTIVITY 6.3

A Year With a Buddy

An excellent way to help students practice humility is to adopt a nearby nursing home or retirement center for the year. Get a picture of the residents to place on the classroom wall and let the students take the lead. Discuss the issues of loneliness and isolation that are often felt by those who live in these communities. Each student can get an individual buddy, or the class can act as one for all the residents. Students write letters, color pictures for the residents' walls, create holiday programs, and do nice things for the elderly to show that they care.

ACTIVITY 6.4

Social Action Projects

Encourage your students to adopt a cause or take up an action project for the year on issues that concern them. This fosters citizenship, builds students' leadership and team-building skills, and aids in building humility and gratitude.

The topic focus can be sparked by current world events or a local community need. Topics should be somewhat organic and develop naturally by interest of the students, if possible. The topic can be the war in Syria, the need for water in Sudan, or climate change, or the topic can be more local like adopting a younger class or a nursing home nearby. Start by having the students identify a problem that needs to be addressed. Brainstorm possible solutions, then narrow down what the students want to do to contribute. Actions can range from letter-writing campaigns, to creation of public service announcements, to service-oriented projects like raising money or volunteering at a local organization to help a group of people. The possibilities and the contributions are endless. DoSomething.org is a great website for sparking your class's imagination.

What can kids do, really? Well, just look what these phenomenal kids have done:

- At fifteen, Shannon McNamara started SHARE, a nonprofit that provides thousands of girls in Tanzania with books and school supplies.

- Neha Gupta began Empower Orphans, her nonprofit, at the age of nine. Her organization has helped more than twenty-five thousand children across the globe.

- LuLu Cerone started LemonAID Warriors at ten years old. Her organization helps other kids make social activism part of their social lives.

- Jonathan Woods created the Under the Tree Foundation when he was twelve after he realized that teens are often overlooked during toy drives.

ACTIVITY 6.5

Excuse Goose

©iStockphoto.com/LordRunar

To help students understand responsibility and not making excuses, introduce Excuse Goose to your classroom. Excuse Goose is always looking for the easy way of doing things, and when someone asks him to take responsibility, he *always* has an excuse or blames someone else. Role-play different scenarios with the students where Excuse Goose lets his family, his friends, and even himself down. Discuss the actions Excuse Goose should take. Make a class commitment to not be an Excuse Goose!

Materials

A stuffed animal goose or a picture of one

Example Scenario

Excuse Goose's mom asked him to let the family dog in when he came home from school, but instead he came home and played video games for hours. When his mom got home, the dog had chewed up the outdoor furniture! His mom was so upset, and she asked him what happened. Excuse Goose said it wasn't his fault. His friend called and wanted him to find a way to slay the dragon in the game. Excuse Goose was just trying to help his friend. What should he have said to his mom? How could he take responsibility for his actions?

Access the website **www.teachingkidstothrive.com** to find more classroom-ready activities, author-recommended videos, websites, and other resources.

CULTIVATING HONESTY AND INTEGRITY IN STUDENT CHOICES

Integrity is choosing courage over comfort; choosing what is right over what is fun, fast, or easy; and choosing to practice our values rather than simply professing them.

—Brené Brown, *Rising Strong* (2015, p. 123)

••• TEACHING INTEGRITY

Teacher: "I see that you copied your paper from the Internet without using quotation marks and without citing the author. You will lose points for plagiarism, and you will have to start over."

Student: "Why? Everybody does it. I didn't hurt anybody."

Teacher: "But what you did was unethical, and it violates our class code."

Student: "I wouldn't have had to copy material if you had given us more time to do the assignment."

(Continued)

(Continued)

©iStockphoto.com/stuartmiles99

Teacher: "I think we both know you would have had ample time to do the assignment if you had started it when it was first assigned. You could have come to me and asked for more time if you needed it."

Student: "I don't know what the big deal is. This wasn't like a term paper or something."

Teacher: "But this is a big deal because you were dishonest."

Student: "I want to know how you caught me. I know of at least three other kids in this room who did exactly the same thing, and you didn't catch them."

Teacher: "So if I had not caught you, everything would be okay?"

Student: "Yes, no one would have ever known, and I'd have gotten my A."

Teacher: "But what would you have learned from the assignment?"

Student: "Look, I just need to get the A my parents expect."

Teacher: "What *I* expect is for you to do your own work. You chose not to do that. After you redo your paper on your own time, I have a Dan Ariely TED Talk I want you to watch; then we will sit down and talk more." ●

Integrity is not an inherent quality. It is fashioned by many facets of the social community including school. In the school environment, students acquire the skills of integrity from their adult role models, from their peers, and through specific instruction about what it means to do the right thing for the right reason (even when no one is looking). To promote integrity and its component parts—honesty, respect, fairness, honor, authenticity, trustworthiness, responsibility, and the courage to stand up for one's beliefs—teachers need to hold their students accountable.

You could say that a keen sense of responsibility leads to personal integrity, and you could say that a keen sense of integrity leads to personal responsibility. Either way, the two dispositions reinforce one another and are generally taught together. Teachers tackle the issue of integrity in the classroom dealing with everything from lying to cheating to apologizing to restorative justice, and to many things in between. Critics of "values education" have argued that it is not within the teacher's scope to talk about such concepts as integrity in the classroom, but our question is, How can we *not* talk about it?

How Do We Teach Personal Integrity?

Accountability: Hold all students accountable for the decisions they make (good or bad). It is important for students to learn that they have the sole responsibility for the consequences of their actions. Learners who believe this are more likely to self-monitor their moral codes.

Feedback: Give positive feedback to students who evidence good decision-making skills. When students feel confident in their judgment, they are not as easily swayed by others, and they are not afraid to act independently based on their own moral code.

Question: Teach students to question when something doesn't "feel right." Learners need to be able to ask the "why" questions of those who are giving commands (be it an adult or a peer). Without being disrespectful, students can evaluate whether what they are being asked to do is the right thing and act accordingly.

In his book *Is It Still Cheating If I Don't Get Caught?* Weinstein (2009) offers five basic principles for those who want to teach students good character and ethical behavior. Following are his rules with our adapted explanations.

"When we think about the kind of character we want for our children, it's clear that we want them to be able to judge what is right, care deeply about what is right, and then do what they believe to be right—even in the face of pressure from without and temptation from within" (Lickona, 2004).

CLASSROOM TIPS

Promoting Personal Integrity

Teachers should

1. **Do no harm.** Say enough to make the point clear, but refrain from saying hurtful things that are not necessary. Be especially sensitive to students who need kindness even more than others including those who fall "outside the mainstream" of their peers.

2. **Make things better.** Create a classroom that is safe and supportive. Lend a helping hand and help students find reasons to feel good about themselves. Never give busywork.

3. **Respect others.** Show respect by telling students the truth, by keeping your promises, and by refraining from listening to or spreading rumors.

4. **Be fair.** Make sure everyone has a reasonable chance for success. Enforce consequences equitably. Gather all information before making a decision. Support students in unjust situations.

5. **Be loving.** Demonstrate compassion and empathy for every student. Let your students know you care about them and their learning as you continue to hold them to high standards for integrity.

How Do We Teach Academic Integrity?

It makes sense that lack of academic integrity is fueled by lack of personal integrity. If students have solid self-smart skills including high personal integrity, it is hard for them to make the internal justification for cheating. Along the same line of thinking, if students have low personal integrity, there is very little reason for them not to cheat if given the opportunity. Teaching, promoting, and acknowledging students' personal integrity with clear emphasis on academics can be helpful. Following are some tips for promoting academic integrity.

High school teacher Paul Richards (2012) finds the most common incidences of cheating in his classes occur in copying homework, lying to miss a test or deadline, and failing to do one's part in a group project. He doesn't see a significant percentage of

CLASSROOM TIPS

Promoting Academic Integrity

- Teach students how to cite and paraphrase correctly so there is no misunderstanding. Teach the difference between the student's original thoughts and work and someone else's original work. Teach students the value of contributing something unique of their own whether that is analysis, logic, commentary, or creative thought.

- Give examples of what is and what is not plagiarism in specific assignments.

- Discuss academic integrity as you present assignments, especially ongoing projects. Describe acceptable and unacceptable behavior.

- Create an environment where students feel they can succeed and are not afraid to ask for extra help when needed.

- If cheating is a problem, give limited subject choices and be familiar with the research and sites related to those topics.

- Create checkpoints so you can see rough drafts and work in progress.

- Create new assignments and projects each year. Avoid using the same project or requirements so students are not tempted to recycle an older sibling's work.

- When giving a quiz or exam, monitor the room.

- If you suspect students of cheating or plagiarizing material, confront them directly and ask questions that will allow them the opportunity to admit or clarify the confusion.

- Make at least part of major projects an oral assessment or include a component that is related to activities from the class.

"copy/paste plagiarism," but he notes that many students fail to cite sources properly. Those problems, however, are not his most unsettling realization:

> Perhaps the most alarming news is that students say their cheating is contextual: based on the teacher, the assignment, or their overall workload. Decisions appear to be based on the extent to which the student can rationalize cheating in a given circumstance. Essentially, the academic integrity scale is a sliding one given the situation at hand, rather than a matter of a person's sense of right or wrong. (p. 97)

"It is a
attentive teache
carefully crafte
assessment
and high-qualit
relationships tha
keep student
honest" (Richards
2012, p. 98,

What Do We Do When Children Cheat?

Cheating—representing someone else's work as one's own—is growing among students who report they do this at least part of the time. Perhaps because of increased pressure on them to do well and score better in order to assure themselves a piece of the proverbial pie (particularly in middle and high school), many learners are cutting corners, copying work, and trying to game the system.

Students often justify their less-than-honest choices with the rationales used by the student in the "Teaching Integrity" scenario at the beginning of this chapter. Candid discussions with students about dishonesty may help curb cheating. Dan Ariely's video on this topic can help students reflect on some of their conflicts of interest that are at play when tough decisions have to be made. It is an insightful resource for lessons. (For a link to Ariely's TED Talk, visit the *Thrive* website at www.teachingkidstothrive.com.) ●

As in the "Teaching Integrity" scenario, teachers need to communicate that learning is the primary goal for every assignment. The teacher in the scenario treats the dishonest behavior as a teachable moment. She wants the student to take responsibility for trying to shortcut the assignment, but she also wants him to reflect on the ramifications of his conduct. She asks him to watch Dan Ariely's TED Talk in the hope that he will rethink his justifications for what he did. She will listen attentively to his thoughts, but she will continue to let him know that dishonesty is never acceptable in the classroom.

The Restorative Justice Approach

Something that involves both personal responsibility and integrity is a program many schools are now adopting called *restorative justice*. Schools approach it in different ways, but the basic model is that students in conflict are brought together to work out their problems. Rather than seeking to punish, restorative justice is more about bringing genuine resolution to hurtful and sometimes potentially violent situations.

When students do something wrong, they are encouraged to use the moment to learn. The learning comes in two parts. First, the student apologizes and thinks about a way to try to make it right with the person who was affected. Second, the perpetrator is asked to reflect on some questions about the incident. "What happened?" "How could I have handled myself with integrity?" Role-playing possible scenarios ahead of time is a good way for students to become comfortable with the process before an actual event occurs.

At High Tech Middle Chula Vista in California, teachers are attempting to implement restorative justice practices to replace the traditional suspensions and expulsions. Their argument is that with their recent focus on project-based learning, a student-centered process that aims at getting kids to invest in and be in charge of their own learning, it seems counterintuitive to maintain a traditional top-down discipline system. Teachers and administrators at this school are trying to view interpersonal and behavior mistakes "the same way they'd frame academic mistakes—opportunities to learn and grow" (Schwartz, 2016b).

••• PREVENTIVE JUSTICE: A "HANDS-JOINED" APPROACH

Inspired by a workshop presented by Youth Equity Stewardship (YES), Jennifer Dines (2016) committed herself to focus on responsibility and integrity not only through restorative justice but also through preventive justice. She recites Luis Valdez's epic poem "Pensamiento Serpentino" daily with her students to reinforce their connectedness to and mutual respect for one another. She says she focuses on maintaining a classroom environment that "feels inviting and encouraging, orderly and relaxed," and is one that gives students structured choices as they are empowered to direct some of their own learning. She calls this environment a "hands-joined" approach and extends it beyond her classroom walls to the rest of the school as well as the entire community. ●

The Courage to Take a Stand

Another measure of integrity is having the courage to take a stand on things that matter to you. Teachers can provide true leadership in this area by letting their students see them taking a stand on issues of importance, especially if their view runs counter to the prevailing thought. Apathy, on the other hand, can actually sabotage integrity. We need to emphasize to learners that having integrity means you will sometimes have to take a stand that is not comfortable or popular at the time. When someone's actions or words go against your moral compass, you have to be willing to stand up. Apathy or thinking something is not your problem can actually diminish your convictions and ultimately your integrity. It takes more than having enough integrity not to steal, cheat, or bully—you also have to be willing not to let those things go on in your presence.

••• A SIMPLE PLAN TO REINFORCE INTEGRITY

In his book *Instant Influence* (2011), Yale professor Michael Pantalon offers a twist on the *implementation plans* discussed earlier in this book. The teacher asks students on a scale of 1 (*very likely*) to 10 (*very unlikely*) how likely they are to behave with integrity in a potential situation (e.g., "On a scale of 1 to 10, how likely are you to steal something that belongs to someone else?"). Then the teacher asks, "Why didn't you pick a lower number?" Students will then justify their number choice (e.g., "I chose 8. Normally I wouldn't steal because it's not right, but if I knew other people stole something in the first place, then I wouldn't consider it theirs. Also, it's not right to steal, but if I was trying to help someone else I might do it. But I'm going to stick with 8 because usually stealing is just wrong, and stealing is not okay in a civilized world"). ●

©iStockphoto.com/Ashrafov

When students begin to explain why they didn't pick a lower number, they are justifying their integrity and actually tapping into their deeply held convictions. They are also reinforcing the idea to themselves about why behaving responsibly and with integrity is important. It is another way to help learners bolster their moral codes.

What Supporting Honesty and Integrity Looks Like in the Classroom

THE TEACHER MODELS HONESTY AND INTEGRITY

As discussed previously, the teacher is instrumental in helping students visualize what having honesty and integrity actually looks like in action.

HONESTY AND INTEGRITY IS NOT A STAND-ALONE LESSON OF THE WEEK

Discussions about what is honest and what is not honest behavior are woven throughout the school year. Teachers regularly point out honorable acts and help students discern what acts are not honorable and why.

VALUES AND FEELINGS ARE VALUED

Teachers are open about existing problems in the classroom or outside the classroom that are affecting students. They provide outlets for student views and feelings through whole-class discussions, small-group interactions, journal prompts, and more.

A COMMON LANGUAGE IS DEVELOPED

The school, department, and/or team develop a common vocabulary across curriculum areas so that literature teachers are using the words *honesty* and *integrity* in talking about traits of fictional characters as coaches are teaching the importance of honesty and integrity in sports.

STUDENTS HAVE A SHARED ROLE

As much as possible, students are involved in making decisions about and sharing the responsibility for the life of the classroom.

Frequently Asked Questions

1. **I find that when I discuss the topic of honesty with my students, they have mixed feelings about what it is and what it is not. They bring up the issue of white lies, telling little kids about Santa Claus, and only telling part of the truth. What do I tell them when I'm sometimes conflicted myself?**

   Obviously, our answer is to be honest about your conflicts regarding honesty. Students appreciate having adults in their lives who acknowledge they are grappling with the same tough issues as students. The Florida Polk County School District's website on character education is a valuable resource for teaching honesty in the classroom. The site provides information and handouts for students, teachers, and community members. In particular, take a look at the "What Honesty Looks Like" poster. You'll find a link for it on the *Thrive* website (www.teachingkidstothrive.com).

2. **I get that teachers should follow the rules, but is it really a big deal if I drink my Diet Dr Pepper in class or take a call from my husband? After all, I'm not a kid; I am an adult, and I sit at the big desk.**

   Major League Baseball players were asked to stop chewing tobacco during games because it sets a bad example for their young viewers. Now they chew gum or eat sunflower seeds, and they deal with it. As teachers, we, too, have an influence with young people, and we need to be aware of that when we model unhealthy food and beverage consumption in front of them.

   Many companies have a policy against taking personal phone calls at work because they know that their employees are often distracted from their jobs both during and after the calls. The same is true for educators. As we have stated several times, the greatest gift teachers can give their students is to be fully present in the company of students. We support a general policy restricting personal phone calls during class time except for emergencies.

We agree that teaching should definitely have its privileges because we are grown-ups who worked hard to get here, and we give it everything we have while we are on the job. And we have given you arguments about why the beverage and phone call policies are in place, but those really aren't the problems here. The larger issue is raised when teachers break school rules that both we and our students know about. How can we ask our students to follow the rules if we don't? Do we want them to grow up thinking it's okay to cherry-pick which rules they are going to follow and which ones are not that big a deal? For the benefit of our students, we have to support the rules, even if we don't like them. It sends a positive message for us to let our students know that we uphold the policies even though we don't agree with them. Then we can be good models and demonstrate how to go through the appropriate steps to try and get the rules changed.

3. **You recommend that teachers take a courageous stand on issues. Given the tension between diverse groups in our current environment, wouldn't it be better to steer clear of controversial issues like Black Lives Matter and access to bathrooms for students who are transgender?**

Certainly you need to consider the age of your students when you decide on the appropriateness of a particular topic, but don't underestimate what your learners are capable of handling. Students have instant access to current news, and they often hear the adults around them discussing tough issues. School should be a place where students can explore issues and feelings in a safe environment. What is the purpose of education if it is not to help students learn to deal with actual matters of real consequence? Exploring controversial subject matter is a way not only to engage students but also to give them a chance to explore what integrity means to them.

Be sure that discussions on sensitive matters are handled with respect and dignity for all parties, and be mindful of the community in which you teach. When in doubt, ask for guidance from your administration. We believe that students appreciate a teacher who is not afraid to tackle the concerns that students have. We also think it is important that teachers do not try to sway or impose their views but rather serve as models for open-mindedness, a willingness to hear all points of view, and empathy for all parties involved.

4. **What are we supposed to do with students who yell obscenities or intimidate other students? I think we may have gone too far with restorative justice. What do we do when our classrooms get hijacked by students who constantly disrupt the learning process for others but keep getting second, third, and fourth chances? How is that fair to students who are playing by the rules?**

The concept behind restorative justice is that instead of automatically suspending or expelling kids, we seek ways to use collaborative opportunities that allow them to make restitution while remaining in the classroom. When it works, it is a win-win policy for everyone. Schools and districts like it because among other advantages student suspensions and expulsions go down. Teachers and parents like it because it gives students a chance to recover from errors in judgment without the risk of getting put into the "pipeline to the penitentiary" with a compulsory expulsion.

That being said, there comes a time when the balance of what is best for one student has to be weighed against the good of the community. We believe that if and when a student's behavior becomes so disruptive that other students are robbed of their right to a calm and safe classroom, something else must be done. Whether it is putting the disruptors in an alternative environment where they can get the special help they need or bringing in specialists to deal with them one-on-one, no student should be allowed to continue to stop others from their chance to learn.

This is not something you as an individual teacher can decide. Work with your colleagues, your administration, parents, and your elected officials to find a plan that is workable for everyone. We advocate a policy that gives students a reasonable chance for success within the context of maintaining a relaxed and sheltered environment for all (including the teacher).

Discussion Questions and Exercises

We encourage you to tweet your responses to @tchkids2thrive.

1. Is cheating a problem in your classroom? What is your biggest area of concern? What steps have you put in place to minimize students taking credit for work that is not their own?

2. Do you agree with Paul Richards that most students see cheating as "conditional"? In what circumstances do your students think it is acceptable to cheat?

3. How do you feel about *restorative justice* as a way to deal with classroom problems? Explain your feelings and justify your response.

4. Do you teach your students to question authority, even yours? Why or why not?

5. Do you regularly talk with students about topics they are concerned about (even the controversial ones)? Why or why not?

6. Describe an event in your classroom that tested your personal sense of integrity. What did you do, and how did you feel about it after the fact?

ACTIVITY 7.1

Find Your Inner Superhero!

After describing what integrity is and how it guides decisions, thoughts, and actions, teachers will explain that superheroes are examples of integrity.

Ask students to name individual superheroes and how they show their true selves in the acts they do in difficult situations. Explain that you believe we all have an inner superhero—we just need to find it! Anytime students are in a difficult situation and unsure of what to do, they can ask themselves, "What would my superhero do?"

A variety of activities can be introduced to support students finding their inner superhero. Students can

1. Name their inner superhero

2. Draw a self-portrait as a superhero, then add the words that represent integrity around the superhero

3. Write a descriptive paragraph about their inner superhero and the qualities of integrity they possess

4. Create superhero capes from either vinyl tablecloths or shower curtains from the dollar store, then write the words that represent integrity on the cape along with their superhero name

5. Create a short story in which their superhero's integrity is tested in a difficult situation

6. Using paper towel rolls and foil, create superhero armbands with the initials "WW_D?" ("What Would _____ Do?") on the armband, filling in the blank with the first initial of the name they gave their inner superhero

To teach students the integrity HEROES acronym, see our handout on the *Thrive* website, www.teachingkidstothrive.com.

ACTIVITY 7.2

Integrity Graphs for Literature and Current Events

After learning the meaning of integrity and getting comfortable with recognizing scenarios where integrity is used, the class will create integrity graphs. During class readings and eventually with individual readings, students are asked to pick a character and graph that character's integrity throughout the story. Teachers can also ask students to use the integrity graph for famous people in history or people in current events. This activity will perpetuate the ideals of integrity and create a deeper understanding of how often our integrity is put to the test.

ACTIVITY 7.3

Integrity Chain

To reinforce integrity throughout the year, cut strips of construction paper and place them in a jar. When students see someone in the class acting with integrity, invite them to point it out and write the act and the student's name on a strip. Then have students link that strip to the class chain of integrity and watch the chain get longer and longer throughout the school year.

ACTIVITY 7.4

Discussion or Journal Prompts: "What Would You Do?"

Give students the opportunity to explore what integrity looks like in real-world scenarios. Doing the right thing can have negative consequences and sometimes feel worse than doing the wrong thing. Kids need to know that it may not be easy to act with integrity.

Ask them, "What would you do if . . . ?" and use these prompts (or create your own) in class discussions or for journal writing:

- You found a $10 bill on the playground
- Everyone was making fun of a new girl behind her back
- You were at the teacher's desk, and you saw the answers to the test
- Your best friend took a new pencil and pencil topper from someone's desk
- You witnessed a classmate being bullied in the hallway at school
- Your big sister said she would finish your project for you

ACTIVITY 7.5

You Are What You Do, an Orange Is an Orange

Some people profess to have integrity but don't always behave that way. This activity is designed to illustrate to students the power of their actions.

1. Before the activity, take an orange and roll it against the counter for about two or three minutes (this will loosen the pulp and ensure that there is plenty of juice).

2. Cut a hole in the orange and cover the orange with a cloth, so students can't see it.

3. Place a clear glass under the orange and then squeeze. Ask the students to tell you what fruit they think you are holding.

4. When students say it's an orange, ask them how they know that. You will hear things like "I can smell the orange" and "I see orange juice coming out!"

5. Tell the students that the store sign said it was a banana. Ask why they do not believe that to be true. Listen to feedback. Say something like "So no matter what the sign said, this fruit is showing its true colors as an orange and not a banana?"

6. Emphasize with the students the conclusion that the action of the orange (producing orange juice) was a more powerful indicator of what the fruit was than the sign at the store. We all want to *say* we have integrity, but it is what comes out of us when we are squeezed that people will see and believe, no matter what we say.

7. Reflection: Ask students to journal about actions they have taken or seen others take that prove they are who they say they are.

Access the website **www.teachingkidstothrive.com**
to find more classroom-ready activities,
author-recommended videos, websites, and other resources.

TAPPING INTO EMPATHY

If you can learn a simple trick, Scout, you'll get along a lot better with all kinds of folks. You never really understand a person until you consider things from his point of view . . . until you climb inside of his skin and walk around in it.

—Atticus Finch in *To Kill a Mockingbird*
(Lee, 1960, p. 33)

●●● EPIPHANY IN A PAPER BAG

After sensing a negative shift in interpersonal dynamics among her inner-city middle school students, Mackenzie Grate (2014) came up with an activity that altered everything for the positive. She handed each student three pink and three green sticky notes. Without signing their names, students were asked to write down on each of the green notes something a classmate had done or said to make them feel happy or special. They folded each note and wrote the responsible individual's name on the outside. On each of the three pink notes, they wrote down something that someone had done or said to make them feel terrible or angry; then they folded each note and wrote the name of the responsible individual on the outside.

On a back table, the teacher had arranged brown paper bags with an individual student's name on each one. The pink and green notes were sorted into the bags according to the names on the outside of the folded slips. Grate reports that most students got a mixture of green and pink comments, but some got

(Continued)

(Continued)

©iStockphoto.com/WendellandCarolyn

an overwhelming amount of one or the other. Every student received at least one note. The brown bags were then distributed to their rightful owners, and students were instructed to read the notes about the consequences of their words and actions. Grate then asked students to journal their thoughts on notebook paper, and she says the writing was teeming with feelings and reflections. After that, she opened a discussion involving how it felt to read about the effects of their actions. A boy who had received dozens of pink notes apologized to his classmates and told them he thought he was just being funny and did not realize the damage he had caused.

Grate says the activity totally changed the dynamics in her classroom to create an awareness of and appreciation for the impact of students' words and actions on their peers. She says that even now, two years later, former students approach her and tell her how that one activity changed them forever. Seeing themselves as others see them was truly an epiphany for many of her middle-level learners. ●

Empathy: What Is It?

In the story above, Mackenzie Grate used a brilliant strategy for introducing her students to what their actions and words cause others to feel. She taught them about *empathy*—an awareness of the feelings and emotions of other people. Empathy is the emotional intelligence that links us as individuals to others and helps us not only to understand their experiences cognitively but also actually to feel what they are feeling. Empathy is what puts tears in our eyes when we watch a Hallmark commercial about a soldier making a surprise visit home and makes us feel joy when we see teachers get honored for their outstanding contributions.

Empathy is more than sympathy. Sympathy is "feeling for" someone; it can be analytical and not particularly emotion stirring. However, empathy is more of a "feeling with" someone, and it is usually felt on a much deeper level. Brené Brown believes that empathy is a bonding agent that strengthens relationships (RSA, 2013). Shawn Murphy (2014) captures Brown's stance on empathy in these words: "It is one human being connecting with another, acknowledging a person's circumstance without diminishing or rationalizing it. Empathy is an acknowledgment without judgment."

Psychologist Daniel Goleman (1998) defines empathy as "sensing what other people are feeling, being able to take their perspective, and cultivating rapport and attunement with a broad diversity of people" (p. 318). Goleman and others believe that empathy is hardwired into the brain. Current research is shedding light on a recently discovered component of the brain called *mirror neurons* (Goleman, 2006; Walsh, 2007). Scientists believe that mirror neurons may be the key to the social and moral underpinnings of the brain. They postulate that when we observe someone's actions or feelings, our mirror neurons fire in chain reactions and stimulate the action or emotion in our own brain.

Mirror neurons also allow us to feel empathy. Every time we observe another person experiencing an emotion, mirror cells activate the same emotional circuits in our own brains. That's why we get scared at movies. When we see someone being abused or attacked, we feel afraid because our mirror neurons are firing. We can get angry when playing a violent video game. For example, a study in the January 2006 issue of *Media Psychology* found that when children watched violent television programs, mirror neurons activated the aggression centers of the brain, making them more likely to be aggressive in real life (Walsh, 2007, p. 53).

There are basically three types of empathy (see Figure 8.1). *Cognitive empathy*, sometimes called "perspective taking," is the ability to identify and understand the emotions in others. *Affective empathy* refers to the feelings we get in response to other people's emotions. *Compassionate empathy* is when we feel compelled to do something as a result of our shared feelings with another person. In teaching children about empathy, Karyn Gordon describes it this way: "The head is the intellectual part of understanding what empathy is and what it does, the heart feels what others are feeling and the hand actually takes action after feeling empathy for someone" (Beach, 2010).

Figure 8.1

Three Types of Empathy

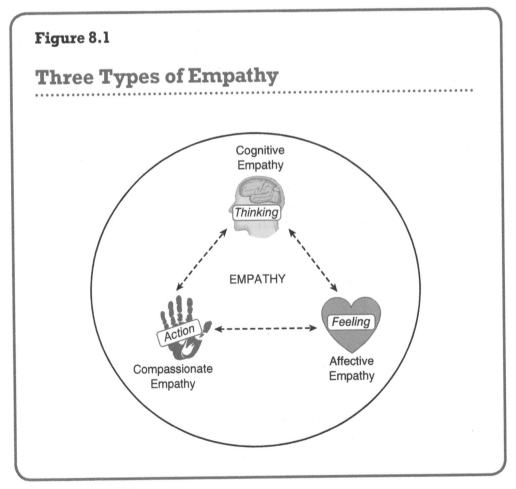

Images source: Courtesy of clipart.com.

©iStockphoto.com/MattiaMarasco

Teachers at Lefler Middle School in Lincoln, Nebraska, took part in a role-play exercise to experience firsthand learning about empathy. The role-play exercise divided teachers into two different groups, each with a packet of information about a fictional (but realistic) family's story. Each person was assigned an identity, told what resources the family had, and given a description of the economic struggles the family faced. Every fifteen-minute period represented a month, and kids went to school while parents waited in line to get food stamps or apply for a job or shop for groceries. They could pawn some of their belongings or get an exorbitant interest loan from a payday lender when they ran out of money. They faced obstacles like losing pay and getting fired for being late to the job when they ran out of bus passes. Teachers role-played what it felt like to live the kinds of lives many of their students faced each day. After the simulations were over, teachers debriefed about what they felt during the exercise. Some said they went from thinking this was a fun activity to getting physically mad about the roadblocks they had to face. Participants got insights into what it is like to not be able to see a light at the end of the tunnel and to have to live from crisis to crisis to crisis. Teachers said the exercise gave them perspective; it enabled them to be more understanding about why parents aren't involved at school, and why kids act out or forget their pencils. ●

Does Everyone Have Empathy?

Goleman (1995) refers to those with a seeming absence of empathy as "emotionally tone deaf." Most researchers, however, agree that with the exception of those with autism, schizophrenia, or some other form of brain development disorder, humans have an inherent capacity for empathy. Toddlers can be observed taking a favorite toy or blanket to another child who is hurt or upset. Most of us have witnessed the "contagious" crying of babies in a public place when one infant sends out a howl of distress. Nonhuman primates have repeatedly displayed empathy in studies, and other species manifest this disposition as well.

Almost all humans, regardless of gender, have the basic ability to cultivate empathy.

There is general agreement that empathy can and should be fostered, particularly in young children. Stanley Greenspan (2007), a clinical professor of psychiatry and pediatrics at George Washington University School of Medicine, believes that the quality of empathy is enhanced by the experience of being *emphasized with*. In the classroom, teachers can help students Thrive by actively listening to them and trying to view things from their perspective. Additionally, helping students understand their own behavior and feelings provides the essential tools for understanding the behavior and feelings of others.

There is a discussion on whether or not gender plays any part in a person's capacity for empathy. Parents and teachers sometimes make the assumption that boys are not as tenderhearted or as caring as their female counterparts. Paul Slocumb (2004) hypothesizes that empathy is impeded in males because they lack the language to express or understand it. In his book *Hear Our Cry*, he argues that because boys frequently have delayed language development (as compared to girls their same age), they have not yet developed appropriate words to express their thoughts and feelings: "Without an emotional language, empathy does not exist" (p. 27). Despite appearances to the contrary, research has shown that men and women do not differ consistently in their ability to detect their own or other people's emotions (Simon-Thomas, 2007). What has been established is that almost all humans, regardless of gender, have the basic ability to cultivate empathy.

What Does Empathy Look Like in Action?

Teachers can easily spot students who lack empathy. These students often seem to have a social blind spot. They either are unaware of others' feelings or don't care how others feel. They sometimes have absolutely no idea about how their actions affect other people. They are unmoved by the circumstances of others and tend to view the world through an attitude of "What has this got to do with me?" They tend to be judgmental and self-centered. Teachers need to be aware that many of these children grew up in environments void of anyone who empathized with them or modeled empathy, and they have not yet learned how to tap that skill within themselves.

Students can manifest healthy empathy in many ways. They may be extremely good listeners who make the time to hear what others have to say. They might always be willing to step in and help no matter the situation. They may demonstrate thoughtfulness and care toward their environment as well as for other people. They might be able to match their moods appropriately to those around them. Perhaps they express great passion toward a call for justice. Or maybe they have the uncanny ability to read people and know just what they are feeling.

Empathy is more than just listening with our ears. Communication research tells us that 90 percent or more of an emotional message is nonverbal, such as "tone of voice, gesture, facial expression, and the like" (Goleman, 1995, p. 96).

An interesting study has been developed to test a person's ability to understand a mood by looking at black-and-white photos capturing only a person's eyes. Teachers and students (both elementary and high school) may want to take one of the tests available in the Resources section on the *Thrive* website at www.teachingkidstothrive.

Why Is It Important to Teach About Empathy?

Barbara Coloroso (2008), an expert on bullying prevention, believes that "empathy is the core virtue around which all other virtues are built" (p. 113). It's an essential skill for what psychologists call prosocial behavior—the actions that are involved in building close relationships, maintaining friendships, and developing strong communities. It appears to be the central principle necessary for developing a conscience as well.

In a recent study of nearly nine hundred youth ages eleven to thirteen, Abbot and Cameron (2014) found that participants with higher levels of empathy were more likely to stand up to a bully on behalf of someone else outside their peer group. This is validated by the research of Hinduja and Patchin (2016), which shows that people who learn about and practice demonstrating compassion and empathy toward others are more likely to establish long-term patterns of positive behavior. In other words, as demonstrated in Figure 8.2, empathy leads to a conscience, which leads to a sense of right and wrong, which leads to integrity, which leads to an ethical adult (Slocumb, 2004).

Richard Davidson at the University of Wisconsin–Madison and his colleagues have been studying the ways that compassionate behavior actually changes the brain. They found that "participants who learned compassion were more generous" and that "greater generosity . . . was associated with changes in the brain's response to human suffering in regions involved in empathy and increasing positive emotions" (Weng, Fox, Shackman, Bussan, & Davidson, 2014). In short, encouraging kids and teens to be kind and caring can result in neurological changes that may lead to expanded and consistent kindness and compassion toward others.

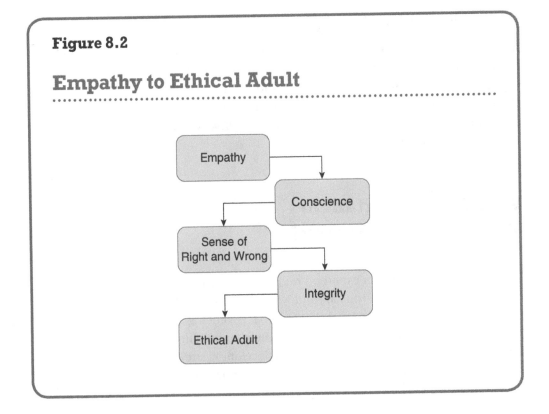

Figure 8.2

Empathy to Ethical Adult

In a project at West Middle School in Grand Junction, Colorado, eighth graders were asked to write their stories of resilience and volunteer to read them in front of fellow students and parents. The hope was that after hearing the stories of their peers, students would realize that many of them faced the same messy life battles and did not live "the perfect life" (as others assumed). About half of the school's 143 eighth graders practiced their stories in class and then volunteered to present them at the Resilience Café at Colorado Mesa University one evening. Stories ranged from a young lady who lost her father to a heart attack when she was twelve and thought of committing suicide to students who talked about the pain of parents' divorces and trouble with stepparents. Many told stories of being bullied to an audience comprising some of the same students who had bullied them. The empathy generated by the stories moved many of the students and their parents to tears. It was a chance for some students to learn for the first time about the challenges their classmates faced every day and to feel a greater bond with them (Hamilton, 2016). •

Modeling Empathy in the Classroom

Hard as it may be sometimes, teachers need to model empathetic reactions with our adult colleagues and administrators at school (no eye rolls, heavy sighs, or other dismissive actions after an encounter with another adult). We have to model the citizenship that we want students to embody. When someone doesn't share the copier, cuts us off in the lunch line, or intrudes on our turn for the computer lab, we need to let our students see us trying to understand the situation from the other person's point of view. When students complain about another staff member, we must be quick to ask, "What do you think that teacher was trying to teach you with that action?" or "Could her intent have been other than something negative?"

We can show students how to resolve conflicts peacefully by modeling empathy in the classroom. Marshall Rosenberg (2015) describes what he calls the four components of nonviolent communication: observations, feelings, needs, and requests. When teachers structure those elements in the classroom, they provide an instructive model for students to follow.

1. **Observe the behavior *without evaluating*.**

   Instead of "You are being so rude and disrespectful!"

   Choose "You just called me an insulting name."

2. **Help the students identify *their* feelings.**

   Instead of "You should be ashamed of yourself for treating me like that. I am so upset that you called me a name."

   Choose "Are you feeling frustrated and embarrassed because I didn't agree with you just now?"

3. **Seek and acknowledge the *real need of the student*.**

   Instead of "What is wrong with you? How do you think this makes me feel? I have gone out of my way to be nice to you, and this is how you respond?"

   Choose "Do you need to know my disagreement with you on that issue has nothing to do with my respect for you as a person?"

4. **Express your *request* clearly and explicitly.**

   Instead of "Okay, that's a time-out for you! You need to leave this class right now, and don't come back until you can show me some respect."

   Choose "I want you to apologize to me for calling me an offensive name and tell me how you are going to make this right with me."

In the scenario above, the teacher is trying to get to the real issue at hand. Rather than just being punitive, she is trying to see things from her student's point of view instead of choosing to be hurt or offended by the action. She is demonstrating empathy not only to the student but also to all the captive bystanders in the classroom.

One program that utilizes many of the nonviolent communication techniques (Rosenberg, 2015) is the Roots of Empathy program headed by Mary Gordon.

We began this book by talking about mindfulness because it is a natural stepping-stone to all the other areas of essential skills including empathy. In order to begin to "radically listen" to another person, students first have to be able to sort out their own thoughts. A good place to start teaching about empathy is to ask students to slow down, take a breath, and pay attention to their own thoughts. Let them know it is okay to disagree with others but that fully listening to

●●● ROOTS OF EMPATHY PROGRAM FOR PREKINDERGARTEN TO MIDDLE-LEVEL STUDENTS

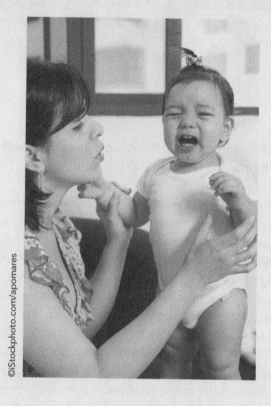

©iStockphoto.com/apomares

Roots of Empathy is being used in about three thousand kindergartens, elementary schools and middle schools in Canada, and forty schools in Seattle. In the program, children get to see a visiting parent and infant interact in the classroom about once a month and watch the foundations of empathy being built. When the baby cries, a Roots of Empathy instructor helps the mother and students think about what might be bothering the baby and how to make things better.

Students are taught that a crying baby isn't a bad baby, but a baby with a problem. By trying to figure out what's going on, the children learn to see the world through the infant's eyes and understand what it might be like to have needs but not be able to express them clearly.

(Continued)

(Continued)

"We love when we get a colicky baby," says Gordon, because then the mother usually tells the class how frustrating and annoying it is when the baby won't stop crying. That gives children insight into the parent's perspective—and how children's behavior can affect adults—something they have often never thought about. "If you look at the development of empathy, one of the key features is perspective-taking," says Gordon. "In coaching that skill, we help them [take the perspective of] their classmates" (Szalavitz, 2010). ●

another person is going to help them learn things they will otherwise never know. Brown and Olson (2015) put it this way:

> An empathetic response does not necessarily mean you agree with the other person or that you avoid tough decisions. . . . Instead, an empathetic response, supported by mindfulness, has a quality of care and kindness. An empathetic response is nonjudgmental. The foundation of mindful action is understanding, kindness, peacefulness, appreciation, and happiness. . . . There is a sensitivity to your own and to another's condition. Empathy is the ability to recognize the emotions of others and to "feel into" them. Since the capacity to understand what someone else may be feeling and sensing is key to maintaining meaningful connection with them, mindfulness helps build our receptivity to this. (p. 166)

In lower (and, yes, sometimes even in upper) grades, teachers can read students' favorite stories or parts of popular books that show characters with empathy or a lack of it. Discussing a character's behavior is a safe way to introduce empathy because it allows students to explore the topic from the safety of a third-person status. Teachers can create a list or an actual library of books for students to read on their own. In general, it helps to have books with well-rounded believable characters. Find stories with feelings that are subtly portrayed and not overly described so that students have a chance to use their own emotions to feel what the character feels (even if the character is making bad choices). Roman Krznaric's Empathy Library has hundreds of empathy-boosting books and films for children, young adults, and adults. See the Resources section on the *Thrive* website (www.teachingkidstothrive.com).

Model the Behavior of Hostage Negotiators

Be aware that in the beginning, students may seem just to go through the motions without really internalizing the feelings of others. That's a good beginning because the practice of using empathetic behaviors can actually lead to empathetic feelings. Adults sometimes do this, too. Cognitive empathy is knowing intellectually you should communicate responsiveness, but you're not yet feeling it. Just listening without judgment can be a signal of an authentic desire to understand and feel what the other person is feeling. The amazing thing is that just practicing the steps, whether they are heartfelt or not, can lead to true empathy. David Swink (2013), hostage negotiator trainer, says that many times officers who are pretending to be empathetic to hostage takers actually find themselves better able to identify with the offenders after only a few hours of imitating compassionate listening. ●

Service Learning Projects

Another meaningful way to teach about empathy is to get students involved in service learning and special projects that reach out to those in need. They can be local or as far away as across the world, but students need to take the responsibility of doing the actual work and sometimes generating the ideas and plans themselves. Instead of awarding treats or ribbons to students who participate in selfless endeavors, though, it is far better to help them realize the positive consequences of their actions. T-shirts and trophies don't compare to a hug or note from the recipient or a photo of a smiling beneficiary. This chapter contains several ideas from many schools. Hopefully, one or more will inspire you to take action with your students. We begin teaching empathy by engaging the head, the heart, and the hand.

Integrating Empathy Into the Curriculum

As with all of the Thrive skills, the best way to teach them is to integrate them into the school culture and across the curriculum. Maurice Elias (2015) believes that in order to understand nuances in emotions, students need a vocabulary to identify subtle differences (e.g., *angry* vs. *enraged*). He supports incorporating social and emotional learning (SEL) skills into vocabulary development and writing exercises. Several of his suggestions can be found in the Resources section on the *Thrive* website (www.teachingkidstothrive.com).

For science, technology, engineering, and math (STEM) classes, empathy has a natural place. It is an integral part of teaching design thinking, which centers on applying creativity to realize and solve problems. In order to imagine or identify challenges to be addressed, students have to put themselves into the lives and circumstances of others. They have to ask themselves, "What is this person feeling?" "What is his situation like, and how can we make it better for him?" They use their insights from those reflections to address solution-based thinking. Through various processes (brainstorming, inquiry, etc.), they identify a specific way they can solve the problem. They design and test their prototype, still thinking about the ultimate user and making modifications with the user in mind. The entire concept of 21st century design thinking is based around the essential skill of empathy.

When history is viewed through the scope of empathy, it becomes more meaningful to students and more relevant as a complex human endeavor. While studying a historical figure, a sports hero, or an artist of any type, ask a student to volunteer to be interviewed as that person. The student takes on the persona and perceived emotions of the figure and answers questions from the class about all kinds of things (e.g., "When did you first realize you had a passion for . . . ?" "How did you feel when . . . ?" "What is it like to . . . ?"). This could be done as a whole class or in small groups with students taking turns to be the interviewers and the interviewees.

Music, art, drama, and dance are used to express deep-seated emotions. Recent studies have shown that playing music together actually boosts empathy in students (Kennelly, 2012). Tapping into empathy helps artists of every sort better hone their craft. Teachers of these aesthetic-driven classes often ask their students to think about what a certain songwriter is trying to say or what an artist is feeling about a subject in a painting. Drama teachers tell students that in order to be believable, they must "get into character," which basically means the students need to identify and assume the same emotions as the character they are portraying on stage. Dance teachers ask students to demonstrate emotions through physical movement.

The Power of Empathy

Empathy not only makes better students; it makes better people. It is a skill that is more than a word of the week to be recited on cue.

It is an essential skill that will make a lasting impression on our students and the school for years to come. We know that empathy can help do amazing things for our class, for our school, for our community and beyond, and for the students themselves. The following are but a few of the examples we've come across in researching this book, but they vividly demonstrate the power of empathy. We welcome hearing from you about what is going on in your school or classroom to help promote this important human quality. Tweet us at @tchkids2thrive.

●●● THE AU-SOME PROJECT

©iStockphoto.com/Mclninch

After reading the book *My Brother Charlie* (2010), written by Holly Robinson Peete and her daughter, Ryan Elizabeth, about their son/brother with autism, Beth Reilly (a preschool special education teacher) and Brenna Lamprey (a fifth-grade regular education teacher) came up with a plan for their respective students. They shared the book with fifth graders and provided them with a chance to spend their recess time with the special education preschool students. Almost all of the fifth graders volunteered. Fifth graders were put

(Continued)

(Continued)

in random groups of threes and began their visits to assist with teacher-led activities such as reading books, singing songs, and helping with sensory and fine/gross motor control stations. Soon the program grew to the point that the fifth graders (the Big Buddies) began developing their own ideas about how to help the preschoolers (the Little Buddies) with plans such as getting them ready for a Special Olympics competition. The fifth graders took it upon themselves to do massive school- and community-wide programs to inform people about the needs and capabilities of children with disabilities. They led students and adults alike on a campaign of acceptance of different abilities and needs. Among other benefits of the program, the fifth graders showed marked improvement on their assessed empathy skills (Lamprey & Reilly, 2016). ●

●●● HUMANS OF MARIN COUNTRY DAY SCHOOL PROJECT

Kyle Redford, a teacher at Marin Country Day School in Corte Madera, California, hoped to broaden her students' understanding of the power of perspective as well as media literacy through a project she and other teachers designed around the idea of Brandon Stanton's Humans of New York project. They solicited adult volunteers from around their campus who typically worked somewhat behind the scenes (e.g., employees from maintenance, lunch and kitchen crews, landscaping, and transportation, as well as business staff, learning support staff, technology specialists, and after-school care staff). They assigned pairs of students to set up times to interview and photograph their subjects. The project culminated with a showcase of the pictures and stories collected by the students. What the organizers had not expected was the powerful connections forged between employees and students. Many employees shared powerful stories about their intimate triumphs as well as struggles related to race, ethnicity, and immigration issues. Some had bits of reflective wisdom for the students. The Humans of Marin Country Day School exhibition drew crowds of people who saw pictures and read about "the invisible" people at the school. Employees reported they had never felt as appreciated as they felt when students later started going out of their way to greet them. Students said they felt more connected to these often unseen adults and began rethinking decisions they made that impacted the jobs of the interviewees (e.g., keeping the common areas picked up, getting to the bus on time). Redford (2016) credits the unanticipated positivity of this project and its profound impact on the entire community to the trust of the adult volunteers who allowed their stories to be told by student photojournalists. ●

Eight-year-old Khloe Thompson passed the same homeless people on her way to school each day. She asked her mom what she could do to help. With her mom's assistance, she came up with the idea of launching her own charity initiative, Khloe Kares, as an organization that focuses on community service and educating other kids about things going on in the world. For her first project, Khloe began handing out bags filled with items like deodorant, soap, lotion, feminine products, and socks to homeless women. Khloe and her grandmother designed durable bags, and together they have created and sewed them. The response to Khloe's initiative has been astounding. Even her friends at school have joined in to help Khloe with her mission. She has her own website (www.khloekares.com) and has gained national attention for her project and the homeless women in Southern California. Now nine years old, Khloe plans to launch a new campaign to collect Barbie dolls and trucks for children who live in shelters. Khloe feels that all children should be able to play with and have their own toys. As Khloe says on her website, "No dream is too small or too big! I want to inspire other kids to be great and to make your mark on this earth. I want to challenge other kids to do something big." ●

What Supporting Empathy Looks Like in the Classroom

STUDENTS KNOW THEY ARE CAPABLE OF DOING BETTER

When students choose a behavior that is not acceptable, it is important to leave their dignity intact. Effective teachers let them know they are not a bad person. Their act may have been contemptible, but their teacher knows they are capable of being a decent, caring responsible kid. The teacher acts on behalf of the classroom community at large while still attending to the members as individuals. They maintain a classroom that feels safe and supportive for all learners. It is hard to focus on the needs of others until we feel we have our own needs met.

EMPATHY IS *FELT*, NOT *COVERED*

Incorporate empathy into the normal ethos of the class. There is nothing worse than schoolifying something that is natural and essential to learning. Empathy needs to be felt and not just dissected, memorized, and assessed with a multiple-choice test. Teachers give students opportunities to talk about and practice their empathy skills. Teachers administer regular surveys (formal and informal) to students to check how well things are going. They allow an open discussion about the skills needed for Thriving. They take students where they are with empathy skills and move them as far forward on the continuum as possible. They are not afraid to tackle tough topics.

THE TEACHER SHOWS EMPATHY TO STUDENTS AND BEYOND

In everything teachers do and say inside the classroom and outside the classroom (where they are still being observed), teachers need to try to model the skills of empathy. They show their students what it means to be open-minded and accepting of other people and their views when they empathize with students and others.

THE TEACHER MODELS ACTIVE LISTENING

Even without specific training, most teachers know the tenets of effective listening and try to use them the majority of the time. We also need to teach these skills to students and give them a chance to practice them in the classroom.

THE TEACHER BUILDS AN EMPATHETIC CLASSROOM COMMUNITY

Relationships in the classroom are valued and promoted. Through team-building activities, small-group work, role play, and whole-group discussions, teachers focus on building connections among classmates. The teacher finds ways for students to discover commonalities with others and share experiences. The classroom is

Active Listening Skills

- Listen to hear what is behind the words
- Pay full attention to the other
- Hold back judgment
- Reflect what you hear (if the situation calls for it)

- Ask for clarification
- Summarize what you heard
- Share your own experiences (if the situation calls for it) ●

treated as a community, and students regularly share their feelings and their concerns with their peers. Empathy is valued as a critical component of forming bonds, and teachers provide both formal and informal opportunities for this to occur.

THE TEACHER STRIVES TO GET TO KNOW ALL STUDENTS

Teachers should make a point to find out about what goes on in their students' lives outside of the classroom. Being inquiring rather than inquisitive, the teacher can ask learners to answer questions that provide insight into their "other selves." It would be enlightening to follow individual students around for a day and record what goes on in their daily lives. If that isn't possible, the teacher can ask a student or two to keep and share an hourly journal of their typical day.

EMPATHY IN ACTION IS ACKNOWLEDGED AND DISCUSSED

The teacher seeks out current events, timeless stories, and local experiences to provide examples of empathy in action. Whenever mishaps or tragedies occur, the teacher asks students, "What do you think would be the most helpful thing to do for those who are suffering right now?" When talking about great literature, teachers can ask, "Why do you think the hero stepped up for those who could not defend themselves? Was that the right thing to do? Why or why not?"

STUDENT INDIVIDUALITY IS VALUED

The teacher values students as individuals with an array of qualities. Middle school expert Rick Wormeli (2016b) reminds us that we need to be mindful of the whole child and not just one aspect about the student. He warns us not to think that because a student is from China she speaks for all Chinese people or that being Chinese is her most important quality. All students have many facets and need to know that we value them and all the factors that make them who they are. Teachers should make the effort to get to know and understand as many pieces about our students' lives as we can.

STUDENTS ARE PROVIDED OPPORTUNITIES TO CONTRIBUTE POSITIVE ACTIONS

Teachers can create opportunities to do good. Doing things to help others is a way to teach students to notice and care about the rights and needs of others, which in turn helps them learn to empathize with others. As teachers, we can sponsor a helping campaign, create time in class for students to work on altruistic projects, and share our stories about our personal volunteer work to help inspire them to consider how to impact people outside their circles.

? Frequently Asked Questions

1. **Isn't teaching empathy going to dilute our students' value systems? How are our parents going to respond when we tell their children they should be tolerant of beliefs that are diametrically opposed to what they've been taught at home?**

   Value systems are a group of strongly held beliefs by individuals and groups. When teaching empathy, the idea is to tell students not that they shouldn't have firmly held ideas but rather that they should be willing to listen to and consider other people's views and actions from the perspective of the other person. It is not a matter of asking anyone to agree with anything he doesn't support. Teaching students to thoughtfully consider the point of view of others should serve to clarify their own belief systems, not weaken them. Certainly, there are families all over the world who believe they have a corner on the truth, and they would prefer that everyone support their beliefs without question. You may get some pushback from some of these parents. In keeping with our anchor question "What do we want students to be like when they leave our classrooms?" we think that having students who think critically, who listen to what others have to say, and who strive to find the human connection in all encounters is exactly how we want them to be.

2. **What do you do with boys who think that showing empathy is weak or unmanly? Some of my male students never want to show their emotions in class or anywhere else.**

   In Chapter 5, we talked about the perception of the "Boy Code" and how many young men are afraid that if they acknowledge or show emotions, they will set themselves up for being ostracized by their male peers. Teachers need to help boys (and girls, too) understand that feeling and expressing emotions is normal. You might start by having them recall positive emotions, like when they finish in first place after a hard-fought battle or have a younger child lift her arms to be picked up by them, and discussing the positive aspects of emotions.

Ask them how they feel when they watch a scary movie or play an intense video game. Offer appropriate books (or movies) featuring an empathetic male character with whom they can identify. Be supportive and encouraging when they start to open up. Focus on the knowledge that feelings are a natural evolutionary part of being a human.

Show them what neuroscientists have taught us about emotions and help them understand that it is actually *abnormal* to deny their existence. When doing classroom activities on empathy, be mindful of students' hesitancy and let them proceed according to their comfort level. Be patient and lead them gently. Use examples from strong male role models who talk about emotions and aren't afraid to show them. Give them lots of opportunities to reflect and share privately (e.g., in journals), and be a good role model by also sharing your feelings with your students.

3. **Some of my teaching colleagues tell the students, "Leave the drama for your mama." Others ask so many personal questions that I feel embarrassed for the students. I don't like either extreme, but I do want to help students fix their problems. What do you suggest?**

While many teachers tell students, "Leave the drama in the hall," empathetic teachers make the time to address the concerns the students bring with them to class. They ask students to reflect on the things going on in their world by listening to them and asking clarifying nonjudgmental questions—not as an examiner, but as an interested inquirer. Instead of judging, evaluating, or trying to fix the problem, teachers can best help the students look beyond their own perspective with thought-provoking "I wonder" statements. "I wonder if she was really upset about something else that had nothing to do with you." "I wonder why he would do something so out of character." "I wonder what would have happened if you had just kept on walking." Getting students to try and view situations from the perspective of someone else shows them what it means to have empathy.

4. **I'm a high school English teacher. I use literature to open conversations about empathy. Recently, one of my students told me I need to "get mortified." Apparently, that has something to do with empathy, but I've never heard of it. Have you?**

Teachers of secondary students are discovering an innovative way to connect with students, but this one takes a lot of courage. Based on a current craze called *Mortified*, teachers are revealing accounts of their own preteen and teenage years by reading their actual diary and journal entries they wrote at that age. *Mortified* is a trend that is sweeping the country as stand-up-and-share entertainment. Along the line of karaoke singing, stand-up comedy, and poetry jam, participants in *Mortified: Share the Shame* stand before an audience and read embarrassing portions of journals and diaries from their prior years. It seems to be cathartic for both the readers and the listeners. Audiences build empathy with the person who shares and also relive some of the anxiety they, too, experienced growing up. *Mortified* has podcasts students can download and hear, but a word of caution is that a few of the narratives dwell on provocative subjects that some schools and parents might consider indelicate for teenagers, so be sure to screen them first. Additionally, listening to these podcasts can help teachers remember their own earlier years and kindle empathy with the students who are that age now.

Discussion Questions and Exercises

We encourage you to tweet your responses to @tchkids2thrive.

1. Have you ever done an activity similar to Epiphany in a Paper Bag (see page 185)? What are the benefits of having students participate in this activity? What might be the drawbacks? Would you give any kind of preparatory comments before beginning? Share your comments and concerns.

2. In your own words, distinguish between *sympathy* and *empathy*. Which one best describes how you feel about students? Which one is the most helpful in terms of helping students cope? Explain your answer.

3. Would you want to participate in an activity similar to the one the teachers at Lefler Middle School did in emulating the lives of some of their students? Why or why not?

4. Do you create opportunities for students in your classroom to do good work inside and outside the classroom? What do you specifically do that provides opportunities for students to contribute to others?

5. Using Rosenberg's four components of nonviolent communication (observations, feelings, needs, and requests), model the best responses to the following situations:

   • Your administrator just stopped by your room and saw a student chewing gum. She demanded that the student spit out the gum and said to you in front of the class, "You know that chewing gum is against school rules! You should not have allowed this student to do it. You obviously aren't paying close enough attention to what goes on right under your nose. I guess I need to come in here more often to help you monitor your students."

- A student is sleeping in your class. You walk over and gently put your hand on his shoulder. He jerks awake and yells, "Get your hands off of me! Leave me alone! I only went to sleep because your class is so boring that I can't stay awake for it. Everyone hates this class, and so do I!"

- In the workroom, a colleague says, "I hear you gave Buster Jones an A in your class. I find that interesting because he's making Fs in everyone else's classes. Could it be that the work in your room is not demanding enough? You're making the rest of us look bad when you give out so many As. It puts pressure on us from the parents."

- Make up your own scenario from real events at your school.

6. Do you consider yourself an active listener? What general practices do you do that make you think you are or you aren't? How could you improve your listening skills?

ACTIVITY 8.1

Empathy Walk Journal

This activity requires students to look deeper as they go about their day, noticing and journaling the things they would normally take for granted.

©iStockphoto.com/asiseeit

1. Have students create a journal with multiple blank pages. They can decorate the cover and title it, "My Empathy Walk."

2. Invite students to spend the day (or week) looking deeper at everything they come in contact with and journaling their thoughts.

3. On the first page of the journal, have them write the meaning of the activity:

   The idea of my empathy walk is to think deeper about the items we come in contact with daily and how they got there. What are the stories behind the items? What is it like to be other people? What are they feeling?

   - *I will use my observation and thinking skills to think and feel like others.*

   - *I will think, observe, and record my thoughts seven to ten different times throughout the day.*

   - *I will have a journal entry for each encounter.*

4. Walk students through what they might encounter on the empathy walk.

   Waking up: Who made these sheets? Where do they live? How do they feel about their job? Who washed my sheets? Who made my bed? How does washing and making the bed make them feel?

   (Continued)

(Continued)

Eating breakfast: Who made sure this milk was at the grocery store? Who stocked it on the shelf? What farmer raised the cows that made the milk? What is life like for those people?

On the way to school: What is the story behind that lady sitting at the bus stop? What do I see when I look at her? Is she happy or sad? Is she tired or rested? Who is that man asleep on the street? What happened to his home? Where is his family? How does it feel to be there late at night?

Arriving at school: Who cleaned our classroom last night? What is it like to be in the school when it is empty? What are their lives like? Do they have kids that go to school here? Where are they, now?

5. After the journal day or week is finished, have students debrief about what it was like to be very aware of the things and people around them. Did they notice new things? Was it sad to think about others? Did they see good things?

6. Have students create a journal entry about how it felt to go on the empathy walk and what they learned from the experience.

ACTIVITY 8.2

Empathy Role Play

Create role-play scenario cards that are age appropriate and have pairs of students randomly select one from the deck. See our scenario cards on the *Thrive* website (www.teachingkidstothrive.com).

1. Have students discuss what is happening in their scenario.
   - What are the characters thinking? Feeling?
   - How do their actions and words show this?
   - Are they being empathetic?
   - How are they not being empathetic?
2. Role-play how to handle the situation with empathy.
3. Create your own scenario card to add to the deck.

ACTIVITY 8.3

"How Does It Feel?" Game

This activity is designed to allow students to see what it feels like to be in different people's shoes. In this activity, students will be assigned one of three roles: Heart, Moon, or Star. Each role has good and bad aspects to it. Encourage your students to explore their feelings in each role.

Materials

A set of stamps, stickers, or cards to designate membership in a group (Hearts, Moons, and Stars)

Directions

1. As students come into class, assign them a role randomly by giving them a card (or stamp or sticker).

2. Explain the roles:
   - Hearts have all the power. They get to sit in desks, and they get to decide what to do for the next five minutes.
   - Moons are basically ignored. They are all to stand in one corner of the room, but they are not to talk or make eye contact with anyone.
   - Stars must sit on the floor and do what the Hearts say. Give suggestions such as "Do jumping jacks," "Tell me how smart I am," "Draw me a picture of a park," "Sit quietly," and so on.

3. Continue for three to five minutes.

4. Then switch roles. Now,
   - Stars have the power.
   - Hearts are ignored.
   - Moons do whatever they are told by the Stars.

5. After three to five minutes, switch roles again:
   - Moons have the power.
   - Stars are ignored.
   - Hearts do whatever they are told by the Moons.

6. Bring the whole group back together. Ask all students to take a minute and do a mindful breathing technique to release any frustrations.

Debrief Questions

- How did the game feel?

- Did each role have its negative emotions?

- Which role was the worst for you?

- Name each role: What did we see physically? What did we hear? What did we feel?

- Do we often experience each of these roles in life?

- Are there times that we ignore groups of people or treat others badly?

- How can we have more empathy for each group in our daily lives?

ACTIVITY 8.4
Peace Table

Montessori schools have been using peace tables in the classroom for years. We think creating a peace area or peace table for students to explore their feelings can be a powerful learning tool. Create an area that is for conflict resolution. Learning to be empathetic with each other will help students gain the tools necessary to work out their problems.

Materials

- A timer
- Several calming methods (a calming bottle, stuffed animals, worry beads, peace signs)
- Handprints painted on both sides of the table
- Discussion prompts for empathetic conversation and conflict resolution
- Guidelines for the peace table posted on the wall

Guidelines

If you need a little peace:

1. Stop, breathe, and get control of your emotions.
2. Sit at the peace table alone or ask someone to join you for a talk.
3. If the person you ask says no, ask her to think about it and maybe you can try again later.
4. If the student agrees, sit at the table with your hands on the handprints on the table.
5. Set the timer for three minutes.
6. Start a discussion (fill in the blanks):

   Prompt: "When you _____, it makes me feel _____."

   Prompt: "You are saying that when I _____, it made you feel _____? Here is how I feel: _____."

   Prompt: "What can we do to make us each feel better?"
7. Have a respectful dialogue about how you can make this issue right and how you can avoid this issue in the future.
8. Shake hands as you leave the table.

ACTIVITY 8.5

History Empathy

As the class studies history, focus on empathy as a way to relate to the people of the time period. Use primary documents, songs of the period, and scenes to evaluate what it might have been like to be alive at the time. What internal conflicts did people struggle with? What were their fears and hopes?

1. **Step into the shoes of a historical figure.** Have students select a historical figure to personify. They should do enough research on the person's life and the events that the person participated in to be able to answer interview questions posed by a fellow student. When answering interview questions, students should express opinions (in character) about the historical events they participated in and how they felt during those events (battle, protest, movement, etc.). What were they worried about? How did their feelings and emotions change throughout the event?

2. **Write a letter to the government.** Ask students to write a letter to the government as if they were a person in a specific time period. In the letter, they should describe what they are experiencing, but also how they are feeling and how their town or family is feeling.

3. **Write a letter to your family.** Pick a significant historical event. Write a letter to your family or a diary entry describing what is happening and what you are feeling.

4. **Take on a leadership persona.** Write a diary entry from the perspective of the leader in power during the historical event. Are you doubting your decisions? Are you confident? Are people upset with you, and how does that make you feel?

Access the website **www.teachingkidstothrive.com** to find more classroom-ready activities, author-recommended videos, websites, and other resources.

Thrive Skills in Action

IT'S ALL ABOUT GRATITUDE

*It's not what you look at that matters, it's what you see—
i.e., compare it to, something worse or better, that determines
whether you are respectively grateful and happy or ungrateful
and bitter.*

—Henry David Thoreau

●●● PAY IT FORWARD

In the movie *Pay It Forward*, Mr. Simonet, a seventh-grade social studies teacher, offers a very different kind of assignment to his students. He tells them on their first day in his class that he wants them to really understand what it means to be *in* this world. He gives them an assignment that asks them to imagine, plan, and implement a change that will make the world a better place. He encourages them to envision a world where people respond to one another with caring.

Eleven-year-old Trevor McKinney proposes the idea of "paying it forward"— that is, doing something good for three people for no reason other than that they need his help. Instead of paying him back, he asks these three people to pay it forward by doing something significant and kind for three more people. He reasons that exponentially his plan has the power to change the world for the better.

(Continued)

(Continued)

The movie focuses on these themes: (1) A single person can influence changes that affect others, (2) there are people everywhere who need help, and (3) most people have a sense of gratitude and are willing to return it in kind or with greater gifts than those they receive. It has inspired "pay it forward" movements in schools across the country. ●

"Pay It Forward" Is Still Thriving

Since the movie was released, thousands of classes and schools have set up programs to encourage altruism, kindness, and gratitude among students. Jeffrey Froh and Giacomo Bono (2012) are some of the first researchers to study gratitude among students in school. Since 2006, they have worked with thousands of children and adolescents across the United States. Though the field is new, they have made some important discoveries regarding teaching gratitude in classrooms. In 2010, they published a study in which they determined programs similar to the "pay it forward" theme contribute more to students than just momentary happiness. They found that gratitude aids in adolescents' development by fostering both a general sense of connectedness to others and a motivation to use their strengths to help the larger community: "It is a positive state of mind that gives rise to the 'passing on of the gift' through positive action" (Froh, Bono, & Emmons, 2010, p. 152). They also conclude that teachers should regularly encourage young students to make public and regular expressions of gratitude.

Robert Emmons, perhaps the world's leading expert on gratitude, goes on to say, "Gratitude is good for kids: When 10–19 year olds practice gratitude, they report greater life satisfaction and more positive emotion, and they feel more connected to their community" (Greater Good Science Center, 2017). He says that gratitude encourages us not only to appreciate gifts but to repay them (or pay them forward). He likens this to what sociologist Georg Simmel calls "the moral memory of mankind" (Greater Good Science Center, 2017).

●●● "PAY IT FORWARD" DAY

In 2016, participants from seventy-nine countries, forty-two states, and forty-eight cities participated in "Pay It Forward" Day. For some examples of "Pay It Forward" Day programs in schools, see payitforwardday.com. You will also find materials to start the program in your school at the site.

Ekstrand Elementary School (San Dimas, California)

Students organized a recycling program at their school and throughout their community to help a three-year-old girl in need of a vital surgery. The students helped raise $9,000 to contribute to Hayley Brang's medical needs and continue to work on behalf of other children who need help.

Southern Regional Middle School (Manahawkin, New Jersey)

Students watched the movie *Pay It Forward* and used Trevor McKinney's plan to calculate the exponential growth factor involved in spreading kindness throughout their school, the state, and the world. For their own "pay it forward" activity, they decorated their school cafeteria to look like a restaurant, complete with place mats and positive character quotes posted on the walls. They prepared "gourmet" meals and served them to their

(Continued)

(Continued)

paying customers, the teachers. With the profits they cleared, the students made donations to various charities they chose. They completed their "pay it forward" initiative by writing letters and stories to incoming students for the next year as well as letters of gratitude to family members and friends who were special in their lives.

Pink Elementary School (Frisco, Texas)

Wanting to help children in need, students decided to make birthdays a special day for children living in local foster homes and women's shelters.

They created birthday boxes filled with everything needed for a birthday party—streamers, balloons, decorations, paper napkins, and more. They also included gift cards for pizza and a birthday cake. The students enclosed a letter explaining the "pay it forward" concept and why they had done what they did to make the recipient happy. They urged the recipient to also pay it forward, even if it was just a simple act of kindness to someone else. ●

Gratitude: What Is It?

Definitions vary somewhat among researchers, but for the most part, experts agree on this general description by R. A. Sansone:

> Gratitude may be broadly defined as "the appreciation of what is valuable and meaningful to oneself. It represents a general state of thankfulness and/or appreciation." (Sansone & Sansone, 2010, p. 21)

Smith (2013) puts it a bit more eloquently:

> Gratitude (and its sibling, appreciation) is the mental tool we use to remind ourselves of the good stuff. It's a lens that helps us to see the things that don't make it onto our lists of problems to be solved. It's a spotlight that we shine on the people who give us the good things in life. It's a bright red paintbrush we apply to otherwise-invisible blessings, like clean streets, or health or enough food to eat.

In *How to Raise an Adult* (2015), Julie Lythcott-Haims differentiates between kindness and gratitude: "Where kindness is about doing, its partner, gratitude, is about recognizing what's been done for you" (p. 282). The book focuses on how to rear children who do not have feelings of entitlement. In *Fall Down 7 Times, Get Up 8: Teaching Kids to Succeed* (2012), Silver discusses her belief that nothing dispels feelings of entitlement as readily as a focus on gratitude and an appreciation for those who made our good fortune possible. Gratitude instills within us a certain humbleness for the gifts we have rather than the arrogance of "Yeah, I have this, and you don't" or "Well, at least I have more than you."

Entitlement can be said to be the opposite of gratitude, but another contrasting concept to gratitude is *scarcity theory*. Rooted in our evolutionary need to survive, part of our nature is to ascribe to the theory that "more is more." Like chipmunks who keep stuffing their pouches in anticipation of a time they won't have enough food, it is easy to become fixated on what we want rather than what we have. We (the authors) often say that teachers are guilty of scarcity theory because we feel there is never enough—time, supplies, materials, clicks on the copy machine—to do the things we need to do for students. (It may explain why we write our names on every single school supply we have.) This feeling is compounded when we hear of other schools or classes that seem to have an abundance of such things.

Likewise, students may look at other students' material possessions or lives in general and feel somehow shorted or cheated. Nothing good comes from such feelings. Scarcity theory extinguishes gratitude, and it can lead to depression, exhaustion, and overwhelming feelings of hopelessness. If students and teachers can learn to turn our attention to the things we already have and be grateful for those things, we can create a feeling in our lives that elevates and energizes us. Practicing gratitude is the skill that helps us to Thrive.

What Research Tells Us About Gratitude

In Chapter 1, we mentioned the current catchphrase "Neurons that fire together, wire together." One of the powerful aspects about gratitude is that it causes a shift away from negative emotions toward positive ones. It is impossible to hold negative thoughts while feeling truly grateful. When we purposefully practice gratitude, we are firing positive neurons. If we do that enough times, we wire that positivity into our thinking, making it easier to practice gratitude on a regular basis.

Humans have preternatural leaning toward the negative. Rick Hanson (2014) says the brain is like Velcro for negative experiences, while it is like Teflon for positive ones. He attributes this phenomenon to our evolutionary history where survival was more dependent on avoiding negative experiences than on seeking out positive ones. Studies have shown these three things:

- In a relationship, it typically takes five good interactions to make up for a single bad one.

- People will work much harder to avoid losing $100 than they will work to gain the same amount of money.

- Painful experiences are much more memorable than pleasurable ones.

Our "implicit memory"—underlying expectations, beliefs, action strategies, and mood—is geared for the negative, but it only takes twenty seconds for neurons to fire and wire together, so actively practicing the positivity in gratitude can literally rewire our brains (Hanson, 2014).

In explaining the importance of gratitude, teacher and author Larry Ferlazzo (2015) talks with his students about their "hot" emotional system as opposed to their "cool" cognitive systems (from Mischel, 2014; see Chapter 2). He explains that one way students can control their negative hot emotions is to "drown out" the negative feeling with a hot but positive emotion. Gratitude is considered to be a hot emotion. Ferlazzo tells his students they can improve their self-control over their hot systems by the simple act of writing down three to five events each day for which they are grateful. ●

The book *Thrilled to Death* (Hart, 2007) discusses various research studies that support the idea that gratitude increases a sense of well-being, and concludes, "A daily intervention of self-guided exercises with young adults resulted in higher reported levels of the positive states of alertness, enthusiasm, determination, attentiveness, and energy" (p. 200). Hart goes on to propose that merely feeling gratitude is not enough to impact these levels:

The second key is to find a way to express your gratitude. It is not enough to just think it or even just to feel it; you must share it with another. Unlike just thinking about your gratitude, speaking about it helps to reinforce the gratitude in your brain and send it far and wide throughout your nervous system. (p. 201)

While recent studies in neurobiology are in their infancy stages, some results regarding gratitude are promising. We now know that the simple act of being grateful floods the body and brain with positive endorphins and emotions (Gordon, 2005). Anecdotally, teachers know that students who exhibit gratitude seem healthier, happier, and more positive. Science is now beginning to explain why.

Why We Should Teach Gratitude in the Classroom

With high-stakes accountability looming and ever-shrinking time to teach to the standards, teachers may question the wisdom of stopping to practice gratitude. Our answer to that is to point out how much impact this relatively no-cost, minimally time-consuming essential skill has on the classroom. Joan Young (2014) sums it up:

> Although teaching gratitude and kindness may not seem to have an obvious place in the classroom, it is a powerful way to create an affirming, supportive culture. Teaching and modeling these qualities even for brief periods can build community, promote positive interactions, and alleviate the negative effects of high-stress events like testing. (pp. 38–39)

Froh and Bono (2012) confirm Young's findings. They write,

> For instance, a recent study of ours found that teens who had high levels of gratitude when entering high school had less negative emotions and depression and more positive emotions, life satisfaction, and happiness four years later when they were finishing high school. They also had more hope and a stronger sense of meaning in life. Another study of ours, which followed students over six months, shows that feeling grateful motivates adolescents to help others and use their strengths to contribute to society.

The positive outcomes of helping students learn to be grateful and to express gratitude not only help their learning community in general but also help them individually. Practicing gratitude on a daily basis has been shown to

- Lessen feelings of social isolation
- Increase joy and optimism

- Enhance acting with more generosity and compassion
- Improve physical health (Wilson & Conyers, 2015)

••• GRATITUDE AS A CHANGE AGENT IN THE CLASSROOM

Owen Griffith (2014), a fourth-grade teacher and blogger, writes about how teaching gratitude to his students has completely changed the culture in his classroom:

> Gratitude has empowered me to teach more effectively, appreciate my individual students, grow in my profession, and enjoy life. Utilizing gratitude, I am able to model one of the most important lessons in life, having a positive attitude, especially about aspects of life that challenge me.

Griffith gives each of his students a composition book and has them start every day by writing five "gratitudes." By the end of the year, students have over a thousand collective "gratitudes." He believes that the physical act of writing a gratitude list helps develop "gratitude muscles," which allow students to better appreciate the benefits of even chores and homework they don't particularly enjoy at the time.

He believes that keeping a gratitude journal on a daily basis helps students achieve the following:

- Higher grades
- Higher goals
- More satisfaction with relationships, school, and life
- Less materialism
- More willingness to give back (Griffith, 2014)●

Gratitude can help students feel a connection to others and to the world in general. It can reduce the risk of depression and increase resilience in the face of stressful situations. "Appreciation transforms the most challenging experience into one that we can embrace" (Stiffelman, 2015, p. 229). In short, teaching about and practicing gratitude in the classroom not only builds a positive classroom culture; it also gives our students lifelong coping skills and helps students to Thrive.

Response to the 9/11 Tragedy

I first encountered gratitude as a powerful classroom strategy in 2001 while I was teaching history to middle school students. September 11, 2001, was a day that shook the world and gave us all a different perspective on everything. My students were visibly preoccupied and felt, like the rest of us, helpless. Studying early American history and ignoring the history being made at that moment seemed to be a disservice to my students. It was a live teachable moment of epic proportions, so I did what I could do—I gave them a venue to talk about it. We had journal prompts; we had lively debates; we tried to put the pieces together the best we could. But from this organic lesson, it was evident to me that my students needed to *do* something. I allowed the students to take the lead, and what developed was truly amazing.

My students organized and created a school and community movement of gratitude for both local and New York City first responders. My seventh graders collected needed items, fund-raised, contacted local fire departments, and got the word out to the community. Those seventh graders were on a mission to show their gratitude. I saw how empowered they had become and how invested they were and decided to take the concept a bit further. We declared it the year of being grateful. My students wrote letters of thanks to people who impacted them, and weekly we wrote down one good thing that happened as an exit ticket out the door. For our current events, we collected only positive news stories. We looked for the good in the world, and we were grateful. I am not sure if it was my perspective that changed or the kids, but my seventh graders seemed a little kinder that year and slightly more mature. (Dedra Stafford) ●

How Do We Teach Gratitude in the Classroom?

As with all the other foundational skills, we believe that classroom implementation starts with the teacher (and other adults at school) acting as models for the skills we want to see in our students. Effective teachers make a practice of showing appreciation for administrators, other staff members, support staff, parents, and students. We make sure our students see us practicing acts of kindness and gratitude, and we are explicit in telling learners why we are doing the things we do.

Moreover, teachers need to let students know the many ways we are grateful to them—how they inspire us, keep us grounded, challenge us to be better, remind us of our purpose, make us laugh, and keep us young. Placing an arm around a student's shoulder and saying, "Thank you—you just made my day," can do wonders for the student's sense of efficacy and well-being. Everyone likes to be appreciated, and knowing they are truly valued by their teachers can make a crucial difference for learners.

Teachers can not only demonstrate gratitude in our daily interactions with students; we can create opportunities for students to actively do the same. In addition to keeping their gratitude journals as described in the story on page 224, Griffith (2014) asks his students to write down "gratitudes" on sticky notes and put them on their classroom door so that they have a positive reminder every time they enter or leave the room. Students tell him they often take this idea home and post gratitude sticky notes around the house.

Once again, we find that mindfulness plays an important role in the other essential skills; it helps with teaching gratitude. The practice of becoming attuned to our environment and being fully present in the moment can greatly enhance our appreciation of and gratitude for ordinary things and people. Mindfulness and gratitude are natural corollaries of each other and can often be practiced together.

As silly as it sounds, playing the Pollyanna Game really works. You may remember Pollyanna as the title character in the Walt Disney movie who taught a whole town a simple game she practiced all the time. Whenever something bad happened to her, she immediately tried to find a least one positive thing to say about it. Teachers can demonstrate this strategy in front of their classes—"I know we're all worn out right now, but at least it's Thursday and not Monday!"—and challenge them to do the same. It's fun, it's inventive, and it plants the idea there is always something to be grateful for if one looks for it.

Like the other Thrive skills we write about, there are hundreds of ideas available from creative resourceful teachers about how to teach gratitude in the classroom. Pinterest is always a good place to look for ideas that spark your own imagination. Our resource sections in this book and on the *Thrive* website (www.teachingkidstothrive .com) are designed to give you some specific tools and strategies to get you started on each skill. Additionally, we have woven activities and strategies throughout the narrative of each chapter. See the Thrive Skills in Action section starting on page 233 for the five most frequently used activities for teaching gratitude.

What Supporting Gratitude Looks Like in the Classroom

THE TEACHER MODELS GRATITUDE

The teacher models gratitude and demonstrates appreciation. Many students report that their parents are more concerned about their own achievement or happiness than whether or not they care for others (Joyce, 2014). Whether that is actually true or not, it is the perception of 80 percent of the students who were surveyed. Students need to have adults in their lives who clearly demonstrate caring beyond themselves. Teachers can post pictures of their volunteer work, regularly talk about outreach programs they are involved in, and communicate to students their willingness to go above and beyond what is required of them in the classroom. We best teach the lessons of gratitude by committing random acts of kindness, pointing out other people's efforts to show appreciation, and manifesting appreciation for the things in our own lives (good and bad).

THE TEACHER CREATES A CARING CLASSROOM

Caring for others is a priority in the classroom. No matter the grade level or content area, it is possible to integrate the concept of caring into the curriculum. Teachers can and should use their subject matter to relate to the human connection and encourage students to be kind. Teachers should frequently acknowledge acts of student caring and provide opportunities for everyone to participate in activities that teach gratitude. The classroom should be a safe welcoming community for every single person who is there.

OPPORTUNITIES ARE PROVIDED FOR "ACTIVE THANKING"

Opportunities are provided for students to practice caring and gratitude. Group activities that feature or at least include practicing gratitude with classmates are instrumental in building trust and mutual appreciation in the class. Here are three simple activities to help: (1) Teachers can provide gratitude journals for every student or just occasionally say to students, "If you are finished with the assignment, please write down three things that happened this week that made you grateful." (2) Teachers can provide a bulletin board for students to place a sticky note that starts with "I am grateful for ____" or "I'd like to thank _____ for _____." (3) Gratitude jars can sit on a counter with blank slips for students to fill out and drop in when they want to acknowledge something good in their lives.

SERVICE LEARNING IS A PART OF THE CURRICULUM

Teachers can invite students to participate in designed service learning projects or come up with their own plans to pay it forward. DoSomething.org is a great place to start.

PRACTICING GRATITUDE IS AN ONGOING VENTURE

The concept of gratitude is revisited frequently. Teaching about gratitude is an ongoing process. It can't be introduced, tested, and then checked off the "did that" list. All of the Thrive skills need to be built and maintained. We need to be realistic with our students and tell them that most of us visit the well of grumpiness more than we would like. Gratitude is not a skill you can develop and rest comfortably on once it is mastered. Studies have shown that the positive feelings made by even the most magnanimous acts begin to diminish over time. Commitment to being grateful is not like charging a battery and forgetting about it; it's more like exercising in that desired results only happen when it is intentional, purposeful, and regular. In order to maintain the benefits of appreciativeness, we have to continue to be responsive and not only think about but actually show gratefulness frequently.

Frequently Asked Questions

1. **How can we ask students to practice gratitude when we are aware of the horrid circumstances some of them come from and go home to?**

   It may seem counterintuitive to expect people to be grateful when they are suffering, but gratitude can actually be practiced in times of stress as well as in times of abundance. One of the gratitude practices is to look at a time when you were hurt or betrayed and try to assign something positive that came from it (e.g., you learned you had more strength than you thought, or you found out you needed to be more cautious in your judgment). Studies have shown that when people do this, they generally feel more closure as well as are better able to move past the experience.

   It has been said, "No matter how bad your life may seem, there are others in this world who would gladly trade places with you." We cannot let our personal feelings of sympathy stop us from teaching all students the value of gratitude. Gratitude helps all of us put things in perspective so that we are not overwhelmed by the sometimes-harsh realities of life. By helping students focus on the things for which they are grateful (and everyone has at least some things), we can help encourage them to tackle the challenges they face. Gratitude can be a deterrent to despair, and everyone's life can be improved by practicing it.

2. **Some of my students find these gratitude exercises a little corny. How do I convince them to try them anyway?**

   We realize that some of the suggestions in this chapter may sound a little hokey and even feel that way to you at first, but we encourage you to give some a try. Later, you may be ready to try something that stretches the class a bit more. Generally, students will react to an assignment or activity with the same attitude the teacher has, so if you treat it as genuine and worthwhile, they are more likely to see it that way.

Be up front with your students and tell them, "I know some of you may feel a little uncomfortable with this for now, but bear with me, and I think you'll see some positive results." It's fine for students to treat the activities with skepticism (we want to teach them healthy skepticism), but not cynicism. If the problem is coming from only one student or a small group of students, you might want to pull them aside and say, "Help me understand why this is hard for you. I want to be mindful of your feelings, but I would really appreciate it if you would give this a try."

3. **It seems like my students today do not know how to give appropriate compliments or receive them. How do you get kids to express gratitude to each other when they are so tactless?**

We (the authors) have experienced this same problem in our classes. Maybe because of the influx of rudeness that students are exposed to on TV, in songs, in movies, in video games, in social media, and so on, they honestly don't know how to give or receive a positive affirmation. Go to a school sporting event and witness the behavior of some of the parents to get further enlightenment on part of the problem. We think it is worth the time to explicitly teach students how to give an appropriate compliment.

Have students brainstorm comments that are truly compliments and those that aren't. Teach them the appropriate words and body language that make a compliment meaningful and positive. Practice with the class pointing out genuine compliments in the classroom and calling out those that are sarcastic and hurtful (including yours).

The second part of your issue is teaching kids to be able to accept a compliment, which is also an art. Brushing off or refusing a compliment is like returning a gift. It is insulting to the giver. Model for and teach students how to thank you in a sincere manner. Teach them how to simply say, "Thank you for your kind words" (or something similar), when they don't agree with the affirmation or feel uncomfortable accepting it. Both giving and receiving compliments are skills of gratitude that can be coached and should be practiced with students.

4. **In the movie *Pay It Forward*, Mr. Simonet tells Trevor he will always care about him. Trevor responds, "Yeah. You're my teacher. They pay you to" (WikiQuotes, 2016). How do we let students know we are genuinely grateful for them without seeming like we are "being teachery"?**

We think kids can spot a phony a mile away, but we understand what you are saying about some kids believing that teachers just say "teachery" kinds of things because it's part of our job. Teachers who use overzealous praise or are too effusive are often perceived as being insincere at worst and indiscriminate at best. They lose the effectiveness of their praise by overdoing it. The best way to combat sounding too canned is to temper your global statements about the whole class with individual expressions to each student. You can write notes (on paper or electronically) to individuals telling them specific things you value in them and appreciate about them. You can pull individual students aside occasionally and thank them for offering a different view in a discussion or reaching out to help another student or for making you laugh with their humor. You can smile when you are standing at your door greeting them to let them know you are honestly glad to see them. You can say things to them like "I was home last night, and I was thinking about how you like to . . ." or "I just read a book that reminded me of you because . . ." or "I was telling my aunt about you, and she said it sounds like you . . ." Students of every age like to know their teachers think of them in contexts other than the classroom. Like everyone else, they like to feel important in other people's lives.

Discussion Questions and Exercises

We encourage you to tweet your responses to @tchkids2thrive.

1. Is it fair to ask a child who has been marginalized, neglected, or abused to practice gratitude? Explain your answer.

2. With your students this year, if you were allowed to teach only one of the Thrive dispositions mentioned in this book—mindfulness, the command and control skills, self-efficacy, persistence, resilience, responsibility, integrity, empathy, or gratitude—which one would you choose, and why?

3. How could your school at large improve the student body's sense of gratitude?

4. In your work, you are in contact with many people. Which ones do you most appreciate? How do you show your gratitude?

5. Think of the one person who had the most impact on your decision to become a teacher. Write that person a letter expressing your gratitude and send it or, better yet, deliver it in person. If that person is no longer living or you don't know how to reach him or her, go with your second choice.

6. How can administrators and colleagues support you as you teach students the Thrive skills? How can you support others who are attempting to do the same?

Thrive Skills in Action

ACTIVITY 9.1
Count Your Good Things

This activity can be done with pencil and paper or an electronic device. Ask students to write three to five good things that happen to them each day. Some teachers have students keep a special journal for recording these observations. Teachers can use prompts (e.g., "Today write about people who make your life more meaningful," "Write about any pets or animals that enhance your life," "List three things that you initially thought were going to be bad but turned out to be positive").

ACTIVITY 9.2

Savor the Flavor

Savor is a gratitude method studied by Quoidbach and Dunn (2013) who found that abstaining from a pleasurable activity for a week (i.e., not eating chocolate) leads to a greater appreciation of the activity when it is resumed. The conclusion from this study is that students need to be taught to slow down and appreciate the simple things around them. We have created the Savor the Flavor activity to allow students to do exactly this.

1. Have students list several things they enjoy and often do (e.g., play video games, eat their favorite snack, jump on the trampoline).

2. Ask students to look up the definition of the word *savor*.

3. Explain to students that there are things that we do so often that we don't enjoy as completely as we used to because we don't always slow down.

4. Examine the phrase "Stop and smell the roses."

5. Ask students to look at their list and select one thing they enjoy, but that they know they don't enjoy as much as they did in the past.

6. Challenge students to take the "Savor the Flavor" Challenge, which is to give up that activity or item for seven days so that they can enjoy it, even more, when it is resumed. See the "Savor the Flavor" Challenge Pledge on the *Thrive* website (www.teachingkidstothrive.com).

7. After the challenge is over, ask students to write about or discuss the following debrief points:

   - Did you complete the challenge?
   - Was it hard to give up the activity or item for seven days?
   - When you finished the challenge and got to resume use of the activity or item, did you enjoy it more?
   - What did you notice? Feel? Appreciate?

ACTIVITY 9.3

Grateful Share Jar

Create grateful thought prompts on slips of paper. Place them in a grateful jar. Students pass the jar around and draw one slip of paper. Students read the slip and take turns sharing their answer to the thought prompt that they drew out.

Possible Thought Prompts

- Name an everyday blessing people take for granted and how your life would be different without it.

- Describe something great that happened to you last year and how it made your life better.

- Name someone you're grateful to have in your life and why.

- Describe something you are particularly grateful for in your life and why.

- Describe something that happened in the past that you didn't feel grateful for at the time, but now think of with gratitude.

- Describe a moment when you were able to show how grateful you are to someone and what that moment felt like.

- Describe something great that happened to you last week that you are grateful for.

- Is there a place you are grateful for? Why?

- Describe something you do that makes you happy.

ACTIVITY 9.4

Silver Lining

If you look for it, there is always something to be grateful for, even in times that are challenging. Encourage students to appreciate the silver lining. Practice scenarios and see if your students can find the silver lining. Use Activity Sheet 9.1, "Can You Find the Silver Lining?" on the *Thrive* website (www.teachingkidstothrive.com) to step through the process.

1. Think about a time when something didn't go your way, or when you were frustrated or upset.

2. In a few sentences, briefly describe the situation in the middle of the cloud.

3. Then, see if you can think of things that can help you see the bright side of this situation. If you get stuck, just ask a friend to help. Write your ideas in the outer edge of the cloud (the silver lining).

can you find the silver lining?

1. Think about the most recent time when something didn't go your way, or when you felt frustrated, irritated, or upset.
2. In a few sentences, briefly describe the situation in the middle of the cloud.
3. Then, see if you can think of the things that can help you see the bright side of this situation. If you get stuck, just ask a friend to help. Write down your ideas in the outer edge of the cloud. (The silver lining.)

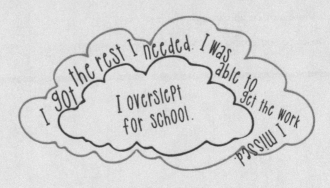

ACTIVITY 9.5

The Twenty-One-Day Challenge

Since it takes about three weeks to change a habit, many teachers like to issue the Twenty-One-Day Challenge. Ask students to go twenty-one days without uttering a single complaint. They can keep track of how they do in their journals, and every time they voice a complaint or whine, they have to start over. You can add to the challenge by asking students to give at least one sincere compliment to someone else each day. They can record the compliment they gave and the response it elicited in their journals. Periodic check-ins and class discussions keep the challenge interesting. When students make their goal, you can give them a certificate of gratitude achievement and put their names on an "I'm a Grateful Person" poster. (For younger students, you can modify this challenge to a week, or in some cases even a day.)

Access the website **www.teachingkidstothrive.com** to find more classroom-ready activities, author-recommended videos, websites, and other resources.

FINAL WORDS

All of the Thrive skills need purposeful ongoing attention to best help students internalize their usefulness. We want to add our voices to those who think schools need to integrate social and emotional learning (SEL) with their own visions of teaching and learning. We strongly urge that Thrive skills be uncompromisingly embedded in the curriculum and actively integrated in daily instruction. Thrive skills should be added to teacher development programs in colleges and universities as well as addressed as a frequent topic for staff development training.

As teachers, we never know the full extent of our influence on our students. We get glimpses now and then when we encounter students years after they've left our classrooms, and they stop to tell us the impact we made in their lives. Some days after a particular student breakthrough or watching students resolve a conflict with a skill we've taught them, we feel a tiny measure of our worth, but for the most part, we do all that we can do every day to ensure the best outcome for students and silently pray that we did enough.

The same can be said about our efforts to teach students the skills to Thrive. Building a strong culture of student-centered learning requires that schools and teachers intentionally help strengthen relationships among teachers and teachers, teachers and students, and students and students. That kind of community building takes a strong commitment not only from administrators and teachers but also from those who shape schools through laws, policies, and financing. Our hope is that all of these parties can come together to help 21st century students learn to Thrive today and in the future.

REFERENCES

Abbot, N., & Cameron, L. (2014). What makes a young assertive bystander? The effect of intergroup contact, empathy, cultural openness, and in-group bias on assertive bystander intervention intentions. *Journal of Social Issues, 70*(1), 167–182.

Ahn, J., Lamnia, M., Nightingale, M., Novak, D., & Xiaodong Lin-Siegler, A. (2016). Motivating students' stem learning using biographical information. *International Journal of Designs for Learning, 7*(1), 71–85.

Alexander, M. (2016, April 13). Who is your warm demander role model? *Edutopia.* Retrieved from http://www.edutopia.org/blog/warm-demander-equity-approach-matt-alexander

Allison-Napolitano, E. (2014). *Bounce forward: The extraordinary resilience of leadership.* Thousand Oaks, CA: Corwin.

American Psychological Association. (2016). *The road to resilience.* Retrieved from http://www.apa.org/helpcenter/road-resilience.aspx

Ariely, D. (2009, February). Our buggy moral code. *TED2009.* Retrieved from https://www.ted.com/talks/dan_ariely_on_our_buggy_moral_code?language=en

Bandura, A. (1985). *Social foundations of thought and action: A social cognitive theory.* Englewood Cliffs, NJ: Prentice Hall.

Bandura, A. (1993). Perceived self-efficacy in cognitive development and functioning. *Educational Psychologist, 28*(2), 117–148.

Bandura, A. (1994). Self-efficacy. In V. S. Ramachaudran (Ed.), *Encyclopedia of human behavior* (Vol. 4, pp. 71–81). New York, NY: Academic Press. Retrieved from https://www.uky.edu/~eushe2/Bandura/Bandura1994EHB.pdf

Bandura, A. (2001). Social cognitive theory: An agentic perspective. *Annual Review of Psychology, 52*, 1–26. Retrieved from https://www.uky.edu/~eushe2/Bandura/Bandura2001ARPr.pdf

Bandura, A. (2006). Toward a psychology of human agency. *Perspectives on Psychological Science, 1*(2), 164–180.

Barkley, R. A., Murphy, K. R., & Fischer, M. (2008). *ADHD in adults: What science says.* New York, NY: Guilford Press.

Baumeister, R. F., & Tierney, J. (2012). *Willpower.* New York, NY: Penguin Books.

Beach, M. (2010, September). Creating empathy in the classroom. *TEACH Magazine.* Retrieved from http://www.teachmag.com/archives/1115

Beck, A. T. (1976). *Cognitive therapies and emotional disorders.* New York, NY: New American Library.

Berger, R., Rugen, L., & Woodfin, L. (2014). *Leaders of their own learning: Transforming schools through student-engaged assessment.* San Francisco, CA: Jossey-Bass.

Bergstrom, C. (2016, January 15). How to practice mindfulness with children—the essential guide. *Blissful Kids.* Retrieved from http://blissfulkids.com/how-to-practice-mindfulness-with-children-the-essential-guide

Bertin, M. (2015). *Mindful parenting for ADHD.* Oakland, CA: New Harbinger.

Bloch, H. (2013, September). Failure is an option. *National Geographic Magazine, 224*(3), 124. Retrieved from http://ngm.nationalgeographic.com/2013/09/famous-failures/bloch-text

Breines, J. (2015, June 30). Four great gratitude strategies. *Greater Good.* Retrieved from http://greatergood.berkeley.edu/article/item/four_great_gratitude_strategies

Brody, J. E. (2010, February 15). Empathy's natural, but nurturing it helps. *The New York Times.* Retrieved from http://www.nytimes.com/2010/02/16/health/16brod.html?_r=0

Brown, B. (2010). The power of vulnerability. *TEDxHouston.* Retrieved from https://www.ted.com/talks/brene_brown_on_vulnerability?language=en

Brown, B. (2012, November 28). The wholehearted parenting manifesto. *The Huffington Post.* Retrieved from http://www.huffingtonpost.com/bren/wholehearted-parenting-manifesto_b_1923011.html

Brown, B. (2015). *Rising strong.* New York, NY: Penguin Random House.

Brown, B., & Olson, K. (2015). *The mindful school leader: Practices to transform your leadership and school.* Thousand Oaks, CA: Corwin.

Buckley, M. A. (2015). *Sharing the blue crayon: How to integrate social, emotional, and literacy learning.* Portland, ME: Stenhouse.

Burns, D. D. (1980). *Feeling good: The new mood therapy.* New York, NY: New American Library.

Carnegie Mellon University. (2014). *Disruptive decorations.* Retrieved from http://www.cmu.edu/homepage/society/2014/spring/disruptive-decorations.shtml

Cascios, J. (2009, September 28). The next big thing. *Foreign Policy*. Retrieved from http://foreignpolicy.com/2009/09/28/the-next-big-thing-resilience

Cavazos, S. (2016, April 6). Schools combine meditation and brain science to help combat discipline problems. *Chalkbeat*. Retrieved from http://www.chalkbeat.org/posts/in/2016/04/06/schools-combine-meditation-and-brain-science-to-help-combat-discipline-problems/#.V8pnWztxKAY

Chandler, A. (2016, September 11). Let's stop grading our kids on responsibility. *MiddleWeb*. Retrieved from http://www.middleweb.com/32690/lets-stop-grading-our-kids-on-responsibility

Claunch, S. (2013, August 21). *Overcoming obstacles*. Retrieved from http://ed.ted.com/lessons/there-s-no-dishonor-in-having-a-disability-steven-claunch

Cleveland, K. P. (2011). *Teaching boys who struggle in school*. Alexandria, VA: ASCD.

Coloroso, B. (2008). *The bully, the bullied, and the bystander* (Updated ed.). New York, NY: HarperCollins.

Conyers, M., & Wilson, D. (2015). *Positively smarter: Science and strategies for increasing happiness, achievement, and well-being*. Hoboken, NJ: Wiley-Blackwell.

Crouch, E. (2014, December 14). Students at gateway elementary aim for new school ties. *St. Louis Dispatch*. Retrieved from http://www.stltoday.com/news/local/education/students-at-gateway-elementary-aim-for-new-school-ties/article_ced783d0-6656-5bf4-bbe7-1dfd3f651f0e.html

Csikszentmihalyi, M. (1990). *Flow: The psychology of optimal experience*. New York, NY: HarperPerennial.

Davies, L. (2008, October 8). Instilling perseverance in children. *Education World*. Retrieved from http://www.educationworld.com/a_curr/columnists/davies/davies006.shtml

Davis, L. C. (2015, August 31). When mindfulness meets the classroom. *The Atlantic*. Retrieved from http://www.theatlantic.com/education/archive/2015/08/mindfulness-education-schools-meditation/402469

Dawson, P., & Guare, R. (2009). *Smart but scattered: The revolutionary "executive skills" approach to helping kids reach their potential*. New York, NY: Guilford Press.

Deak, J. (2010). *Your fantastic elastic brain: Stretch it, shape it*. Belvedere, CA: Little Pickle Press.

Deci, E., & Flaste, R. (1996). *Why we do what we do: Understanding self-motivation*. New York, NY: Penguin Books.

Deresiewicz, W. (2014). *Excellent sheep: The miseducation of the American elite and the way to a meaningful life*. New York, NY: Free Press.

Dines, J. (2016, September 12). Youth equity in stewardship series: Connecting stewardship to restorative justice. *Corwin Connect*. Retrieved from http://corwin-connect.com/2016/09/youth-equity-stewardship-series-connecting-stewardship-restorative-justice

Duckworth, A. (2016). *Grit: The power and passion of perseverance*. New York, NY: Scribner.

Duckworth, A., Peterson, C., Matthews, D., & Kelly, D. R. (2007). Grit: Perseverance and passion for long-term goals. *Journal of Personality and Social Psychology, 92*(6), 1087–1101.

Dweck, C. (2000). *Self theories: Their role in motivation, personality, and development*. New York, NY: Psychology Press.

Dweck, C. S. (2006). *Mindset: The new psychology of success*. New York, NY: Random House.

Dweck, C., Walton, G. M., & Cohen, G. L. (2011). *Academic tenacity: Mindsets and skills that promote long-term learning*. Seattle, WA: Bill & Melinda Gates Foundation. Retrieved from https://ed.stanford.edu/sites/default/files/manual/dweck-walton-cohen-2014.pdf

Einstein, A. (n.d.). *Quotes*. Retrieved from http://www.brainyquote.com/quotes/quotes/a/alberteins106192.html

Elias, M. J. (2015, July 7). SEL and the Common Core, part two: Why emotion vocabulary matters. *Edutopia*. Retrieved from http://www.edutopia.org/blog/sel-and-common-core-part-two-why-emotion-vocabulary-matters-maurice-elias

Elmore, T. (2014, April 21). From entitled to empowered: Building four virtues in students to combat entitlement in the classroom. *The Huffington Post*. Retrieved from http://www.huffingtonpost.com/tim-elmore/from-entitled-to-empowere_b_4804516.html

Emmons, R. (2013, November 21). Five myths about gratitude. *Greater Good*. Retrieved from http://greatergood.berkeley.edu/article/item/five_myths_about_gratitude

Falk, B. (2013). *The resilient farm and homestead*. White River Junction, VT: Chelsea Green.

Farrington, C. A., Roderick, M., Allensworth, E., Nagaoka, J., Keyes, T. S., Johnson, D. W., & Beechum, N. O. (2012, June). *Teaching adolescents to become learners. The role of noncognitive factors in shaping school performance: A critical literature review*. Chicago, IL: University of Chicago Consortium on Chicago School Research. Retrieved from https://consortium.uchicago.edu/sites/default/files/publications/Noncognitive%20Report.pdf

Ferlazzo, L. (2015). *Building a community of self-motivated learners*. New York, NY: Routledge.

Fine, S. M. (2015, October 7). Deeper discipline demands deeper pedagogy. *Education Week*. Retrieved from http://blogs.edweek.org/edweek/learning_deeply/2015/10/deeper_discipline_demands_deeper_pedagogy.html

Frankl, V. E. (2006). *Man's search for meaning: An introduction to logotherapy* (Mass market paperback ed.). Boston, MA: Beacon Press.

Froh, J. J., & Bono, G. (2012, November 19). How to foster gratitude in schools. *Greater Good*. Retrieved from http://greatergood.berkeley.edu/article/item/how_to_foster_gratitude_in_schools

Froh, J. J., Bono, G., & Emmons, R. (2010). Being grateful is beyond good manners: Gratitude and motivation to contribute to society among early adolescents. *Motivation and Emotion, 34*(2), 144–157.

Gallup. (2015). *Gallup student poll: 2015 results.* Retrieved from http://www.gallup.com/services/189926/student-poll-2015-results.aspx

Ginsburg, K. (2011). *Building resilience in children and teens: Giving kids roots and wings.* Elk Grove Village, IL: American Academy of Pediatrics.

Goleman, D. (1995). *Emotional intelligence.* New York, NY: Bantam Dell.

Goleman, D. (1998). *Working with emotional intelligence.* New York, NY: Bantam Dell.

Goleman, D. (2006). *Social intelligence.* New York, NY: Bantam.

Goleman, D. (2013). *Focus: The hidden driver of excellence.* New York, NY: HarperCollins.

Gollwitzer, P. M. (1999). Implementation intentions: Strong effects of simple plans. *American Psychologist, 54*(7), 493–503.

Gordon, J. (2005). *The energy bus.* New York, NY: Wiley.

Grate, M. (2014, November 12). Bullyproof your classroom with brown paper bags. *MiddleWeb.* Retrieved from http://www.middleweb.com/18809/a-strategy-improve-classroom-culture

Greater Good Science Center. (2017). *What is gratitude?* Retrieved from http://greatergood.berkeley.edu/topic/gratitude/definition

Greenland, S. K. (2010). *The mindful child: How to help your kid manage stress and become happier, kinder, and more compassionate.* New York, NY: Free Press.

Greenspan, S. I. (2007). *Great kids: Helping your baby and child develop the ten essential qualities for a healthy, happy life.* Boston, MA: Da Capo Press.

Gregoire, C. (2014, May 22). Why children need mindfulness just as much as adults do. *The Huffington Post.* Retrieved from http://www.huffingtonpost.com/2014/05/22/why-children-need-mindful_n_5354143.html

Gregoire, C., & Resmovits, J. (2015, May 7). How mindfulness has changed the way Americans learn and work. *The Huffington Post.* Retrieved from www.huffingtonpost.com/2015/05/07/mindfulness-schools-workplace_n_7085718.html\

Gregory, G., & Kaufeldt, M. (2015). *The motivated brain: Improving student attention, engagement, and perseverance.* Alexandria, VA: ASCD.

Griffith, O. M. (2014, November 17). Gratitude: A powerful tool for your classroom. *Edutopia.* Retrieved from http://www.edutopia.org/blog/gratitude-powerful-tool-for-classroom-owen-griffith

Gritz, J. R. (2015, November 10). Mantras before math class. *The Atlantic.* Retrieved from http://www.theatlantic.com/education/archive/2015/11/mantras-before-math-class/412618

Guare, R., Dawson, P., & Guare, C. (2013). *Smart but scattered teens.* New York, NY: Guilford Press.

Hamilton, A. (2016, May 11). Students learn empathy at the resilience café. *The Daily Sentinel.* Retrieved from http://www.gjsentinel.com/news/articles/students-learn-empathy8232at-the-resilience-cafe

Hanson, R. (2014, June 1). Do positive experiences "stick to your ribs"? *Take in the Good.* Retrieved from http://www.rickhanson.net/take-in-the-good

Harris, E. (2015, October 24). Under stress, students in New York schools find calm in meditation. *The New York Times.* Retrieved from http://www.nytimes.com/2015/10/24/nyregion/under-stress-students-in-new-york-schools-find-calm-in-meditation.html?_r=0

Hart, A. D. (2007). *Thrilled to death.* Nashville, TN: Thomas Nelson.

Hattie, J. (2012). *Visible learning for teachers: Maximizing impact on learning.* Thousand Oaks, CA: Corwin.

Hattie, J., & Timperely, H. (2007). The power of feedback. *Review of Educational Research, 77*(1), 81–112. Retrieved from http://education.qld.gov.au/staff/development/performance/resources/readings/power-feedback.pdf

Hattie, J., & Yates, G. (2014). *Visible learning and the science of how we learn.* New York, NY: Routledge.

Heick, T. (2015, February 10). Teaching empathy: Are we teaching content or standards? *Edutopia.* Retrieved from http://www.edutopia.org/blog/teaching-empathy-content-or-students-terry-heick

Henderson, N. (2013). Havens of resilience. *Educational Leadership, 71*(1), 22–27.

Henriques, G. (2015, February). What is mindfulness and how does it work? *Psychology Today.* Retrieved from https://www.psychologytoday.com/blog/theory-knowledge/201502/what-is-mindfulness-and-how-does-it-work

Hinduja, S., & Patchin, J. (2016, April 19). Ideas to make kindness go viral. *Corwin Connect.* Retrieved from http://corwin-connect.com/2016/04/ideas-make-kindness-go-viral

Hoffman, J. (2013, February 22). Self-regulation techniques for children. *Today's Parent.* Retrieved from http://www.todaysparent.com/family/education/self-regulation-techniques-for-children

Jackson, R. (2009). *Never work harder than your students.* Alexandria, VA: ASCD.

Jacobs, T. (2015, September 25). More evidence that mindfulness breeds resilience. *Pacific Standard.* Retrieved from https://psmag.com/more-evidence-that-mindfulness-breeds-resilience-b45582745bcb#.8il8hwnwk

Jain, R. (2013, March 8). Filling in thought holes: An invaluable social and emotional learning lesson. *Edutopia.* Retrieved from www.edutopia.org/blog/SEL-filling-in-thought-holes-renee-jain

Joyce, A. (2014, July 18). Are you raising nice kids? A Harvard psychologist gives 5 ways to raise them to be kind. *The Washington Post.* Retrieved from https://www.washingtonpost.com/news/parenting/wp/2014/07/18/are-you-raising-nice-kids-a-harvard-psychologist-gives-5-ways-to-raise-them-to-be-kind

Kabat-Zinn, J. (2012). *Mindfulness for beginners: Reclaiming the present moment and your life*. Boulder, CO: Sounds True.

Kamenetz, A. (2016, January 4). We're thinking about ADHD all wrong, says a top pediatrician. *NPREd*. Retrieved from http://www.npr.org/sections/ed/2016/01/04/459990844/were-thinking-about-adhd-all-wrong-says-a-top-pediatrician

Kennelley, S. (2012, June 8). Does playing music boost kids' empathy? *Greater Good*. Retrieved from http://greatergood.berkeley.edu/article/item/does_playing_music_boost_kids_empathy

King, M. L., Jr. (1960, May). "Keep moving from this mountain," address at Spelman College on 10 April 1960. *Spelman Messenger*, pp. 6–17. Retrieved from https://swap.stanford.edu/20141218225553/http://mlk-kpp01.stanford.edu/primarydocuments/Vol5/10Apr1960_KeepMovingfromThisMountain,AddressatSpelmanCollege.pdf

Klemm, W. R. (2012). *Memory power 101*. New York, NY: Skyhorse.

Kohn, A. (2014, April 6). The downside of "grit." *The Washington Post*. Retrieved from http://www.alfiekohn.org/article/downside-grit

Krznaric, R. (2011). *The Wonderbox: Curious histories of how to live*. London, UK: Profile Books.

Lamprey, B., & Reilly, B. (2016, July 6). Project Au-Some: Building empathy and collaboration. *Edutopia*. Retrieved from http://www.edutopia.org/blog/project-au-some-building-empathy-collaboration-brenna-lamprey-beth-reilly

Le, C., & Wolfe, R (2013). How can schools boost student's self-regulation? *Phi Delta Kappan, 95*(2), 33–38.

Leder, M. (2000). *Pay it forward* [Film]. Hollywood, CA: Warner Bros.

Lee, H. (1960). *To kill a mockingbird*. Philadelphia, PA: Lippincott.

Levy, D. M. (2016). *Mindful tech: How to bring balance to our digital lives*. New Haven, CT: Yale University Press.

Lickona, T. (2004, February). Teaching respect and responsibility. *CYC-Online, 61*. Retrieved from http://www.cyc-net.org/cyc-online/cycol-0204-lickona.html

Lipoff, B. (2015, November 4). Blue valley mentor program fosters "new kind of bond." *The Kansas City Star, Overland Park & Leawood Edition*. Retrieved from http://www.kansascity.com/news/local/community/joco-913/overland-park-leawood/article42937662.html

Lippmann, S., Bulanda, R. E., & Wagenaar, T C. (2009). Student entitlement. *College Teaching, 57*(4), 197–204.

Long, R. (2013). *Room to breathe* [Documentary drama]. San Francisco, CA: ZAP Zoetrope Aubry Productions.

Lopez, S. (2013). Making hope happen in the classroom. *Kappan Magazine, 95*(2), 19–22.

Lumpkin, A. (2008). Teachers as role models teaching character and moral virtues. *Journal of Physical Education, Recreation & Dance, 79*(2), 45–49.

Lythcott-Haims, J. (2015). *How to raise an adult: Break free of the overparenting trap and prepare your kid for success*. New York, NY: Holt.

Markham, T. (2014, December 18). What believing in the possibilities can do for learning and teaching. *Mind/Shift*. Retrieved from https://ww2 .kqed.org/mindshift/2014/12/18/what-believing-in-the-possibilities-can-do-for-learning-and-teaching

Matthiessen, C. (2015, October 30). Life after wartime. *Great! Schools*. Retrieved from http://www.greatschools.org/gk/articles/life-after-war

Meiklejohn, J., Phillips, C., Freedman, M. L., Griffin, M. L., Biegel, G., Roach, A., . . . Saltzman, A. (2012). Integrating mindfulness training into K–12 education: Fostering the resilience of teachers and students. *Mindfulness, 3*(4), 291–307. Retrieved from http://link.springer.com/ article/10.1007/s12671-012-0094-5#/page-1

Mindful Schools. (2017). *About*. Retrieved from http://www .mindfulschools.org/about/our-story

Mischel, W. (2014). The marshmallow test: Why self-control is the engine of success. New York, NY: Little, Brown.

Mizerny, C. (2015, April 5). Misconceptions about mindset, rigor, and grit. *MiddleWeb*. Retrieved from http://www.middleweb.com/21699/our-misconceptions-about-mindset-rigor-and-grit

Mogel, W. (2010). *The blessings of a B minus: Using Jewish teachings to raise resilient teenagers*. New York, NY: Scribner.

Monson, T. S. (n.d.). *Quotes*. Retrieved from http://www.brainyquote.com/ quotes/quotes/t/thomassmo297244.html

Motivating students' stem learning using biographical information. *International Journal of Designs for Learning, 7*(1), 71–85.

Murphy, S. (2014). Empathy and good managers. *Switch & Shift*. Retrieved from http://switchandshift.com/empathy-and-good-managers

Nagaoka, J., Farrington, C. A., Ehrlich, S. B., & Heath, R. D. (2015). *Foundations for young adult success: A developmental framework*. Chicago, IL: University of Chicago Consortium on Chicago School Research.

National Scientific Council on the Developing Child. (2014, January). *Excessive stress disrupts the architecture of the developing brain: Working paper no. 3* (Updated ed.). Retrieved from http://developingchild .harvard.edu/wp-content/uploads/2005/05/Stress_Disrupts_ Architecture_Developing_Brain-1.pdf

Neu, T. W., & Weinfeld, R. (2007). *Helping boys succeed in school: A practical guide for parents and teachers*. Waco, TX: Prufrock Press.

Nietzsche, F. (1888). *Quotes*. Retrieved from https://en.wikiquote.org/wiki/ Friedrich_Nietzsche

Nottingham, J. (2017). *Challenging learning through dialogue*. Thousand Oaks, CA: Corwin.

Oettingen, G. (2014). *Rethinking positive thinking: Inside the new science of motivation*. New York, NY: Penguin Random House.

Pantalon, M. (2011). *Instant influence*. Terra Alta, WV: Headline Books.

Paul, A. M. (2013, June 10). Eight ways of looking at intelligence. *Mind/ Shift*. Retrieved from https://ww2.kqed.org/mindshift/2013/06/10/ eight-ways-of-looking-at-intelligence

Pay It Forward Day. (2011). *Ideas 4 paying it forward in schools*. Retrieved from https://payitforwardday.com/wp-content/uploads/2011/02/PIFD_Schools_Kit-2011.pdf

Peete, H. R., & Peete, R. E. (2010). *My brother Charlie*. New York, NY: Scholastic.

Petlak, L. (2013, October 22). Classroom management miracle: Executive functioning. *Scholastic Teachers*. Retrieved from http://www.scholastic.com/teachers/top-teaching/2013/10/classroom-management-miracle-executive-functioning

Piper, W. (1930). *The little engine that could*. New York, NY: Platt & Munk.

Price-Mitchell, M. (2015, May 20). Does your classroom cultivate student resilience? *Edutopia*. Retrieved from http://www.edutopia.org/blog/8-pathways-cultivate-student-resilience-marilyn-price-mitchell

Quoidbach, J., & Dunn, E. W. (2013). Give it up: A strategy for combatting hedonic adaptation. *Social Psychological and Personality Science, 4*, 563–568.

Quy, L. (2016, August 17). 6 ways FBI agents increase their resilience. *Smart Brief*. Retrieved from http://www.smartbrief.com/original/2016/08/6-ways-fbi-agents-increase-their-resilience

Redford, K. (2016, May 9). Sharing stories to enrich school culture. *Education Week Teacher*. Retrieved from http://blogs.edweek.org/teachers/reaching-all-students/2016/05/sharing_stories_to_enrich_scho.html

Responsive Classroom. (2012). Want positive behavior? Use positive language. *Information Library*. Retrieved from https://www.responsiveclassroom.org/want-positive-behavior-use-positive-language

Ricci, M. C. (2013). *Mindsets in the classroom: Building a culture of success and student achievement in schools*. Waco, TX: Prufrock Press.

Richards, P. (2012). Academic integrity: A case for good teaching. *Independent School, 71*(4), 96–98.

Riest, M. (2016, August 10). Lefler teachers spent an hour in the shoes of their students, learning empathy. *Lincoln Journal Star*. Retrieved from http://journalstar.com/news/local/education/lefler-teachers-spent-an-hour-in-the-shoes-of-their/article_61eec6e0-a457-5527-9158-86d82eaef7b8.html

Rosenberg, M. (2015). *Nonviolent communication: A language of life* (3rd ed.). Encinitas, CA: Puddledancer Press.

Rowling, J. K. (2008, June 5). The fringe benefits of failure, and the importance of imagination (text of Harvard commencement speech). *Harvard Gazette*. Retrieved from http://news.harvard.edu/gazette/story/2008/06/text-of-j-k-rowling-speech

RSA. (2013, December 10). *Brené Brown on empathy*. Retrieved from https://youtu.be/1Evwgu369Jw

Ryan, T. (2012). *A mindful nation: How a simple practice can help us reduce stress, improve performance, and recapture the American spirit*. Carlsbad, CA: Hay House.

Sansone, R. A., & Sansone, L. A. (2010). Gratitude and well-being: The benefits of appreciation. *Psychiatry, 7*(11), 18–22.

Schwartz, K. (2013, February 5). Age of distraction: Why it's crucial for students to learn to focus. *Mind/Shift.* Retrieved from http://ww2 .kqed.org/mindshift/2013/12/05/age-of-distraction-why-its-crucial-for-students-to-learn-to-focus

Schwartz, K. (2016a, March 30). What changes when a school embraces mindfulness? *Mind/Shift.* Retrieved from http://ww2.kqed .org/mindshift/2016/03/30/what-changes-when-a-school-embraces-mindfulness

Schwartz, K. (2016b, July 12). Why discipline should be aligned with a school's learning philosophy. *Mind/Shift.* Retrieved from https://ww2 .kqed.org/mindshift/2016/07/12/why-discipline-should-be-aligned-with-a-schools-learning-philosophy

Searle, M. (2013). *Causes & cures in the classroom: Getting to the root of academic and behavior problems.* Alexandria, VA: ASCD.

Segal, J. (1988). Teachers have enormous power in affecting a child's self-esteem. *Brown University Child Behavior and Development Newsletter, 4,* 1–3.

Seligman, M. E. P. (1975). *Helplessness.* San Francisco, CA: Freeman.

Seligman, M. E. P. (1990). *Learned optimism.* New York, NY: Vintage Books.

Seligman, M. E. P. (2006). *Learned optimism: How to change your mind and your life* (2nd ed.). New York, NY: Vintage.

Shoda, Y., Mischel, W., & Peake, P. K. (1990). Predicting adolescent cognitive and self-regulatory competencies from preschool delay of gratification: Identifying diagnostic conditions. *Developmental Psychology, 26*(6), 978–986.

Siegel, D. J., & Bryson, T. P. (2012). *The whole-brain child: 12 revolutionary strategies to nurture your child's developing mind.* New York, NY: Bantam Books.

Siegel, R. D. (2014). *The science of mindfulness: A research-based path to well-being.* Chantilly, VA: The Great Courses.

Silver, D. (2005). *Drumming to the beat of different marchers.* Chicago, IL: Incentive Publication by World Book.

Silver, D. (2012). *Fall down 7 times, get up 8: Teaching kids to succeed.* Thousand Oaks, CA: Corwin.

Simon-Thomas, E. R. (2007). Are women more empathic than men? *Greater Good.* Retrieved from http://greatergood.berkeley.edu/article/ item/women_more_empathic_than_men

Slocumb, P. D. (2004). *Hear our cry: Boys in crisis.* Highlands, TX: Aha! Process.

Smith, J. A. (2013, November 20). Six habits of highly grateful people. *Greater Good.* Retrieved from http://greatergood.berkeley.edu/article/ item/six_habits_of_highly_grateful_people

Smith, T. (2014, March 17). Can focus on "grit" work in school cultures that reward grades? *Mind/Shift*. Retrieved from https://ww2.kqed.org/mindshift/2014/03/17/can-focus-on-grit-work-in-school-cultures-that-reward-grades

Snel, E. (2013). *Sitting still like a frog: Mindfulness exercises for kids (and their parents)*. Boston, MA: Shambhala.

Souers, K., & Hall, P. (2016). *Fostering resilient learners: Strategies for creating a trauma-sensitive classroom*. Alexandria, VA: ASCD.

Sparks, S. D. (2015, June 2). "Nation's Report Card" to gather data on grit, mindset. *Education Week*. Retrieved from http://www.edweek.org/ew/articles/2015/06/03/nations-report-card-to-gather-data-on.html

Sprenger, M. (2015, May 28). The importance of working memory. *Corwin Connect*. Retrieved from http://corwin-connect.com/2015/05/the-importance-of-working-memory

Stahl, B., & Millstine, W. (2013). *Calming the rush of panic*. Oakland, CA: New Harbinger.

Stamps, L. (2006, August 28). Responsibility: Raising children you can depend on. *Gifted Today*. Retrieved from https://blogs.tip.duke.edu/giftedtoday/2006/08/28/responsibility-raising-children-you-can-depend-on

Stiffelman, S. (2015). *Parenting with presence: Practices for raising conscious, confident, caring kids*. Novato, CA: New World Library.

Strauss, V. (2016, May 10). The problem with teaching "grit" to poor kids? They already have it. Here's what they really need. *The Washington Post*. Retrieved from https://www.washingtonpost.com/news/answer-sheet/wp/2016/05/10/the-problem-with-teaching-grit-to-poor-kids-they-already-have-it-heres-what-they-really-need/?utm_term=.eda8c58c3f67

Swink, D. (2013, March 7). I don't feel your pain: Overcoming roadblocks to empathy. *Psychology Today*. Retrieved from https://www.psychologytoday.com/blog/threat-management/201303/i-dont-feel-your-pain-overcoming-roadblocks-empathy

Szalavitz, M. (2010, April 17). How not to raise a bully: The early roots of empathy. *Time*. Retrieved from http://content.time.com/time/health/article/0,8599,1982190-2,00.html

Tartakovsky, M. (n.d.). 10 tips for raising resilient kids. *Psych Central*. Retrieved from http://psychcentral.com/lib/10-tips-for-raising-resilient-kids

Thompson, K. (n.d.). *Khloe Kares*. Retrieved from http://www.khloekares.com

Thoreau, H. D. (n.d.). *Quotes*. Retrieved from http://www.azquotes.com/quote/787737

Tomlin, L. (n.d.). *Quotes*. Retrieved from http://www.brainyquote.com/quotes/quotes/l/lilytomlin153964.html

Tomlinson, C. A. (2001). *How to differentiate instruction in mixed-ability classrooms* (2nd ed.). Alexandria, VA: ASCD.

U.S. Department of Education. (2013, February 14). *Promoting grit, tenacity, and perseverance: Critical factors for success in the 21st century.* Retrieved from http://pgbovine.net/OET-Draft-Grit-Report-2-17-13.pdf

Vander Ark, T. (2015, December 21). 10 tips for developing student agency. *Education Week.* Retrieved from http://blogs.edweek.org/edweek/on_innovation/2015/12/10_tips_for_developing_student_agency.html?qs=Vander+Ark+2015

Vasicek, B. (2010, December 25). Integrity. *Scholastic.* Retrieved from http://www.scholastic.com/teachers/classroom_solutions/2010/12/integrity

Vygotsky, L. S. (1980). *Mind in society: The development of higher psychological processes.* Cambridge, MA: Harvard University Press.

Wallace, K. (2016, February 9). Calming the teenage mind in the classroom. *CNN.* Retrieved from http://edition.cnn.com/2016/02/08/health/mindfulness-teenagers-schools-stress

Walsh, D. (2007). *No: Why kids of all ages need to hear it and ways parents can say it.* New York, NY: Simon & Schuster.

Wang, A. (2015, January 6). Preschool kids can have fun building the crucial life skill of self-regulation, research shows. *The Oregonian/Oregon Live.* Retrieved from http://www.oregonlive.com/kiddo/index.ssf/2015/01/preschool_kids_can_have_fun_bu.html

Weiner, B. (1980). A cognitive (attribution)-emotion-action model of motivated behavior: An analysis of judgments of help-giving. *Journal of Personality and Social Psychology, 39*(2), 186–200.

Weinstein, B. (2009). *Is it still cheating if I don't get caught?* Irvine, CA: Flash Point.

Weng, H., Fox, D., Shackman, A., Bussan, D., & Davidson, R. J. (2014). Changing your brain and generosity through compassion meditation training. *Center for Healthy Minds.* Retrieved from http://centerhealthyminds.org/science/studies/changing-your-brain-and-generosity-through-compassion-meditation-training

Werner, E., & Smith, R. (2001). *Journey from childhood to midlife: Risk, resilience and recovery.* Ithaca, NY: Cornell University Press.

WikiQuotes. (2016, September 21). *Pay it forward.* Retrieved from https://en.wikiquote.org/wiki/Pay_It_Forward

Wilson, D., & Conyers, M. (2015, September 30). Unleashing the power of positivity in your school. *Edutopia.* Retrieved from http://www.edutopia.org/blog/unleashing-power-positivity-your-school-donna-wilson-marcus-conyers

Wolkin, J. (2015, September 20). How the brain changes when you meditate. *Mindful.* Retrieved from http://www.mindful.org/how-the-brain-changes-when-you-meditate

Wormeli, R. (2013). Looking at executive function. *AMLE Magazine, (1)*1, 41–43.

Wormeli, R. (2016a, May). Teaching students responsibility. *AMLE Magazine.* Retrieved from http://www.amle.org/BrowsebyTopic/ WhatsNew/WNDet/TabId/270/artmid/888/articleid/639/Teaching-Students-Responsibility.aspx

Wormeli, R. (2016b). What to do in week one? *Educational Leadership, 74*(1), 10–15.

Wright, T. (2013). "I keep me safe." Risk and resilience in children with messy lives. *Phi Delta Kappan, 95*(2), 39–43.

Young, J. (2014). *Encouragement in the classroom.* Alexandria, VA: ASCD Arias.

INDEX

Frankl, V. E., 116

Frequently asked questions:
    culture of responsibility and, 156–159
    empathy and, 204–206
    executive function skills and, 57–58
    gratitude and, 229–231
    growth mindset/self-efficacy and, 82–84
    integrity and, 176–179
    mindfulness and, 23–25
    perseverance and, 104–106
    resilience and, 131–133

Froh, J. J., 218, 219, 223

Frustration zone learners, 73 (figure), 74

Game playing, 44, 226

Genius Hour movement, 103

Goleman, D., 12, 187, 190

Gollwitzer, P., 42, 47, 54

Gonzalez, A., 18

Gordon, K., 188

Gordon, M., 194, 196

Grate, M., 185, 186

Gratitude, 217
    active thanking opportunities
        and, 227–228
    adolescent development, connectedness/
        positive action and, 218–219, 224
    appreciation, expressions of, 226,
        227–228
    brain function and, 221–223
    classroom instruction in, 223–227,
        229–230
    classroom/school programs in, 218–220
    classroom support strategies for, 227–228
    Count Your Good Things activity
        and, 233
    definitions of, 220
    entitlement beliefs and, 221
    environmental risk factors and, 229
    frequently asked questions about,
        229–231
    giving/receiving affirmations, practice
        with, 230–231
    Grateful Share Jar activity and, 235
    healing power of, 225
    Hebb's rule and, 221
    hot emotions vs. cool cognition and, 222
    kindness and, 220–221
    mindfulness and, 226
    modeling gratitude and, 225, 227
    Pay It Forward Day programs and,
        219–220
    paying it forward concept and, 217–219
    Pollyanna Game and, 226

    positive emotions, shift towards,
        221–222, 223
    positive outcomes of, 223–224, 229
    practice of, 221, 223–224, 228
    public expressions of, 219, 222
    research on, 221–223
    Savor the Flavor activity and, 234
    scarcity theory and, 221
    service learning opportunities and, 228
    Silver Lining activity and, 236
    supportive/caring classrooms, creation
        of, 223, 224, 227
    teacher demonstration of, 225–226, 231
    The Twenty-One-Day Challenge activity
        and, 237
    See also Empathy

Greater Good Science Center, 219

Greenspan, S. I., 190

Gregoire, C., 18

Griffith, O. M., 224, 226

Grit, 4, 96, 98, 104–105

Grit Scale, 98

Gritz, J. R., 19

Growth mindset, 68, 75
    classroom support strategies for, 81–82
    development of, 78–80
    Fabulous Fails activity and, 91
    Failing Isn't Final activity and, 89
    fixed mindset/entity theory and, 76, 77,
        78, 83–84
    formative assessment and, 81
    frequently asked questions about, 82–84
    grading practices and, 83
    Growth Mindset/Fixed Mindset
        Preassessment and, 77
    growth mindset/incremental theory
        and, 75
    growth mindset instruction and,
        79–80, 83–84
    Lenox Academy Brainology program
        and, 80
    Me Me Me activity and, 88
    mindset theory and, 76
    mistakes/failure, opportunity of, 78,
        82, 89, 91
    productive effort, focus on, 78
    Redo Request activity sheet and, 78
    risk taking, modeling of, 81
    Rolling From Fixed to Growth Mindset
        activity and, 90
    struggle, appreciation of, 73, 77, 82
    student agency and, 77–78
    teacher feedback practices and, 82–83
    thinking process, encouragement of, 81